BOEOTIA

• *Thebes*

MAINLAND
GREECE

Corinth

Athens

Mykene

ARGOS

gos

Salamis

Aegina

CAPE
GERAESTUS

CAPE
SOUNION

CDAEMON

CAPE
MALEIA

Kythera

1 CENTIMETER = 14.5 KILOMETERS
1 INCH = 22.8 MILES

25   50KM

25   50MI

N

· THE PENELOPEIA ·

JANE RAWLINGS
THE PENELOPEIA

ILLUSTRATIONS BY HEATHER HURST

DAVID R. GODINE · PUBLISHER

BOSTON

First published in 2003 by
David R. Godine, Publisher
Post Office Box 450
Jaffrey, New Hampshire 03452
www.godine.com

LIBRARY OF CONGRESS CATALOGING-IN-PUBLICATION DATA

Rawlings, Jane
The Penelopeia / by Jane Rawlings ;
illustrations by Heather Hurst.– 1st ed.
p.   cm.
ISBN 1-56792-206-6 (alk. paper)
1. Penelope (greek mythology)–Poetry.
2. Mothers and daughter–Poetry. 3. Women–Mythology–Poetry.
4. Women–Greece–Poetry. 5. Oracles, Greek–Poetry.
6. Greece–Poetry. 7. Twins–Poetry
I. Title
PS3618.A95P46   2003
811'.6–dc21   2002041666

First Edition
PRINTED IN CHINA BY EVERBEST PRINTING CO.
THROUGH FOUR COLOUR IMPORTS, LTD.

· CONTENTS ·

CONTENTS

CONTENTS

CONTENTS

· PREFACE ·

Did you know that Penelope had two shining daughters by Odysseus, after he had sailed for Troy? I suspect not; after all, that was not part of Odysseus' story. Even the Gods did not choose to tell him of it.

What *do* we 'know' of Penelope from *The Odyssey*? We know that she wept and lamented her husband's long absence, and that she waited faithfully for his return. She even held off a house-full of rowdy younger suitors by a ruse, until that was uncovered. But there is more to her than we tend to remember. If we reread *The Odyssey*, we find much upon which to build her story. Especially as Odysseus' journey was coming to a close, Penelope was revealed as his match for strength and wiliness.

What of Penelope's own journey? She too 'journeyed' through life, although she ostensibly remained at home on Ithaka. She, too, coped with misfortune and practical diffiiculties for twenty years. Yet the epic was written about her husband, a man, as were all the epic tales. Penelope's story has also been an epic tale, one lived by unsung women for thousands of years.

Who would 'sing' of this woman now, in the twenty-first century, when women are valuing and appropriating men's lives? Who would consider Penelope's reactions to encounters with the same people her son and husband met on their journeys? Who would engage with Helen of Troy and Penthesileia, Queen of the Amazons, from the point of view of a very different woman of their time?

And who would 'sing' of those matchless daughters, or the kindredship between women, of the subtle psychological interplay between father and daughters, mother and son (and daughters' suitors!), brother and sisters, wife and father-in-law? Or of a woman's feelings as she launches her children on their own life-journeys?

Without stretching too far, or violating, what we 'know' of the events of Penelope's time, I would.

· THE PENELOPEIA ·

· I ·

Now, PENELOPE, *shining among women and men who praised you
only as circumspect wife of godlike Odysseus, speak.
It was you who kept for him his homecoming to his high-roofed palace,
his crowding herds, fields and estates, his thralls and family.
You in your heart devised the tears and lamentations, the contests,
the schemes, forever weaving and unweaving to keep the indolent
unworthy suitors near you, guarding your halls and balancing
one against another in rivalry and strength. Now you,
who brought your children to their coming of age — Telemachos
and the two matchless daughters — complete the story.*

When Odysseus again stepped over the stone threshold
of the great hall, I was on hand for appropriate welcome
as befits the wife of a king who is queen by her own right.
For did I not prove to be a woman of many ways as I struggled
for my own life and that of my loved ones, journeying alone

3

though seemingly always near home? And was I not destined
soon to make my own far journeys? But in this I am ahead
of my story, and it is important that this tale be told well.

Before Odysseus had come the herald Medon, who called to me saying
that peace was accomplished and there would be no more clamor
of strife between the men of Ithaka and their lord, although my husband,
returned home after twenty years of struggle and wandering,
had killed many of their haughty sons. He did it in his wrath
because they were living recklessly off the provisions of his own
herds and flocks, his orchards and vineyards, wasting away
the inheritance of our son Telemachos and showing evil
intentions and indignity in courting me, his untiring wife.

And so I called to all my remaining servants and handmaidens
and set them to polishing the claw-footed tables and chairs
and setting out the stores of bronze vessels edged
in gold, the platters and bowls marvelously wrought in silver
for mixing sweet wine. Also the two-handled cups,
pitchers and golden plates for feasting that I had hidden
in inner chambers until his homecoming. I sent some women
to gather fragrant grasses and herbs, and shining blooms
to adorn the great hall, whose tall bronze doors
I now had these women throw open to the stirring air.
For suddenly, it seemed, the springtime of our youth was returning also.
And I sent Medon swiftly on my own errand.

I called for Aktoris, lame daughter of a manservant, whom once
I asked to bring with me out of my father's household
because she was scorned there. She bathed me and anointed me with oil,
unbinding my hair so it fell about my neck and shoulders.
We arranged it loosely, in the way I wore it before my beauty
and figure were ruined with the passing of years and the constant devising
of schemes to keep my household and estates well settled.
I put on my sheerest and most elaborately woven robe
and came down from my upper chamber to see all
the chairs covered in fleeces, the cressets alight
and a great fire burning for when my husband and his men should return
to sacrifice and roast the choice thigh pieces for our feasting.

4

Now when Odysseus entered the hall he was amazed.
As a man who has been walking in a mist and suddenly the mist clears,
he looked about him. He turned and spoke to me, saying:
'Surely some one of the gods has been with you for you
have changed. Lately your eyes were red with weeping, your face
had a long sadness upon it. But I remember well
how you looked when I went away in the hollow ships with the Argives
and now all that youthful magnificence has returned.'

    And both our eyes filled and overflowed
but I could not keep a smile within me, so I turned
my face aside so that none might see it. Now Telemachos
stepped between the high columns and looked in amazement
for he knew me not as I was now, but remembered me weeping
and lamenting as I showed myself throughout his youth. Odysseus
called to him, to Eumaios, the staunchly faithful swineherd,
and aged Dolios, together with his loyal sons, and to all
his eager henchmen. He bade them kill and sacrifice
the best of his flocks, fat sheep, a towering ox,
goats and swine. The men stepped quickly and did
his bidding, prepared for joyous feasting with full abandon
as had not been known in the palace during my husband's absence.

    Now came also Laertes, respected father of Odysseus.
He had always preferred to stay away on the estates
tending his bounteous orchards with his own hard labor
and skill. I kissed his head and eyes and made much of him.
I drew him to the most elaborate chair beside the high throne
of his regal son. Odysseus spoke to me, saying:
'You are so strange. On the way returning with my father
there came my herald Medon, who would not return with us
but said he was bound on winged feet to do your bidding.'

    I took my place by the pillar that supports the well-joined
roof of the lofty house and answered him with measured words:
'Great Odysseus, much longed-for husband and lord,
do not be angry with Medon, nor scold me. You have been
long away from Ithaka and our besieged household.
Of all your servants, he has been the most loyal

to me, beside faithful Eurynome, my own Aktoris
and beloved nurse Eurykleia, who knew you first by your scar.
Now, as you came with your noble father and the good men
of Ithaka for sacrifices, feasting and libations to the gods,
I sent Medon out again to our wide-spread estates
and bade him return with all the maidservants thereabouts
to replace those traitorous women of your household who died with the suitors.
For I would have this homecoming be truly fit for the hero
returned to relieve his household with such glorious dispatch.'

    Medon came in with twelve women from the country and these
carried with them sweet-meats and dried fruits, nuts
and curd and strained honey, and they joined the work willingly.
I signaled to steadfast Eurynome who with the women,
clad in their finest robes, brought around pitchers
to pour water over the silver bowls for the men to wash.
They brought in baskets piled with loaves, and olives
and many savory provisions that we had kept hidden, locked
behind the barred doors of a high storeroom while the arrogant
suitors were a plague in my household. Telemachos looked on
in puzzlement, but Odysseus laughed and nodded. He called Medon
to him and spoke to him and sent his herald on his own errand.
When the men had roasted the meats and offered sacrifices
to the gods they poured wine from the mixing bowls and pitchers
of silver into the handled goblets, and each guest
drank and ate as he wished. Then began the music.

    But when it was time for the dancing to begin, Odysseus signaled
the singer Phemios to stop his playing. He spoke, saying:
'Good friends, you ask me to recount to you the story
of my long years away from Ithaka's shores, of the great deeds
of the Achaians who hurled our strength from the hollow ships
for ten years against the walls of Ilion, until
with wiles and cunning far surpassing the seers' warnings
we beguiled open the gates and stormed her from within.

    'And I would tell you also the tale of my long years
of voyaging, of the wonder-filled shores, cities where language
upon language is spoken, the seas wide and treacherous

6

with many strange islands and inhospitable coasts
where with my companions I labored mightily and resourcefully
always for our homecoming to our own Ithaka. But
the gods had willed it otherwise, setting before us obstacles
and sharp calamity, sweeping the men relentlessly away
with ships and spoils and gifts of tribute and glorious hospitality.
As a great stallion who heedlessly grazes the meadow
pricks his ears to the buzzing of flies around his flanks
and he flicks his tail ceaselessly lest they settle on him,
but with each sweep he dashes to the ground many, lifeless,
so the gods in their wrath smashed the breath from my companions
singly and they were sent down to Hades in piteous swarms.
This will take many an evening to tell and enliven
torch-lit hours after the sacrifices and feasting are done.
For though I have told it before this, yet it is sweet
to tell, and I will tell it gladly, for now it is over.'
At these words from my hero's lips I could not keep
my secret joy within me, and turned aside to smile.

    'I alone have returned to steep-rising Ithaka, but not
empty-handed. Even now comes my herald, Medon,
returned at his lord's bidding with wondrous gifts and prizes
from my journey's last adventures. And these far exceed in richness
all those which I and my companions carried with us
as our share of the spoils from Troy's abundant storerooms
when we had sacked her. These I have brought to the shores of our own
light-mantled Ithaka where I put them away in a secret place.
So now, herald Medon, bring on the treasures you have fetched.'

    Now here, returned, was faithful Medon, standing
at the bronze threshold of the thronged hall before his master.
He entered, leading a string of retainers bearing
a seemingly endless procession of great cauldrons and tripods,
shining bronzes of fine quality and craftsmanship,
deep jars in strange shapes with quantities of oil and wines,
finely wrought wine sieves and ladles of silver and gold,
fleeces, hinged chairs, and lengths of cloth. Medon himself
brought in a chest tied with its complex knot. This

I recognized, for only Odysseus and I knew its design.
      I stepped forward then, ready to help with the knot.
But he held me back, and seizing his sword he cut it quickly.
He raised the lid to reveal a trove of surpassing splendor –
silver and bronze edged in gold and the lovely cup
presented to Odysseus by King Alkinoös himself. He drew them
out triumphantly, setting them in front of Laertes, Telemachos
and all present. Then he turned to me and spoke, saying:
'My queen, yours is this robe wrought by Alkinoös' queen
with her daughter, Nausikaa, and laid by the queen's own hands
inside.' He lifted it out of the chest, a beautiful robe,
fine-woven and richly worked. He held it toward me,
but then looked back into the deep recess of the chest.
      'This is so strange,' he said wonderingly. He reached
again into the coffer. He drew out two robes,
delicate and diaphanous as the webbed fin of a small fish
or a butterfly's wing, and sea-colored. One was light, the other
darker, and together they dazzled the eye with color and design.
'Surpassing strange. For in my own sight did Alkinoös
and the queen, his wife, put away the splendid gifts in this chest.
Yet never did I see, nor with my ears heard I account
of these beautiful robes. And can they be for you? For they
would become you better were you still the young bride I left
when I went away in the ships nearly twenty years ago.'
But he put them into my hands, together with the wine-dark robe
from the hands of the queen and Nausikaa, and I took them, wondering to myself.
      Then Telemachos, son of our youth before his father
departed with the Argives in the black ships for the siege of Ilion,
stood before us and spoke in wonder and amazement, saying:
'I too have abundant treasures to show to this assembly.
For when I journeyed from home with Mentor to seek news
of you, illustrious Father, I came into the halls
of Nestor, breaker of horses, glory of the Achaians.
And there, well provided with chariot and horses and escort,
I traveled even to the courts of great King Menelaos,
shepherd of the people and beloved by Zeus, father of Helen.

She, of the fair cheeks and white arms, shining
among women and goddesses so that men and gods, cities and countries
have vied and perished for her, sat radiant beside her husband,
both returned from Ilion and restored each to the other.
He, out of the abundance of his echoing palace, splendid
as that of the gods on Mount Olympus, gave me gifts.
And Helen herself sent a robe of lovely design, the finest
of many she had woven on her loom. She spoke to me, saying:
"Take this also, a gift from my own hands to remember me by.
Keep it for your wife to wear on the lovely occasion of your marriage."
       'But when I, along with my good companion Peisistratos, son
of Gerenian horseman Nestor, was returning homeward in our chariot,
we took refuge at sunset from the darkened ways in the hospitable
house of Diokles, as we had done on the outward journey.
And this man's wife, Narcethe, skilled with the distaff, questioned me
endlessly to learn of lovely-haired Helen. She would not rest
until I drew from the chariot's traveling basket the robe
that was placed in my hands by the far-sung queen herself
so she could admire and finger its figured border.
Because she in her house had received us so heartily, generous
with her provisions, I thought to loosen the robe from its folds
so that she might see and wonder at the fine weaving
and surpassingly lovely design. And it fell from my hands and shimmered,
dazzling us all. But here is a puzzling thing. From within it,
softly as a dove's feather molting, fell two robes
besides, also finely woven, like those brought you
by my noble father. But I think that these also are unsuitable
for you, my mother, although lately you are much improved
from your stooping and long face. So I wonder, deep in my spirit,
who the two young maidens are for whom these are intended
and what the gods mean by this strange coincidence?'
For once Odysseus was struck dumb. He looked to Laertes,
his wise old father, in a questioning glance. Perhaps
he had seen how that venerable's eyes were fixed on me.
       So I went and stood by the pillar that supports the high roof
of the house in all its joinery and spoke, smiling to them and saying:

'Great Odysseus, noble and long-awaited husband,
and Telemachos, son of his youthful vigor and worthy heir,
you have both returned to these halls having accomplished much
in your journeying and manly deeds and with excellent treasures
of surpassing worth and usefulness, delightful to behold.
For my part, I have spent the years waiting here,
watching long over the provisions and careful maintenance
of these halls for your safe homecoming and your maturity.
But I too have treasures to present and bestow upon you,
and I think that you will find these richer, lovelier and more delightful
by every measure than any you might in your hearts imagine.
My husband, my son, here now are my treasures.'

° II °

FROM BEHIND watchful Laertes, where he turned to draw them forth
with his own regal hands, came two lovely maidens
out of those twelve brought to augment my serving women.
These easily outshone all the others in beauty,
stature and in womanly poise, and all present saw it
and were sending them admiring glances and whispering. Telemachos
had been struck hard. Even Odysseus leaned toward them.
I mounted the platform with joy in my heart ready to burst
from the cage of my breastbone on soft-feathered wings or a shower
of petals, like bubbles rising to froth on a tumbling stream.
    'Noble Odysseus, my husband and father of our son Telemachos,
here are your own twin daughters, born to us
in your absence and waiting dutifully always for your homecoming
and lordly recognition. I name them Nerianne and Ailanthis.'
My daughters, standing gracefully by his right hand, were overcome
at his godlike stature and majesty. They knelt before their sire,
finally returned to know them and bestow his fatherly blessings.
I reached to them with my hands and stepped between them, saying:
'Telemachos, these are the sisters you have not known before.'
    All who were present in the hall were stricken to a silence echoing
as when the great blood-red sun is lying on the hills;
then the tall cedars close to the well-joined eaves of the house,
where a thick tumult of sparrows has been seething and settles
with wild cries, are suddenly hushed. The ear hears
the raucous noise as if for the first time, although flown,
together with the strange quiet. Throughout the house
with its flares and cressets vying with shadows in a wild dance,
light darted from gleaming bronze and silver vessels edged
in gold and the glowing russet wine of a hundred cups

11

halted between polished table and shining lip. Light flashed
from the cloak-pins and belts of the warriors, ear-pendants and girdles
of the women, from my son's dark curls and rings,
and my husband's sandal thong, silver-handled sword and wrist-cuff.
It glinted from the widened whites of his eyes. All were stilled.
Odysseus' eyes held mine in a deeply pondering look
while none moved. Not one spoke or turned,
or sank to chair; no notes played from Phemios' lyre,
no footfall or sip was heard in that space.
    Now Laertes, Odysseus' proud old father,
kindly and respected by all, stirred. Bearing himself erect
and lordly as ever I saw him, he approached Ailanthis,
of the gray eyes and sparkling wits, nearest him. He took
her outstretched hands, raised her up and conferred her to me.
He next inclined his look to Nerianne, gold of hair
and golden, too, of voice, though speechless now, fearful
in her father's gaze. I took her hands besides, and dear Laertes,
stepping back, signaled his son to greet them
and accept their bow. He had to, for each bore features
that startled his fatherly gaze as if from the smoothest mirror
of polished bronze. Odysseus stood, and from those eyes which had seen
so much of the world and its wonders, its trials and terrors, danced
the brightest of lights in all the now resounding hall.
He took them both into his great embrace and kissed each gently.
He held them forth and looked, then kissed again.
    The rise and fall of wonderment became a tumult. Then he spoke,
saying: 'You are so surprising, my queen. But you spoke rightly.
For surely this must be the greatest prize
a man could encounter upon return from voyaging, his treasure
multiplied. Not twice, but thrice the youthful riches
await his approving eye at his homecoming as he reassumes
his throne. Telemachos, my son, bestir yourself! Come
stand beside me. Greet my daughters, your beautiful sisters!'
Telemachos, the wondering on his face changed suddenly to delight,
sprang to his feet, and gave his sisters a brotherly greeting.
    Now all in the palace marveled and exclaimed aloud,

and the joyful rise and fall of their wonder and merriment flickered
like the catching of fire in freshened cressets and new-brought torches
so the shadows seemed to dissolve in the laughter and all was bright.
Odysseus glanced at his smiling father and stepped forward
to silence the jubilant throng. He gestured, making ready
to speak. But, while no tears flowed down his glowing cheeks,
as would ill befit the hero returned to claim his household,
no words would rise to his tongue, so caught was my great
wandering seafarer in the net of his own emotions.

 It was Laertes, our mainstay, who quieted the throng, saying:
'Hear me now, you loyal and steadfast friends of my house,
its sons – and daughters! For these are indeed the daughters
of this house. I myself cared for them and raised them in secret
on the estate, together with Antikleia my departed queen.
We did not bring them in to the city, and this was according
to the wishes of their prudent mother, Penelope, and our plan with her.
But I think that this is a story which she can tell best
since it is a tale of her designing. Sit, good people.
Pour for them more of the sweetest wine of twenty years,
you heralds and serving women, for even I, who know this story,
will gladly enjoy it in the telling when it is fully told by her.'

 They did as he bade them although they stared and whispered, amazed
at so astonishing a turn. And all around I heard
the scraping of chairs pulled closer, settled into, creaking,
as I drew my breath and pondered how to speak, seeing
Odysseus' fine eyes full upon me, questioning,
from his high seat. Telemachos then, at his father's signal,
placed gra-eyed Ailanthis in the chair beside her father
that had been his. He drew another close for Nerianne
and himself sat at the feet of their father as I stirred to speech.

 For had I not known deep in my breast and my mind
that this time would come? Had I not often rehearsed
this moment in my dreams, journeying toward this light in my spirit,
restless as my husband's as he made his way home?
Had I not uttered before these same words, which echoed
inside my ears and behind my brow as I raised my eyes,

stood tall, and spoke in a soft voice, which nevertheless
reached far into the corners of the chamber, saying:

'Odysseus, what you have heard is true. I tell you now
the rest. For as you climbed aboard the black ships
with those men willing to sail for Troy in their eagerness
for glorious deeds, honor and booty, you never imagined
how long and treacherous, hard and unpredictable the outcome
of such undertakings is. Nor could you know you had already
sown two far greater triumphs to be sung of, along with
Telemachos, your first born. I did not know it then myself,
and took the signs for grieving's wrack on my body. I lay
so ill, so wretched, finally I feared my strength would fail
and leave your son uncared-for, his heritage to spoils
and you supplanted in the halls reserved for your return.

'So I went to the estates with Laertes. There your mother, Antikleia,
guessed my state. She, from whom your shrewdness came in part,
divined the measure of it soon – that two should be born together.
This is rare, so strange a portent that we feared
to show it to the people lest they rise in terror or make of it
some pretext of scandal for punishing our house and seizing
your power. How we felt your absence then, for their sake.
As soon as they were born I left them to be governed by your mother
and steadfast father. I returned to these courts with our unwitting son,
eager to retain for him his birthright in this palace
where already some usurpers thought to sit. Only your old nurse,
loyal Eurykleia, knew of it, she who recognized you when you returned
by that scar you received on Parnassos' slopes as a youth
but she kept your return secret for you. She returned with us to care for
Telemachos and succor me with wise counsel and cheer
in the running of your house. And she governed things well, especially when
I managed to slip away to visit our unlucky daughters,
cruelly separated from family and birthright by chance and the fate
devised for them when the gods denied their father's homecoming.

'For without their powerful father, who would be able to keep them
from the bondage of the unprotected, the whims of suitors? You know
most of the story of the years since the fall of Ilion when all

the other heroes returned with their ships, their men and plunder
and still you did not return to your waiting family and lands.
Your mother despaired of you at last, and died grieving, though not
before she had bestowed upon your daughters knowledge, graces and manners
equal to a prince's, equal to your son's. I raised him myself,
and did all I could, with Eurykleia's help. For she guarded
my honor when the suitors filled the palace, with their pressing arrogance.
Together we kept them competing, one against the others, for the merest
glimpse of me behind my veils or descending the tall staircase to appear
at their rabbling feasts upon enough occasions to keep them hoping.

‘And she gave out that tears and lamentations were filling my days
and nights, while in secret I went to my girls. But then some ruse
was suspected – it was necessary to allow the suitors to find me
unraveling my weaving, for they had begun to suspect deceit
far closer to the truth and more dangerous to our concealment
of your daughters. For who could have long held back three of us
from those men for whom despoiling your substance, the provisions
of your house, were but foreshadowing and palliative to lust?
For these daughters I had in mind better things of my own devising.

‘From this time it was impossible for me to leave the palace.
So alone your stately father, skilled in the growing of vines
and cultivation of orchards and knowledgeable of all green-growing things,
had charge of these maidens. They learned well, and they comforted him,
and he them, for the loss of your mother now in Hades.
But I, caught at last in the knot of my own tale,
was constrained now to remain here in the city, in these halls
filled with the endless feasting and raucous strutting of men
repugnant to me. I felt more alone than ever, and finally
began to live my ruse, so that tears and lamentations were lately
more real than before. Meanwhile, Phemios, skilled with the lyre,
was called to the estates to console Laertes with the gift
of singing. Only he could go back and forth. He,
who is gifted with knowing deep in his spirit, guessed our secret.
He saw the likeness in the brows, the set of the eyes or chin,
the shining intelligence of the two lovely young maidens
who were favored in Laertes' household. He comforted them greatly, singing

and carrying messages between us all. For he was also the singer
for those haughty suitors and had to return often.

    'But his songs fell on swine ears. Only I
was attuned to the new sadness in his tales and despaired.
This brings my story nearly to these last few days. How
I sorrowed and truly wept when Telemachos also left
you may surmise. But all seems now like shadows, deepened
throughout the night while the evening fires dwindled and died,
but dispelled at sunrise.' Telemachos again sprang up to say:
'So these must be the maids for whom those robes from Menelaos'
Helen were sent. I give them gladly to my sisters. But, hear
now, hard Mother, how is it you chided me
for journeying, for leaving you alone without your knowing,
when I was come of an age to look after my father's business
and that of my own house? For you have kept secrets from me –
these sisters, the delight and comfort they would have brought
while you were far away on other long journeys.'

· III ·

THUS HE SPOKE, and I was amazed. I stored his words
away to ponder in my heart later, and spoke to him quickly,
saying: 'My dear son, you speak as though you had a cause
for bitterness in your heart. It is true you were never able to know
your sisters, nor they you, save for one visit to the estates
when you were still a child. Even then you were struck
with their charms as you were tonight; but of course you have forgotten it.
While we were gone, evil plotters found our absence
the excuse to lay troubles at the gateway of your father's house.
Never again could you, the heir to his power and substance,
be absent. Nor could I leave the city openly
to visit your father's aging parents in the country.
If there is bitterness in your heart for being left
out of the secret let it loose to run from you never
to return, like a fleet-footed dog that has proven untrainable.
For consider that you have been here, recognized as your father's

17

heir, respected and tutored in all disciplines and delights
by the best counselors, never lacking in comforts and amusements.
You always had power and possessions to look forward to
while they received second best. Nor could they know you.

   'As for long journeys on my part, you are mistaken.
My journeys were made within the span of only days.
And under wise Eurykleia's schemes and watchful eye
you almost never knew I was not here lamenting
and wetting the soft coverlets of your father's bed with tears.
I think that now you are speaking out your childhood imaginings.'
Next my perceptive husband, with grace about him like a god,
rose and clasped our son's shoulder, and spoke to him, saying:
'Surely this must be so. It is painful to me, now
I am returned, to hear how all of you have suffered.
And who can say which among us has suffered more than the others
until now, when the gods have brought about our happy union?

   'I see that these well-crafted robes, fashioned
by Alkinoös' queen herself with her daughter, and laid in secret
under my own knot, are also destined for you,
O my daughters, shining among my treasures, loveliest
among all maidens around the wide-ridged seas.
Telemachos, my son, you must let me examine your mother
in the ways that a man and woman have to know each
the secrets of the other. For I see that she has been sorely tried,
and the spirit within her scarcely knows how to assay
the silver of this moment against her woman's heart,
leaden so long. Come now, let us all go forth,
to the well-leveled courtyard. It is time for the music to begin,
for the well-tuned lyre to ready your hearts for singing and dancing.'

   It was a rapturous evening, and perhaps what has been told
in the past, of the gods holding back the chariot of the rising
young Dawn so that we mortals might savor some moment
of particular sweetness, was true. For while no night
could be long enough to contain the full unraveling of so much
delight, intricately woven with the tissue of hopes and fears
and pricked with suspense, I had a sense of the time

behind us, and therefore of time ahead, which would unspool for us.
    And I spoke to my husband, much-enduring Odysseus, and told him.
But he shook his head – too much had unwound too quickly; he did not
wish to witness the flickering, one by one, of the torches,
nor to see the smoke wraithing from gray ashes before dawn.
Well before the sky gave up its deepest black, the stars
still suspended across the billow of night like the knots
of a net, my lord signaled an end to the dancing, saying:
'Dear friends, it is time to offer to the gods the sacrifices due them.
May the gods grant to us all favor and an end to hardship,
good reputation and, to these, my beautiful daughters, husbands,
lordly and among the noblest sons of those we would so favor.
Soon I will make the hecatombs, one hundred oxen for the gods
who have counseled and protected my household in my absence,
and have led me at last to this joyous feasting. Now, to rest.'
    Odysseus rose and descended from the dais to lead the way
for each to return to his own dwelling place to sleep.
I had a bed prepared for Laertes on the deepest side porch
and Eurykleia attended him. I had also made arrangements
for my daughters to sleep in my old high chamber.
Here was where I spent so many hours at the distaff and loom
while pondering their fate and lamenting their necessary exile,
their father's long absence, the threats to his household
and to their inheritance, while weaving my strong designs for their future.
I had beds made for them, covered with the finest cloth
in two shades of Dawn's own purple. And these
Eurynome covered with the softest fleeces, and with them
yet another fine-textured covering from my loom.
For this was my daughters' first night under the high roof
of their own strong-founded house. This was their first night
spent with their father, mother and brother here in the palace.
And they went up like brides on their father's and brother's arms,
following as I led the way up the high staircase with Eurynome.
Then Odysseus, their true father, set a watch over them
before he led me to our own deeply cushioned marriage bed.
    And this was a night like none before it. Surely

some goddess or other spirit cast a spell about us.
For it was as if my powerful hero had been graced with an aura
of manly beauty, of prowess and firm bearing matching
that of our first night of lovemaking long ago.
Alone together, within the hidden recesses of rich
hangings and deep-folded fine cloths, with many
soft fleeces laid under and arrayed over, and drifted
about with the fragrance of hyacinths and lilies
I had strewn around the wide and handsome marriage bed
Odysseus himself built and joined tightly to the earth
by the strong bole of the olive tree, he and I
both felt desire urgent upon us as never before.
It was at once heavy as the scent of flowers on the evening dew,
yet lifting us as lightly as the wings of swallows rising
on blue spirals of the sun's devising. He whispered to me secretly
and softly, ceaselessly and strong within the dark warm
folds of the night – that I was for him as he was for me:
both young and matchless in form, as in our youth,
until the ageless Dawn slipped in her cool fingers and drifted
sleep over us, quiet, restful and breathing contentment.

    Yet when we had had our fill of sleeping side by side
and were refreshed, by some magic the day was still new.
Our children had thought what to do next, and their minds were as one.
They persuaded Laertes to remain with us here in the palace
to lend counsel to his son. For much was needed to restore
order in our house, in the council halls, and in the populace.
Already my daughters had busied themselves, with Eurynome, seeing
to the order of the house after all the feasting. My son, with Eurykleia,
had made ready rooms for Laertes on the shaded side of the house.
Laertes and Ailanthis were gone out of the gate to the gardens
lying nearby on the slope of the valley, and were seeing to their care.
Telemachos was receiving deputations for his father. Nerianne
was in a far corner of the great house with Phemios, her teacher.

    Odysseus was amazed. He spoke to me somewhat harshly saying:
'I see that this house has been too long without its master.
For never in times past would the herald have failed to awaken me.

Now the young Dawn has fled and Helios has set his dominion
in the sky, cleared of early mists before I ever set foot
outside our chamber.' But I spoke to him quickly saying:
'Do not be angry with me, dear husband, and do not chide
faithful Medon. You lingered in sleep at my request.
You have been long away, tossed on the wide seas;
you have suffered griefs and endured hardships as no man
has before you. Nor do I think that any other
could return to his country and his house and, finding it besieged and unruly,
dispense so quickly with so many foes, and these
so entrenched. I remember well how your old wound begins
to sap your strength and hinder you after great trials.
I wanted you to taste the sweetness of a well-earned rest.'
    Odysseus gazed in thoughtful silence for some moments.
Our son Telemachos approached us then. My resourceful lord
then laughed loudly and turned toward me saying:
'You are so strange, my matchless queen. I see that there is still
much I need to examine you about when next we are alone.
It seems that when a man returns home after long years
away he has more to do than I imagined to master again
his own household, nor did the gods reveal it to me.
But here comes my worthy son. It is time for him
and me to exchange counsels and plan what is best to do next.
I leave you to look after my possessions, my father and my daughters.
Come now, my son, tell me what good men
are left, and tell me about them, so I can know how many
there are to help me establish my power again. But first
it is right that you greet your resourceful mother before she withdraws
to her high chamber to take up again her distaff and her weaving
with your lovely sisters, and soon they will match her in craftsmanship.'
    But Telemachos held back, so I spoke to him, saying:
'My thoughtful son, you have been deceived and hurt
by my scheme, deprived as you were of the knowledge of your sisters.
Within days of his homecoming, your long absent
father learned of his daughters. Far away he could not
have heard it sooner, but was told even as you were, who suffered

those years of trials and uncertainty with me. And never
would you say the word to send me away back to my father.
Nor did you force me to marry and leave our house and our hopes.
Your sisters, your grandparents and I took comfort and strength
from each other, but you had to test your strength alone
against the arrogance of grown men who beset our house.
Often I wished I could tell you. Can you understand this?'

    'Oh heartless mother, since you speak of it, I will be truthful.
I wish you had told me. It is hard to think that during those days,
while I suffered the taunts and insults of outrageous suitors plotting
my undoing, I was denied the knowledge that would have kept
my spirits high. Already I sense in my sisters kindred spirits
I sorely missed. It is hard, Mother, for me
to understand why you did not tell me when I
had come of age. I think that perhaps I never shall.'

So I HAD much to ponder in my heart and mind as I climbed
the staircase again. But this time I awaited the light-heeled steps
of my daughters, and soon Nerianne came to me, saying:
'My brother sent me to you, dearest Mother. Is this not a dream
made real? For all your hopes, for all your faith and strength,
I sometimes did not even dare to think about this day.
Now we are here. All home. We are together. Does
your heart not sing like mine, and can you keep from dancing
as you walk these smooth floors? Oh, Mother, do I annoy you
with my joyous babble? At last I have such happy songs
within my heart, and you nearby to hear them!'
    I embraced her then and kissed her head, and from my eyes
the warm tears flowed, and from hers also. But when
we had put aside our desire for weeping, I spoke to her saying:
'Sing you may, trusting daughter, and soon. Your father,
noble Odysseus, has said that he will question you with Ailanthis
today as we feast. I, too, am eager to hear your songs.
For too long have I only had reports from Phemios.
I would hear for myself now, but will share this treasure of yours
with your father. Tell me, my child, are you not distressed
that I kept you away from your splendid home for so long?'
'Dearest Mother, how can you think it? I see that your design
was the only way it all could be accomplished. For did not
the goddess herself approve all that you devised? And thinking
of this matter, will it not be hard to make the journey
we must undertake and leave this joyful house
and family, so newly found and bound together? How
will this happen? How will you bear to leave?' I answered her saying:
'There is time, now, for all to be accomplished, though we cannot

presently see the way. I will speak to your father soon.'
Then we two continued to converse on many matters
pent up in our hearts while events had kept us apart.

    Soon the banqueters came in, driving the sheep before them.
The men piled faggots high, slaughtered the sheep, and prepared
the spits for roasting. The women brought food with them
and maidservants set the benches, chairs and tables close
and brought the mixing bowls, wine, cups and platters,
baskets of bread and other provisions for the generous feast.
And the hour of gathering brought us together again in the great hall.
I descended the tall staircase with Nerianne, delight
singing in my heart for her close companionship beside me.
There we encountered Ailanthis, returning with beaming Laertes.
Next came Telemachos, walking now with his father's bearing.
Now came Odysseus, parting a way among the men
and women, both again under his powerful sway like small
boys playing in a courtyard, who stop their games
to make a pathway for an older, taller youth
since he deigns to speak to them and not to jeer or chide.
Odysseus had the servants place two chairs beside him.
And in them he placed our two shining daughters.

    And I noticed that he leaned first to one side and then
to the other from the moment when the serving women first
brought in the basins and golden ewers and held them out
for him to wash his hands until the last libation was poured.
Until the last notes of Phemios' lyre had died away
and the guttering torches were lifted high to lead the last
knots of revelers out of the wide portal and to their couches
he attended each daughter equally. And this tenderness
cast for me an aura of grace around him surpassing
any man, even the firm-loined youths of Ithaka,
Telemachos' friends, and even our handsome son himself.
I felt the heart in my breast swell, and could scarcely
hold within me the desire to be his again, alone in our chamber.

    When we had put our hands to the good things before us,
Ailanthis turned and spoke aloud to her father, saying:

'Father, you have questioned us about our years
on the estate with our grandparents, Laertes and Antikleia –
how I wish she could be with us still. Now I, for one,
am eager to hear you tell the tale of the wanderings
you spoke of, the more since I have been raised away in the country.
For while Phemios sang to us the latest tales of the battles and deeds
of the heroes in far Ilion, I wish you would tell us
of the many lands you visited, the people who greeted you there,
whether their customs were like ours and whether you spoke to them
easily and were well received.' Then Laertes, Telemachos,
Nerianne and all assembled agreed and urged him to tell it.
    So he began and all in the hall were silent, straining
forward on benches and chairs, from fleeces piled near the hearth
and standing beside the columns and in the doorways, enthralled.
And he spoke so movingly and well that we who heard him
felt the full drama of it, the excitement, valor, comradeship,
the horror, tedium and misery of the ten long years
before the walls of Troy, and then the glory of victory,
the pleasure in the spoils. We felt how eagerly the Argives set
their sails for the journey home. We marveled at the seas' capriciousness,
at the numerous islands and far coasts with strange peoples
and stranger beasts and monsters, at my ever-resourceful hero's courage
and endurance. And we wept for those companions lost through misfortunes
and their own recklessness, along with so many strong-benched ships
and all the plunder. We lived it fully, hearing even
the creak of the oarlocks and the wheels of Nausikaa's shining chariot.
We tasted the bitter medicines of Circe's island, felt
our skin pucker in the chill of the sea and the salt scurf,
heard waves dash cliffs at Scheria and longed for Ithaka,
nearly won when the thrashing seas snatched our men
away from the sight of our own bright fires to punish
them for years longer. Some of the listeners would have had it
go on and on, and to them the end seemed abrupt. All
sat in stunned silence for some moments, still
enmeshed in the story's spell. Then, as if stirred by the strokes
of a silver wand, we returned to our own minds and purposes

and again took up rejoicing for his story's desired end.
　　This bright occasion also folded its wings
and then we two were lighted to our inner chamber, torches
before and the cressets already lit to lick the walls
and ceiling with dancing tongues of light and fragrance
from the heady incense brought by Odysseus from the Queen of Scheria.
After we had taken our pleasure in each other's bodies,
our minds were also as one in the desire to exchange our thoughts.
Odysseus began it, when we could hold ourselves back no longer,
saying: 'You are so strange. I remember well how you were
when I left in the strong-benched ships for Priam's Troy.
In your beauty and stature you shone above all women. I never
saw any woman like you for poise or for steadfastness.
But you amaze me. I never thought more easily to vanquish
your scheming suitors than to take up the steering-oar in my own household
and be its helmsman again. You are full of surprises.
These daughters I cannot deny are mine, for they have
my features and my father's word on it. Nor would I wish to,
for they shine among all women. But I was far away
and sorely tried with all my travails. Therefore, though I wonder
at it in my heart, no rumor concerning them ever came to me,
for the gods did not wish to burden me with their fatherless plight.
But as for my son, who was with you all the while, he
was growing into powerful manhood. Surely he could have been told.'
　　I went to my curved-leg table of smoothest ebony
and held before me the mirror of polished bronze finished
in silver and worked with intricate designs on its reverse. I let down
my hair from the bands that held it high on my crown this night
and spoke to him saying: 'As for the gods, I cannot say why
they choose to reveal some things but keep others
hidden. I do know that I often considered telling our
son about his sisters' existence. I wished for them all
to be brought together. But you see Telemachos now,
when he has already become stronger and bolder
on his journey with Mentor, to Nestor, Lord of Gera,
and to King Menelaos and Helen in Sparta, to search for you.

From your example he has already grown in bearing
and confidence, and now he is not as I knew him before.
Although our household was his to inherit, it was mine to govern,
since he was cowed by his youth and by the numbers of raucous men,
and was confused in his duty to me. How could I be certain
he could withstand their bullying and follow my wishes to keep
his sisters unmarried until your homecoming? It is
a complicated matter, raising a son without a father's help.

   'Do you think it was easy to manage alone for all those years?
I did what I did because I had to.' I felt hot tears
pricking my eyelids and was amazed I could feel anger
toward my splendid husband, whose still glorious stature glowed
in my raised mirror by the light from the lamps. I saw him turning
toward me and a thoughtful look replaced the hardness tightening
his jaw. He looked over and saw my desire in the mirror. He laughed
and spoke soberly, saying: 'I think that there is much we have
still to learn from each other concerning these matters. O my lustrous,
my queen, Penelope, my shining one, we will speak more presently,
but for now let us return to our deep-corded marriage bed.'

   I turned, pretending still to be angry: 'And what, my Lord,
of *my* word?' My stately warrior, standing before me
in all his vigor, was resourceful as ever: 'You had only to tell me
here, looking into my eyes, they are my daughters,'
he said, and I melted. 'Besides, Ailanthis' eyes are gray.'
We both laughed then. And, lingeringly, we loved each other again.

   And when the young Dawn appeared, golden-tressed
and sparkling, with birdsong weaving the air between the eaves
of our well-built house, each of us was ready to part from the other,
to take up the distaff or the rod, the lyre, the keys to the storerooms,
to hold council and receive tribute, to oversee henchmen
or serving maids, or to order the day's observances and tasks.
And when all this was done, or humming in the doing, I climbed
the staircase to wait again in my high chamber for Ailanthis.

   'Dear Mother, you must be pleased now all
has unfolded as you hoped. How wise you were, and both you
and noble grandfather shine before us all, for strength

and courage like my father's. I told my father so last night.
He questioned me then about my powers – my virtues he called them.
He seemed amazed by my knowledge of growing things.
But I was careful, Mother, not to mention the plans
we have devised for our journey. I could see he knew nothing of it yet.
I think you must tell him soon, for he will be hard to persuade
if he has no hand in this, or if it comes up suddenly.'
      I answered her, saying: 'Have patience, dear. It will take time
and tact to bring about our appointed journey. You must
be mindful that, although you are young and eager to go out
into the world, I have two desires that must
be balanced. My spirit urges me to start on our journey, but my heart
would have me stay. Your father has just now enjoyed
his longed-for homecoming. How can I ask him to let us go
so soon? And also, I would stay for a time within
the encircling cords of his love and strength, before I yield
to that other purpose.' And she, always eager to put her days
to good use, spoke again, saying:
'Then, Mother, you must help me to persuade my father
that I must go out to the fields daily with my grandfather,
and even into the places among the high crags
away from the shore where hawks soar and no asphodel
grows, to glean from him all I can. For he is grown frail,
and I think that he may not live to see our next homecoming.'
She spoke heartily, and her eyes were bright with tenderness and zeal.
I was amazed and stored these serious words away
deep in my heart, where later I had cause to ponder them.
      I drew her to the high window where so lately I had sighed
and prayed for my relief, and spoke to her further, saying:
'Now that we have at last some time to speak together,
tell me something of what father Laertes has passed on to you
and what you make of it. For every generation builds the world
anew and you will find new worlds besides. I, too,
would know something of these matters.' And she was pleased,
and willingly told me all she could, while the sun blazed
its high hush over the myriad angled roofs

with tall cedars thrusting skyward among them and down
toward the courtyard where again the men began to prepare the fires.
    As always my women were smoothly performing their tasks within
the portals of the house, pouring water from the great jars,
grinding the grains from the storerooms, forming loaves
on their smoothed work stones with oil and water and salt
from my house's own salt pan facing the dry winds
from far Aithiopia. They were plucking the tenderest leaves of thyme
and mint to join with the meats, and young grape leaves,
taking olives and oil from jars and dried fruits
and spring greens so our house would be generous with its provisions.
    For my lordly husband had counseled with his revered father
and also with Telemachos, who added youthful strength
and daring to his father's fabled statecraft, while he studied closely
every subtlety of Odysseus' dealings with men.
In this my son was like a woman of the village who has been
to a distant well for water from the source, and arriving home
she drinks deep draughts to quench her thirst.
Now my husband drew to his council sessions the best men
in Ithaka and the neighboring islands, Same, Zakynthos, Doulichion.
This was to re-establish his power and dominion
over the land. My daughters and I, meanwhile, held
our own council, and by late afternoon we knew each other's minds.
Then I descended the staircase to preside over the last preparations
for that evening's feasting in my well-ordered household.
    And soon, with all in readiness, my serving women brought in
the bowls for our guests to wash and poured the water over their hands
from the silver pitchers. Then they began to distribute breads
from their baskets, and the other good things from our careful provisioning.
My husband sacrificed the choicest thigh pieces to the mighty gods
who had finally granted him favor and a glorious homecoming.
When all had feasted and drunk as much as they desired, Odysseus
looked down from his platform to Phemios. He signaled, and spoke, saying:
'Singer, let us hear again the new songs that circulate
among the listeners. For although there is much that is always sad
to my ears, yet would I still hear over and over

the glorious deeds and the names of my comrades among the Achaians.
Come, good Phemios, bring out your lyre and begin.'
Phemios came near, carrying the marvelous lyre
Odysseus had presented him from among the treasures
given by King Alkinoös and his queen among the Phaiakians.
He bowed before Odysseus, but then he gestured to Nerianne.

◦ V ◦

Nᴇʀɪᴀɴɴᴇ sᴛᴏᴏᴅ and turned to her father with her eyes cast down.
Raising them and the chin that was molded from his own likeness
she spoke to startled Odysseus softly, yet with a resonance
that carried to the farthest corners of the hall where heads turned,
all motion halted as all the guests, the serving maids,
the stewards, petitioners and torch-bearers just now reaching
their faggots to light the cressets in the darkest corners, all
ceased their chatter. Nerianne looked into Odysseus' eyes
calmly and smiled, and I did also. She spoke to him, saying:
'Illustrious father, have you heard the people saying
that I have been blessed with the voice of a singer? And when you have asked
where I was in the house and how I busied myself
while the household was bent toward preparing the day's feasting, have you not
been told I was gone to a far chamber to sing with Phemios?
Still I think you are not prepared for the excellence of the singing
I have learned from him. Nor was it difficult for me to study

in secret far away from the city with the end of it as shrouded
in the distant future as the cliffs of high-echoing Neritos
in the morning mists. But it is hard to stand as a woman before
the greatest in the land and their consorts to chant men's stories.
And I never intended to do it without your pleasure in it.
Will you not give me your blessing, and ask me to sing for you?'

    Quick-minded Odysseus, stricken also to silent wonder
as serene Nerianne began her plea, needed no sign,
no help this time from Laertes, but rather sprang quickly,
almost like a youth, to his feet and answered her graciously. He had to.
'Oh beautiful daughter, you who are matched for youthful charm
in all the world only by this other goddess, your sister, sing.
For I would know you, take pleasure in your splendid treasure first,
as is my fatherly right, before bestowing it far
or near. Sing your songs for us, full and clear,
and hearken, all you Ithakans, and wonder as you hear.'

    Whereupon from behind the platform came stately Mabantha,
wife of Phemios. She held high her husband's clear-toned lyre,
the one he had carried with him often to the country estates.
She stopped at the edge of the platform. Her dark skin gleamed,
her singular headdress and robe of rich browns swirled
in strange borderless design and her red-gold bracelet
in the form of a serpent coiled around her upper arm.
As always she awed the company with her calm assurance and grace.

    She stood beside Phemios, holding the lyre she had brought him
and offered it to Nerianne who was stepping down to meet them both.
Nerianne stopped and raised her hands to her face, glowing
with pleasure, for this was a prize without price, the finest
Phemios had ever found in his youthful wanderings. He now
struck up Odysseus' even finer one, and began. He sang
of the black ships filling with hot-blooded men,
of the myriad journeys over tossing seas converging
on that one dark shore where so many great heroes,
husbands, fathers, grandfathers, sons and secret sweethearts,
urged each other on to their brave, foolhardy deeds
while the years rolled onward like the wheels of a well-built chariot.

Parts of his song we had heard before, the tales of those
long returned that the singers first circulated
among the listeners. But Phemios was no ordinary singer.
　　Already he had joined my hero's tale to the songs
of the others, artfully intertwining as if they made a tapestry
of sound and color, and in this he was aided by clear-voiced Nerianne.
She joined in the singing, sometimes in concert with her master.
At other times her voice, gaining always in richness
and assurance, was interwoven with the notes of the lyre alone
and it was impossible to tell whether this was by instinct or by design
worked out between them during the daylight hours, so intricate
was the pattern, so alternately bold and sweeping, then intimate,
complex and simple, triumphant then humble, exultant then sad,
colorful, full of motion and perfectly pitched to the ears
of each listener thrilling to this first hearing. And none
was more amazed than my husband who sat entranced, forgetting
his lordliness in the sway of the song's unwinding, and wondering
at its marvelous fabrication. But then the song changed.
　　Nerianne sang it alone, and it was haunting and sinuous as fine
tissue running between the fingers like a cool stream.
And suddenly my majestic husband's face drew taut; suffering
cast its network of lines across his brow. He stirred,
twisted in his silver-studded throne and reached to signal us,
disturbed, amazed, and pained so that we all turned toward him,
afraid he was ill. Nerianne stopped her singing and questioned him,
saying: 'Dear Father, are you tired, or rather does our song
sadden you because so many of your dear companions were lost?
Shall we leave off our singing for tonight and take up the lyre again
tomorrow?' But my resilient hero recovered at once and noting
her perplexed tone, the disappointment brimming in her eyes,
spoke brightly, saying: 'Oh lovely one, look on this as nothing.
It is true that I am tired after my wanderings and grieve for my companions.
But I was enjoying your song from the moment Phemios first
struck the deep-toned lyre from Alkinoös' queen.
It rings deep within me, as if I were singing with you,
or as if an unseen goddess were playing with you on her own

other-worldly instrument. Consider it nothing. Continue.'
  Nerianne's face had softened as her father's frame relaxed,
at ease again. She looked to Phemios, who swept a chord
and nodded. Together they took up again the voyage
to Thrinakia from Circe's island. Once again we stirred
to their mingling voices, the lyre's delightful strains dissolving
all our thoughts, our cares, in thrall of the tale they wove for us.
Next Phemios, his lyre, then Nerianne's faded from sense
like breezes dying before a fiery sunset, and again we were enchanted,
leaning forward from every studded chair, rapt.
  But then a moan shattered the dusk. 'No more!
Stop, I implore you, stop!' Again Odysseus, our king,
my husband, warrior and hero, writhed in his throne. He gripped
its arms and turned his head first to the side, then
to the sturdy beams supporting the well-joined roof.
I was beside him quickly with Ailanthis and Laertes
when he spoke: 'That was the Sirens' song – you sang the song
the Sirens sang to lure me, taunt me, haunt me. How?
Who told you, taught you, since all men die who hear them,
drawn to those bone-heaped shores enchanted, never more
to leave. And only I survived, of all the heroes
returning with me to Ithaka who heard these maidens,
sea-witches who enchant weak and foolish men with their cries.
I heard the Sirens sing. It was music like this – infinitely
sweet, yet shaded with pain – that grips and haunts me still.'
  He shook his head, looked out steadily again, and then rose.
He swept his hand above the crowd for calm, and spoke,
saying: 'I think that this is playing and singing for another time.
For now, lovely daughter, be assured it is not your honeyed voice
I would stop from delighting the multitudes, but only this song. . .'
  Then Laertes moved to rise, but first Telemachos
was on his feet with princely grace and motioned to the heralds.
'Hero that my father is, he is a man and tires
as lesser men do also. You have heard his wracking tales
of glorious deeds, long trials and hardships driving
over the treacherous sea-ways raised always against him

34

by raging Poseidon. I think that the god is angry still
and demands further sacrifice. It is for me, as the son
of Odysseus, and my grandfather with me, to mix the wine,
ten measures of water with it only, and to pour a libation
before each man departs for his own house
to sleep there until clear-eyed Dawn calls
us together in the council chambers.' He spoke thus, descending
the steps of the high platform with a regal grace about him.
He motioned to Medon, our faithful herald, to go before
and to the stewards to bring the great mixing bowls and jars
of sweetest wine and measures of water out through the throng.
And they followed in his footsteps willingly. For all admired him, marveling
at his manly poise, and turning to discuss it one with another
they raised a babble as they clamored to follow him out
to the eave-framed courtyard. So skillfully did he turn
their attention to the next delightful ceremony they did not see
my husband avert his furrowed brow from Nerianne.

    She was stricken as by thunder itself, and stood like a hare
surrounded by eager hounds, whose slightest quiver may release
the next fury upon her. But Ailanthis rushed to her side
and held her, with Laertes. And he gently took from her hands
the inlaid lyre and returned it to Mabantha, Phemios' lady.
My hero groaned. Laertes motioned all away,
then nodded to commend him to my care and left us alone.

    I remember so well the retreating tumult, then
the murmuring voices of those dearest to me and my love
falling gently away and eventually severed by the clang
of the great bronze doors closing in the high portal.
I remember how dark the room seemed, how alive with shadows
leaping and reaching toward us from the wavering flames of torches
and lamps and the many cressets of well-worked bronze,
which hardly seemed to light the hall now it was empty
of the oiled faces, the shining ornaments and glinting movements
of women and men who had carried all gaiety away with them.
I remember that the flames hissed in the cressets and torches
so the lamps burning on the polished tables seemed eerie

in their silent flaring. It fell so quiet I could hear a slight
clink from a cauldron-chain still swinging from a tripod, and so lonely
that the flashing bats were as welcome as swallows in the courtyard at dusk.
    We sat for some time in the silence and our hearts were pondering.
I took my beloved's hand and soothed his body with my touch
until I felt the tension drain from his limbs and shoulders
as from a sickly child who resists sleep but yields
to caresses, then sinks at last into his fleeces.
Finally I spoke to him, saying: 'You are so strange.
It seems that you left out some parts in telling of your journey.
Scarcely did I hear you mention these Sirens; rather you passed
quickly from the end of your long detention by the fearsome hag
Circe to the grisly man-eaters on your way to Thrinakia's shore.
You are rightly acclaimed for your mastery in story-telling. I think it is not
like you to shrink from telling the whole of a story even
to me, although you have told it over before. Was it so horrible?
Were you so terrified you had to withhold the telling even
from me?' I spoke lightly, but even so his wrath was stirred.
    'Do you suppose, my queen, there is only one way
to tell a tale, and all of it in one telling? I told you
more than I can tell these men who need to know
that I am still the best among them if I am to be their King,
far more of my grief and suffering and pitiful drifting at the whim
of the jealous gods. For you are my wife, and tenderness
fills you to hear of my anguish. But I think there are some parts
of my journey which are best left untold, no matter who the listener
may be. And besides, I think that you also withheld
some parts when you recounted to me the years of your waiting
for my return.' I was confused and could only stare.
    He continued, saying: 'O my matchless queen, what
of Telemachos' tale? What of those long journeys of yours,
of the long days and nights he remembers being alone
in the halls but for Mentor and the thralls around him. These
are not easily explained away, since he was an observant child
who looked about him and saw how things were. And what
of the robes – two shining robes, priceless for beauty

and design, from the hands of Helen herself, although our daughters
were unknown even to the gods? And there are also the robes
from Alkinoös' queen, which she sent hidden at the bottom
of the chest I sealed with my own knot.' He sat erect
now on the studded throne, and stared intently, gray
eyes blazing into my bewilderment. I answered him, saying:
  'I have questioned also these things you speak of.
For they are beyond my understanding. Do you think
I could have left these halls, the watchful eyes
of all those eager suitors long enough to visit Helen,
longer still to venture to the shores of far Scheria
where Arete reigns with great Alkinoös? And what
of the singers – could no word escape the shroud of secrecy
over such journeys, neither make its way
among the sea-routes, down the plains, along the sky-winds,
nor echo on the rocky cliffs to reach the ears of the singers?
And would no jealous goddess or god have whispered it to you?
As for Telemachos, our son, he was a fanciful child
always. I think that he must be mistaken in this.'
  My thoughtful lord leaned toward me, saying:
'Penelope, my queen – my devious one – you forget
that no gods ever thought to tell me of these daughters either.
I think that there must yet be some way they mean
to punish me, some test or hardship I must yet endure.
For you have been hard with me, my wife, although circumspect,
by all accounts around the wide-ranging sea.
Yes, hard. And I know you have never told me all
that is in your heart. For answer me this. How is it you could name
Alkinoös' queen, Arete of the succoring heart, when I
have never named her to you? I think that no god
whispered this one detail from my story in your ear.'
The furrows on his forehead deepened but around
those gray eyes I saw soft lines of questioning.
  The heart within me fluttered wildly like a caged dove
before the deathlike grip of the captor's hand of bronze.
'Do not doubt me, Odysseus. Have you not told

us all the story of your stay in Scheria, how Alkinoös, Nausikaa
his daughter and his grateful queen received you kindly, welcomed you
and sent you on your way in their unerring ships with precious gifts?
I think that you have spoken her name, and this more than once.'
    I spoke thus, but I shuddered with strong doubts as I looked
into the glare of triumph on my husband's face. 'O Penelope,
do you think me so addled by wandering and hardship
I do not know what I have said? I never named her, and the heart
within me bounded when you did, like a doe's as suddenly the hunter
rises from behind a crag before her, so close
that all her senses sharpen to the dangerous lull before
as well as to the dodging ahead. At once I thought about how
to question you, and this seemed to me to be the best way –
I spoke to you again just now of the glorious robes from Helen
and Alkinoös' queen. I did not speak her name, yet you
were again enmeshed in your guise of guilelessness. You named her easily,
as if you had been with me. I think that there is more you have to tell me.'
    His eyes burned dark fire. He leaned toward me
nearly out of his throne, and as I had seen him many times
during the telling of his journey, he reached to his side
for the handle of his great bronze sword. This was too much.
My husband, my glorious hero, my lord – for whom I waited
and yearned, tossing in my bed where I clutched the cushions
to my breast and endured the longing that crept into my loins
for the best of the fresh young suitors who could have delighted me –
my Odysseus had found me out in my secret's maze and would not
be denied an explanation. I could no longer hold it within me,
nor stop the sudden burst of tears and lamentations
its suppression had cost me. And although I could feel the anger still hard
within him against my body, my Odysseus took me by the arms
and held me till the violent shaking that seized me drained from my limbs
and left the heart in me slack. 'Do not be harsh with me, Odysseus,
you who are the most understanding of men. What you say
frightens me terribly, for how then could I know it unless –
unless there is truth in what I am about to tell you, unless –
though it seemed to happen only in my darkest dreams – I have

betrayed you and my son. . .' He thrust me from him roughly, and descended the steps of the platform to their mid-point with heavy tread. There he sat, half turned away, to hear me.

· VI ·

'ONE NIGHT, and only one, – it seems a dream to think it –
once. . . But you will never understand unless I tell you how he won
my favor. This was a man unlike the rest, and differing
greatly also from you. In this he was attractive to me,
for I wished you had not gone with the Argives, and I cried out
endlessly my rage against our fate. O, I was not some sweet nymph
who would have held you here for pleasure only,
against your will and the dictates of Ithaka's honor. But still
I resented your decision to go. And sometimes it seemed,
in the darkest nights, in the third part when the stars burned sharp before
the early morning mists that shroud the couch from which
tremulous Dawn arises, I wakened as if in a dream, and I longed
for a different kind of a man. And it seemed that one
was close at hand. Among the suitors, arrogant shoats
from papless sows, not half-men by your measure, I had one friend.
He listened and was thoughtful. When he spoke he was discreet
and made good sense. It was he who held the others from their plotting
against us more than once, and he gave me strength. Oh,
I knew he too desired to win me over in his way,
by this sympathetic stance, and later . . . later he proved it.
    'But then he began to enter my dreams. You had been long away –
his face supplanted yours, and while I curled around your absent strength,
asleep in our strong-boled marriage bed, he came to me often.
At first he was a shadow, only someone strange, unknown,
who, when I woke, I could not name nor find
among men, like my youthful dreams of ideal princes lost.
But then the shadow took his form and name, and then he came.
How often I was tempted and about to yield to sweetness.
Then I would awaken, shaking in my disordered linen,

trembling for my near escape, for desire, and for your returning.
    'Then one night – Melantho, she, I discovered later,
who first betrayed our household, lying with Eurymachos and spying
for the suitors, had arranged it – he came to me unbidden in my chamber.
And this is how she accomplished it; she busied Eurykleia first
with our son, whose cup she filled brimful too often or with some
foul potion, felling him with sweating and a sickness. Next
she cast a potion into mine, so that I dragged myself, heavy with sleep,
along the corridor to our own bedroom and never cared
that Aktoris was not yet there guarding my door.
And whether this happened while she was still making her way
to me to guard me, or after she took up her post
I cannot tell, for she, too, was treacherously drugged.
Otherwise how could she fail to come to my cries and entreaties
yet be there when first dove called to the sky-mounting sun?
Yet he came to me in my bed, and this is how I knew it;
I chanced to find a cloak pin with the curved horn of a ram,
exactly like one he wore, lying in a fold of my coverlet.
He came to me, strong, overmastering, and I, in my drowsy state,
could scarcely tell whether I dreamed it, or perhaps
it was no dream but a waking vision. I screamed
and struggled, pleaded with him . . . then, it seemed, I submitted sweetly
as never before and dreamed no more until early light.
    'I remember the doves, the first call before light, the soft
answer in the hush when the owl had settled with a rush of wings
and the bats returned to hide under the wide frieze
of the cornice. I was awake and knew and didn't know
what seemed a dream. But I know this. I never dreamed
of him again. My only longings were for you and your homecoming,
only stronger than before.' I paused. My throat felt dry and tears
came unbidden to my eyes and wet my cheeks. The hall was dim.
    The cressets had gone dark, the lamps and torches guttered.
No light reflected from the scattered chairs, the pitchers
and basins of gold and silver, the mixing bowls. The nails
in my husband's stately throne, the sword at his side,
his dangled cup, and his handsome eyes were dull. He turned

and looked at me steadily and terribly with a hard set to his brow.
'O my queen, this is a breaking tale you tell me. I think
it is not easy to know what is the truth of the matter. And yet,
no rumor of this ever reached the ears of gods or men,
no singer ever sang but of my circumspect wife,
nor did he claim you, and thereby put an end to the suitors' siege
of my household. It is hard for me to understand how this
was accomplished. But you tear my very heart inside its coverings.'

    'Do not turn from me, O my long-lost love. Neither
hate nor blame me in your suffering. Do not turn from me as from
some weak woman who has willingly shamed and betrayed her husband.
I betrayed you only in the dream, of this I'm sure.
But even as to the dream's substance I am uncertain.
And I will tell you why, and you must judge it. Once only,
that day, he appeared without the clasp, but I
had already thought what was best to be done. I already
had one master, and wished to accept no other.
I descended the tall staircase to join the feasters that very day,
letting there be no sign on my face, nor
in my walk or manner to suggest that anything unusual stirred me.

    'I continued to favor Amphinomos just as before, no less,
no more, and met his gaze with calm, nor did I let
the color rise to my cheeks nor recognition flicker
on my brow. Neither did Amphinomos make any sign, so I wondered,
deeply amazed, at my dream. Except he did not wear
the clasp. And then, my husband, on the next day the clasp
again appeared, high on his left shoulder. We spoke
and, as usual, he was calm and sensible. And I – you would
have been proud of me then, my devious one. This was
the hardest moment in all those grievous years, this or one
that came soon after, which I will recount to you presently.
This time I was caught completely unguarded
like the dove who pecks in the courtyard at dawn for strewn barley
from last night's sacrifice, and the sun is not yet up and the mist
hides the owl returning to his nestlings in the tall cedar
with empty talons so that without warning she is forced to face

his approach. I drew on all the fibre those years of hardship
had stiffened within me and showed no sign, no change
of tone, no halt to my words, no hesitation in my steps
as I approached him also. Did he look into my face
with the hint of a question? I could not tell for sure.

'My husband, what that moment cost me – may you never
feel or know it. I think I could never relive it or the heart
within my breast would stop its beating. But it seemed to me
the only way to meet the trial. And I am certain it was,
for I was never beset by him again. He for his part
never acknowledged the moment either. So did it ever happen?
When I went to the footed bronze casket where I thought
I had secreted the clasp, it was gone though the box still lay
in the polished chest, the knot still tied as I kept it. No
sign of a clasp. Did I dream this, also? Could Melantho
have been so skillful she could pass Aktoris again,
Eurynome and Eurykleia also, whom I set guarding our room
day-long?' Odysseus strode up the steps to stand
over me. He spoke in harsh words now, saying:

'But you forget, my queen, my *circumspect* Penelope –'
he spat the words at me like sharp spears toward my heart,
'this woman, this Melantho, was the creature of Eurymachos. How,
then, could this be accomplished if that one and the others knew nothing
of it? I think they would not let the matter rest in silence.
They were too eager to force you to choose among them. . .'

I stopped him almost before I thought: 'O ingenious one,
don't you see how this was not necessary? Often
one man among them would begin to claim advantage.
The others would then deny his position, or they would let me
do it through some ruse of my own devising. I think
that as loudly as these lusting men claimed that they wished me to end
their constant attendance, their wasting away of our substance in suit
of me, rather they wished to prolong it. For they had grown soft
with luxurious living; no longer were they fit, nor did they yearn
for hard work in their own fields, nor tending their goat herds
and sheep flocks, nor for sitting in councils. But whether all

43

conspired against Amphinomos' chances, or perhaps it was he
for his own designs postponed them, quickly I was to endure
the trial that I told you was still to come. Within the span
of that new young moon's swelling from crescent to full,
those insolent men, the loudest and most unrestrained among
that rabble, the ones most strongly balanced among themselves
to keep the household in thrall, burst in upon me
all at once in my high chamber, torches held burning,
and seething for retribution. I was at my loom as I was nightly,
unweaving my glorious shroud for Laertes. Only Helen. . .'

· VII ·

'HELEN? What name is this that you allow to escape your lips?
What Helen do you mean, and what has she
to do with this story?' He spoke now in puzzlement. Confusion
replaced the stern anger in his stance and he took
his seat beside me again heavily. He clapped his hands
then, and from the end of the dark hall the tall doors
creaked on their fastenings. A spear of light sprang across
the threshold and leaped along the polished stones toward us
before the torches of Phemios and Mabantha, who carried in
jars of oil. They moved in all that dark space
like starry messengers from the gods, weaving about us with filaments
of light as they filled the lamps and re-lit them one by one.
Eurynome, bearing provisions for our strange vigil, was with them,
and Medon mixed fresh wine with many parts water
for our refreshment. It was clear they knew our need
to finish our hearts' confiding that very night. In silence

45

we let these good people attend us. The night sounds drifting
from the now-deserted courtyard beyond mingled to reach us
with the hiss of kindled cressets, the melodic pulse of thick oil,
trickling wine and coursing water. The lip
of the silver pitcher clinked on the rim of Odysseus' cup,
and sandals scuffed among the dry rushes and mints.

    At length we were roused by a firm clang of echoing bronze
on bronze. We awakened as if from a dream into light
that had slowly dissolved the wide shaft from the open door
just as the dawn melts the halo of a sleepless lamp.
Odysseus began, and I ate also. When we had satisfied our hunger
with the good things set before us, and slaked our thirst,
I spoke again, saying: 'Now I can tell you my greatest secret,
one I have dared tell no one before this. I tremble to tell it
even now after all I have told you this far
for fear you will end believing nothing I've told. For again
this was all dreamlike. Rather it seemed that it happened only
in dreams. But since you and our son have returned from your journeying
each with two robes, exquisitely suited to your then
unknown daughters, and since Telemachos insists that he missed me
far longer than my short absences to the country estate
could account for, I no longer know thought from truth, light
from the darkness of a cave, the journey from the dream. You, my husband,
you must travel it with me, help me to unravel the slub
from the strand and discover the way to pull the threads together.

    'It was Helen – your Helen, Menelaos' Helen, Helen of Sparta, she
of Troy, of Egypt, then again of Lakedaimon, Telemachos'
Helen. Long before the night I've told you of I dreamed
another dream. I dreamed I journeyed long and far, but this
was in secret. I dressed in the robe and veils of a Cretan dancer
and with Phemios and Mabantha went down to the wide harbor.
There the merchant ships bench their oars and lay in to disgorge
their grain from Doulichion, cattle and swine from the grazing plains
on the mainland, iron and flax, and the strange bands of seafarers,
all from distant lands I knew of only in the tales
of the singers that Phemios brought to our house. I dreamed

that Phemios searched the ships for a steersman he knew until he found him.
Then he stood close to this man and spoke quietly to him, saying:
"These women are sent as prizes from the young lords
of Ithaka to glorious Menelaos, King of Lakedaimon, leader
of the Danaans and all those many heroes and men gathered
on far Ilion's shore. But since there is bitter division
in this country because the lord Odysseus' homecoming is ruined
or delayed, we must travel in secret." And in my dream
Phemios led us down among the stores between the benches
of the oarsmen, away from the ordinary travelers above.

    'O my love, how well I seemed and to taste with you
your desperate hours tossing on the churning seas, to sense
your raw fear as the winds toyed with you and slapped you down,
lashing out again and again with monstrous waves
as you told it in your tale. I dreamed I smelled the sweat of the oarsmen
between the ranks, the salt on the sails and the filth that sloshed
at their feet. I heard the creak of the oars in their fittings, their slap in the scurf,
the groan of heaving timbers and the quivering song
the winds played in the straining halyards. But our helmsman
was strong and our way was not your long one over wide seas
between here and Troy. I dreamed we made landfall safely
by Nestor's Pylos. Here Phemios judged we should avoid
the high citadel, eager though he was to listen
to the stories that Nestor, your stately companion at Priam's walls,
could have told him. He feared that some one of the people
always gathered in such a house to supplicate or to pay service
to great men, or to feed off their bounty with no thought
of repaying save by their fawning, some one of these
or one of their sharp-eyed women might notice me and know
my bearing modest, my beauty and stature strange for a common dancer
who roams the far reaches of all the seas.

    'Besides I was ill. The tossing of the sea left me weak
and wretched so they laid me down in the chariot on piles of fleeces.
The journey passed like a dream within the dream
and I thought I was at home. Telemachos came to me sobbing in grief
over his first swift bitch's death. For this was

the sleek hunter grown from the brindled pup you
placed in his arms the last moment before you boarded
your great-oared ship bound for Troy, leaving
your dazed son bereft except for his pup and me.
And now I comforted him, though I was reft myself and knew not if
I dreamed or woke. I told him that although his favorite was gone
from him forever, still she gave him pups, and some of these were bitches
and had pups themselves. So he did have many ties to you,
his absent father, all around him when he set out gaily
with these fleet-footed companions eagerly flocking and baying
at his heels, myriad chips off of one great flint,
all sharp to do his bidding, to return his tender care.

   'And I taught him that he was such a link for me to you,
and that this is the way that men make the most of themselves and their portion
on earth – this is all we truly make that will live on
past our time, our houses, our studded thrones, our ships
and cities and the glory of our empires and wars. Then it seemed I woke again
before the great door of Menelaos' splendid palace,
roused from a daze clear-eyed. I descended from the chariot easily
as if on the arm of the goddess herself. I walked amazed
across the great stones of the courtyard to the high portal
of bronze heavily worked by Hephaistos and surmounted
by the high roof of the house with its carnelian frieze,
a wonder to set the summoned and the suppliant alike to marveling.

   'But then my eyes were undazzled in the shade of the high porches
at the wide threshold, and there she was; she of whom all men
have sung and whose mystery all women have weighed,
measuring themselves as shadows against her blinding light. And she,
starting as if from some dream of her own, knew me at once
as I did her, and came to me. She set aside her distaff
and footstool, and stood as I entered. A knowing look passed
the length of the distance between us as we walked to our meeting,
she stately, graceful, fully aware of the figure she made.
She was light on her feet and delighted as a girl who lives with brothers
when her girl-cousin comes from the next village for a wedding or feast day
to visit, and they talk long into the night after the scrabbling boys

and hard-drinking elders have tired and fallen
onto their fleeces to sleep heavily without dreaming.
She smiled, and there was love in her smile, a kindled warmth
as if for a long-lost friend, and her eyes shone blue,
like the palest sea shallow, the sky above the rising dawn
or just as night comes on. As she moved she seemed
to shed all manner of veils, fine-woven and shining
and finally reached me clothed in her own simple handiwork.

    'She came and took me by both hands and we kissed like sisters.
Then she turned to Menelaos, stern upon his studded throne and spoke
with fullness in her throat and brightness in her eyes, and said to him:
"Here she is, Menelaos, come at last." And to me, "Dear friend,
welcome, for my heart tells me you are she who will be
my friend, she whom I awaited and I knew she would come.
But, dear husband, favorite of Zeus, my father, our guest is tired
from her travels. I know you will wish me to see to her wants myself,
queen to queen, for her fame goes out over the lands
along the journeying ways and over the seas in the tales
of the glorious singers even as mine does." And indeed,
she led me herself from that marvelous hall whose richness and radiance
were fit for the palace of one of the goddesses herself. Yet Helen
herself was so gracious, so exceedingly kind and tender,
she outshone all. Thus it was I was drawn after her,
as she led me up the staircase to her own chamber.

    'There she bathed me herself and poured into her silver bathtub
brought from Egypt fragrant oils that Alkandre of Thebes
had blended for her only. Never were my body and spirit
so soothed, never after bathing did I feel so like a goddess,
for she dressed me in a robe of her own handiwork, finely woven
and edged in purple with silver threads in a design
of stars on a clear night. And the girdle was worked in silver
also, and the sash was of spun gold and delicate stuff
such as even I had never woven. And gladly she shared
her wisdom with me, telling me the whole of her wild enchantment,
the nightmare that followed, her heart torn between one man
beloved and respected and that new, exciting man who made himself

49

her master. It was she who counseled me from her heart how to shutter
my eyes against meeting the look of him who had pleased me,
but never to lower my eyes; for by this he could know
my loins' turmoil. Such moments come without warning to women
and men, without their willing them, and woe to her who would be reticent
if she ever acknowledges him who would have her against her intention.
For he will woo her with subtle means and if he take her, whether by force
or by sweet entreaties, she is bound to be his while in his power.
And it was Helen who showed me how to restore my dignity
when my pride and stature and reputation were threatened.'

    Odysseus looked at me sharply. He would have spoken but I stopped him,
taking his hand and saying: 'Hear me out. For she also shared
with me her most secret crafts, her weaving, the fine embroidering
and the spinning of delicate silver threads, her perfumes and oils,
all but her potions and medicines and the knowledge of them. "For these,"
she spoke to me, saying: ". . .these are the secrets one daughter will seek
and make her own wondrous craft. And when you make
your appointed journey with your daughters, bring that one to me,
for I shall. . .'"' Here my husband thrust away my hand
and stood before me, terrible in outrage, his lips pursed
to a tight line in his beard that shook with suppressed fury.

    I knew that this was a shocking prospect, but again I smiled
within me. For I had not known what manner of occasion, what moment
of conversing together would open the hour for me to reveal
my whole purpose, the last hard secret between us.
He spoke to me, resourceful and full of guile, saying: 'You are so strange;
O wife, here is the proof of the wildness of your dreaming.
To think such a thing is the very substance of dream.' I looked up
at his overmastering stance and manner and summoned to me all
the dignity of bearing wise Helen had struck into my heart.
'My Odysseus, I think that although you do not wish to believe
my story, yet I am telling it as well and as truly as I can.
For this was not the only dream journey I took, to return
as on the wings of a goddess with cloud horses straining
to bear me over mountains and valleys and rocky crags
flecked with foam from the jealous seas. For it seemed I also visited

Arete of the consoling ways, who sits beside her husband
in all his councils with the best of their men. And she is free
to walk about their city and to counsel and be heard, even
as he is. But tell me this, Odysseus, since some parts
of your story have confused me. For although she is highly esteemed
and sought by many, she does not exalt herself. I never heard her send
greeting such as you told them when you spoke of your sojourn with her
and Alkinoös in Scheria.

                    'For I dreamed I went there also, sped
lightly over wine-purple seas, gently buffeted along
by playful waves creaming behind a matchless ship.
It carried me gliding on what seemed its own purpose,
like a dolphin leaping from crest to crest on the frothing ridges
of the sea, and lulled so I scarcely remember how I reached her.
But next it seemed I awakened in the lush gardens of the palace
and was led to the silver doorway by Nausikaa herself.
And when I came to the inner room, that high-roofed hall
where Arete sat with her husband, Alkinoös, holding session
with the leaders of the Phaiakians, she knew me at once. She came to me
and took me by both hands and we kissed like sisters. Then
she turned to Alkinoös, and again to all the company assembled,
saying, "I give you a woman's greeting from the heart of understanding
that is ours." Later, before I was sped homeward
on the wings of the wind as if on the back of Pegasus himself,
she spoke to me saying, as I hear her say always in my heart:
"When you make your appointed journey, I think that you will see
Helen again before you come to me. Speak to her
from me saying: *Arete gives you a woman's greeting*."

    'That was how she said it in my dream. My husband, I ask you,
and you must give me an accurate answer: how did she send
her greeting? For as you told it she sent me "a queen's greeting."
I think that perhaps if this was so, the truth of the matter
can be known.' My hero turned away his face, but not
before I saw a war break over it from deep within,
a battle fierce as ever he fought before the walls
of far-off Troy, but not with arms or massed ranks

but cool craftiness amid storms of temperament.
I saw it in the set of his shoulders, the slight drop of his head,
the clench of his fists, the taut muscles in his calves loosening
before he turned and spoke to me, saying: 'O my queen, my Penelope,
I no longer know whether you are mine or not. But see,
I will answer truthfully what you have asked. First you
must answer me this. What is this journey you speak of?
How is it these far-distant women, of whom you seem
to know so much, although I think it is not possible you have
visited them even in dream, can prophesy some journey for you?'

'Dear husband, my dearest lord, I ask
in turn how they could *not* have known, for each of us
must make her own journey also. But whether, in the end
this was substance or the stuff of dream, the journey is one
I cannot evade. For when our splendid daughters descended
into my life as gifts from the gods, they were not freely given.

'O, I had fought the one dread battle that women
must face alone, despite their sisters near at hand
and kindly intentioned, even as men are, in the end,
lone warriors in the grim fighting. And even though
I fought it then again without you nearby
in bearing you these daughters, and later it was
with painful hardship that I cultivated and hid their talents like lights
under a basket, still a debt is outstanding to the goddess.

'For one night in the seventh year after you had departed
and still you had not returned, I despaired. I was just returned
from a visit to the country where your father and mother stayed with our daughter
I faced another string of days in charge of our household alone.
Telemachos was now an insistent boy – he too
was lonely in this house and always begging me to bring him companions.
And there were those here who heard his pleas and urged
me to do it for his sake, until I had no strength or arguments
left. In the last third of the night, after I had truly wept
and lamented and lain down often without the relaxation
of sleep, I arose and washed and laid white barley
into the basket and with it the silver distaff I brought

from my mother's house. "Hear me, Atrytone," I prayed to Athene,
"Hear me, daughter of Zeus, if you ever accepted gifts
offered in your honor, and answered the prayers of a suppliant, come
to my aid and help me to fend off these torments which trouble me."
    'Then Athene herself came to me shining in the glory
of her godly stature and beauty, and bearing her golden staff.
"Penelope, you have always been so steadfast that the singers
have spread your reputation far beyond the seas to distant shores.
Yet now you seem to be giving way to your fears.
I have no doubt that you can provide for the safety of these daughters.
With the help of Antikleia and Laertes you will bring them to their full maturity.
Few are the daughters of even the greatest heroes
who can match them for accomplishment. I myself will see to that,
but with one provision. You must pledge your solemn oath
that before Ailanthis and Nerianne come to the age of majority
you will have them make a journey, one that is urgent for them.
They must go to Pytho, to the Nombril Stone itself
and there give thanks for my protection. And there Apollo will also
hear their thanks, and give them, through the words of his high prophetess,
advice and help with what they must do next. Promise!"
    ' "O Goddess, I pledge it. But you who know the skein
of the future before it is unwound for men, won't you tell me
of my absent husband's fate? Will he prevail in the hardships
of battle and journeying? When he will return to his home and family?"
"I cannot tell you this, for nowhere it is written in your destiny to know it
now. But soon you must go back to your bed and rest, knowing
that I will order things for you as you go forward and you will know
when I am helping you. But because I move over earth and the seas
with many things to concern me, do not expect to see me
again, for you will be able to fulfill much on your own."
So she spoke, and an owl called as dove-rustling Dawn arose,
lifting the dark pall from my spirits.' Thus I told Odysseus.
    Now again an owl called, and a dove answered, signaling
an end to this longest night. I took Odysseus' hand
to descend the steps of the platform. He held back a moment but did not
withdraw it and allowed me to lead him out beside me

to a window facing the courtyard. There the first light was showing
over the enclosing walls of the palace, only faintly
where the stars halo the dark hills, and these slowly
gave way to deep blue, then plum, and soon the golden heralds
of Dawn herself announced the new day, breaking
a pathway for glorious Helios. We watched long in silence,
each wrapped in a cloak of thoughts. His hand,
when he withdrew it, left my hand so cold it seemed that warmth
had never sheltered there that night. I was alone facing a new day.
I did not see Odysseus that day, nor indeed for many more.
I felt heavy as I climbed the tall staircase to my upper chambers
and lay down in the anteroom next to where my daughters slept.

    Next Eurynome, the old housekeeper came in, touching
my shoulder and gently rocking me. She spoke to me saying: 'Dear child,
you must wake. For your husband has sent Medon, and he has a message,
of grave import, for you alone. Only first you must
arise, wash and anoint your face, for this is seemly for a queen.'
A tightness clenched the heart in my breast, and I started like a hare.
Then I sank to the fleeces once more. 'How can you speak
of such trivial matters as washing and adorning my body when Odysseus
has left? For this must be the reason he sends a herald to me.
Give me only my hero's mantle to wear, and call Medon
to my chamber, for I wish no others to hear my husband's words
until I have heard them first and know what to do next.'
    Then the kindly housekeeper stood still, amazed.
She said nothing, but turned reluctantly toward the gaping doors
and hurried away. I wrapped Odysseus' mantle around me,
the rich one that had been a gift from the loom of Arete herself.
He had wrapped it around my shoulders before, but unconsciously, not
realizing he touched me tenderly, when I shivered in the cold window.
Now the spring pushed violets from the earth, and shoats
from the sows, and sparrows to gather bits of straw from the dung heap
and wool from my basket to weave their nests, but his robe would be well-worn
when next he claimed it. Medon entered, saying:
'I come, my queen, from Lord Odysseus. The king himself

bade me greet you thus and tell you officially that he leaves
to see to his flocks' and herds' replenishment by Ithaka's lords
and also Zakynthos' and Doulichion's. His son goes with him. You
he leaves in charge of his household, stores and your glorious daughters.'
    He spoke with a tone so hard that I knew my husband
had impressed it on him. So I answered him harshly in turn, saying:
'Well then, Herald, is this all? You do not mention
when Odysseus plans to return.' He spoke then more thoughtfully,
saying: 'That, my queen, was the whole of his message as he was minded
to send it, and he ordered me to tell it carefully in his words.
I do not know what god has moved him, but although his words
were stern, I could see that the heart within him was sorely divided.'
'Medon, I thank you for this, your twofold message. I thank
you also for your loyalty both to me and to Odysseus, for although
it is a painful matter to deliver such news, you have rightly understood
that loyalty to each is loyalty to both and does not betray.'
    While we were conversing thus, Eurynome had gone through the palace
for Mabantha. She of all my women was the one most kindred
to my mind and spirit, and she came to me, knowing I would be bereft
because of Odysseus' sudden departure. She entered the doorway
and stood framed by the tall door-posts. Her figure was imposing
as always, her carriage splendid, with black hair swept
from her strong forehead into a striking wind of cloth.
She closed the doors as Medon departed and spoke, saying:
'Dear friend, Penelope, Eurynome is saying Lord Odysseus is leaving
and you remain again. Can this be the way of it? Where is it he is going?'
'Dear friend, it has happened just as you say. My herald has said
although he left with heart divided, he has not given word of return.
So while I have spent my days in waiting and yearning for my life
to begin again, and now it had begun, he would leave me. . .' Here
I could not finish, for my strength and fire were quenched as if
in a rising stream at spring flood. She held me then
to her copious shoulder while I shook with strong surges of grief
and fruitless rage besides. And when I had finished with weeping,
when I had released the storm within my heart, when the tears
no longer came and I relaxed against her, she began to rock.

Then she hummed to me softly. She sang an old melody
that always stirs and comforts me. But I was amazed that she,
from far Aithiopia, knew it. So when I took the sponge
she handed me to wash my burning face and cool my wrists,
I spoke to her, asking: 'Tell me, dear friend, wherever did you learn
this song of my childhood and how did you know it would comfort me?'

∘ VIII ∘

SHE WAS about to answer when a terrible cry clove the calm
of the morning. Now Eurykleia came in, moaning
so wildly I feared Odysseus' aged father Laertes
was taken from us. But behind came Eurynome leading Nerianne.
She walked haltingly, as if encountering unknown terrors
and behind them came Phemios, the two precious lyres
cradled in his arms, but nearly forgotten. He spoke, saying:
'O my queen, please do not ask me how this has come to pass
for there is nothing I can see as the cause of it. Never in all my journeying
have I encountered this in a singer, and I do not lay the blame
on her sex. This is the work of some jealous god; she is voiceless.'
     I think that had my daughter not been there before me, silent,
bewildered as a gosling when her mother has been snatched by some ill-trained dog,
I would have shown the clutch of fear upon my heart. And were it not
for those gathered with me, my most loyal servants, I might
have felt unbidden tears prick my eyes and let
the desire to weep overtake me again. But strength came to me
and with it calm, so that even now I saw where all events
were pointing. I spoke to my daughter kindly but firmly to remind her
who she was, saying: 'Nerianne, my daughter, although you are grieved
to find that your father has departed again, you are Odysseus' daughter
and mine as well. He will return, and we must bear up
and be ready.' She shook her head, then stepped away from the nurse.
She spoke thinly, saying: 'O, Mother, how can this be true?
If my song has displeased him so gravely that he has left your house, what more
can strike me? For what Phemios tells you already happened, and I did not
know that he was gone. My voice has left me, though you hear me speak.
I can no longer sing.' She dropped to the low footstool
before me and lowered her covered head so that golden curls

escaping the intricate coils hung toward her knees as she hugged them
to her. Mabantha went to her and knelt and held her but then
drew her upright so that even before Ailanthis flew to her
across the room from the threshold Nerianne's head was high.

    My bright Ailanthis with her father's eyes turned to me, saying:
'Surely, it cannot be true. No man who has just returned
after years of wandering will leave his family soon again
and stay away, especially this glorious father, Odysseus.
I cannot believe it will be for long. Sister, hear me. I think
it was not your song that drove him from us. Some other thing
has done it. Don't you agree, Mother?' All turned to me then
and though I suspected the design behind these things, no smile
was in my heart, for the way ahead was too uncertain and the testing
severe. Nerianne spoke next, asking: 'Mother, what will this mean
to the plans for our journey? For always you have vowed to wait for our father
to return and grant his permission. I think that now it will delay us
too long.' Ailanthis added: 'But since he has been home, perhaps
you have asked him, and whatever has come of it we must be released to go.'

    While we were conversing, I saw that Phemios stood back
amazed with Eurykleia and Eurynome, stricken motionless like stones.
'You, Phemios, with Mabantha, will journey with us when our day
of departure finally comes. Dear nurses both, do not be
shocked at my bold speech nor the plans it reveals. For these
are Odysseus' shining daughters, and theirs are not ordinary fates.
Yes, my always astonishing daughters, what you guess is true;
I have spoken to him. Since he has not agreed, I shall keep to my vow
for I believe he will return quickly. He too will see this as a sign
the goddess has sent and know that he must let us journey to Pytho
to speak to the prophetess, and also to seek the return of Nerianne's voice.

    'This is how I see it. But we do not have to wait idly.
You, Phemios, must go down to the harbor to search
among the strong-benched ships for a helmsman you know well
from your early years of voyaging. He must be a man you can rely on
to carry the women in our party, who are both accomplished
and young, with beauty and bearing that can attract
evil attentions. And if such a ship and her helmsman are found

only on the seas beyond the cutwater, then you must wait
for her to glide into the port to alert you that here is our conveyance
for the sea leg of our journey. Eurynome and Eurykleia,
dear trusted friends, you will stay here in charge
of the women of the household and the stores as you have always been
before now. My husband and son will have need of your ministrations,
and godlike Laertes also. But you must now
help us to prepare for the journey. So in our hearts and in yours
also you will make the journey with us. You are the only ones
who may know this, but you, Eurynome, must have ready hard loaves,
many measures of barley stitched in strong leather bags, and oil,
wine, dried fruits and meats and whatever else
is needed for journeying. These you will secretly set aside,
with stored-up bolts of cloth from my own handiwork.
You, Eurykleia, know well the hidden storeroom where these
have been kept. We will take them only, for gifts of handiwork
are the best gifts from woman to woman. I have woven
many shimmering robes for the women I will meet on my travels.
    'You must fold them away carefully with the other provisions in secret
and tie the chest with my own knot which only we three
know. Now go out and appear again in the household so none
may guess our plan. Send word of Nerianne's plight
to my husband. I think he will return sooner.' Ever faithful,
they followed Phemios down the staircase. I turned to my daughters
who stood amazed. I spoke to them firmly, saying:
    'Do not be dismayed, my dears, thinking that our journey will be long
put off. I know you are anxious in your hearts to begin it, and perhaps
you fear that your father will not return soon. But I remember
well what he was like before he went away to never-to-be-mentioned
Ilion, and I must tell you that sometimes a man can act
just like a boy. So much has happened in the long years
since he left that many things have changed. Besides, he and I
are not the same man and woman we were once.
He needs to find out what is still his to govern and what
he has relinquished, for gain or loss, to those who have kept supple
his fair sandals while he was dallying elsewhere. I am sure

59

that we will be journeying before the first winds of summer.
And I see, Nerianne, that your distress must be
merely the working out of some plan by the goddess.
It will be the last proof your father will need that he must
allow you to go, and me with you. Go now, both of you.
Only a measure more of patience is required.' Ailanthis
thought to speak, but with a meaningful gaze I gestured
toward her stricken sister. She raised her eyebrows in that way of hers
that indicates shared understanding better than words.
She embraced Nerianne and gently pressed a hand on her spine.
    Nerianne straightened and looked into her sister's face
for a full moment. Then she linked a white arm
in Ailanthis' sun-burnished arm. Leaning their heads
slightly together, they went out through the doors which Mabantha
closed firmly behind them all. I sank into my chair,
feeling the spirit draining from my body like yarn unraveling
on its own from a tightly wound skein. Mabantha spoke to me, saying:
'You were magnificent, my friend. Always you were saying
perfect words to persuade their hearts and giving them cheer.
Queen Antikleia would be very proud.' She pressed my hands
but I felt strong again. There was much for me to prepare
for our journey also, much to think about. I spoke, saying:
'My friend, I thank you. I could never have borne the snarls
and pricks of these years since she died had you not come.
You have been more than a sister to me. But still I wonder
about the things you have never told me about yourself and your country.
    'Many times I have asked you this, about your parents,
your city and your girlhood, for I think it must have been very different
from mine. Yet although I sense in you a kindred spirit, still
you always seem to withhold these answers from me
by design. But now I am even more eager to question you
and you must give me an accurate answer. This song
you sang to me was always my comfort, always the balm of my childhood.
For when I was a little girl in the palace of my father, Ikarios,
my mother was the last to leave my room each night. She would set
a molded lamp with its measure of oil burning in it

in a corner protected from the sly gusting of night's Zephyr
so I always felt safe. And outside my door she set Admete
to playing the lyre, which she had learned in secret. She always
played that song, which my mother walked away singing
down the stone staircase into my father's cavernous halls,
singing sweetly until I left when I was still a bud of a girl.

'And I have not heard this song since – except when my daughters
were living in secret with Queen Antikleia and good Laertes
on the estate. Then I would sing it to them and leave them
with two burning lamps to guard them in my long absence.
But you sang it moments ago, and brought back to me memories
so strong and bittersweet that dealing with present griefs
was an easy matter after I had mastered a longing for my youth.
But come, answer me this truthfully, for you sang it expertly
and in just the words I learned, so I think that you must have learned it
from the same source, not from some chain of singers passing it
from palace to palace, city to city, country to country
like a design that is changed when handed from household to household.

'My friend, I need for you to be truthful regarding this now
for I could not easily contemplate this journey without you
and Phemios to accompany us as you said you would be ready to do
after my husband's return. And besides this, I am eager
to know why the measure of your sojourn here was always
the elusive homecoming of my lord whom you had never
seen, even after Phemios made you his wife, and despite
your obvious delight in the joy granted you two together.'
My friend now took my hands and led me into the anteroom
where a bath was prepared for me in my fluted tub.
She helped me to undress, releasing my sashes and loosening my robe.
Then she bathed me herself, mixing ever warmer water
into the bath so it was just as I wished it. She poured
her own blends of fragrant oils into the water
and soothed away the tension from every aching sinew
of my body with her knowing hands. Then she dried and anointed me with oil,
which seals the skin against the chafe of dry winds.

And all the while she told me her astonishing tale:

'My friend, Penelope, you who were making your way in this life
by staying near to home and banking hearth fires
of a secure holding, I am telling you now the story of some different one.
For also I was nursed on this song. It had come
to my country some long-time past from Same,
the country lying next to your Ithaka, by a singer blown
to the Southern shores of the great sea. And this one, Kamylos,
he named himself, slipped from the ship that was unwelcome to the peoples
along green Aigyptos and found his way to tall-pillared
Thebes-Astride-the-Current. Soon his strange singing
was taking him from house to greater house, and then to the palace
of Pharaoh. There he found favor and was content
to forget his island in the sea garlanded with olives and pines
and to linger by the lotus pools among the lifted columns.

'But there was then in Pharaoh's service a chariot driver,
a handsome youth with smooth, well-oiled limbs, slim-loined
and quick, skillful at driving the horses. This one had caught
the appraising eyes of Pharaoh, but also Kamylos loved him
in secret. And these two would be often resting together
in the courtyard of the palace in the heat of the day while the slaves were fanning
the drowsing Pharaoh in his darkly shaded bedchamber within.

'Then came a summons from Pharaoh, the kind this driver was fleeing
time upon time across all the lands from Phrygia
to Helios' rest. Janys was his name, and now he spoke
to his lyre-bearing friend and named him and touched him, enflaming
his hiding passions so Kamylos was ready to do at once
as he was asking. These two set out in Pharaoh's chariot,
running beside the river along the journeying ways on the shelf
above the red bluffs by moonlight and stars, and the sheen
of the river between its dark green sleeves was leading them.

'That Janys, driver of horses, had chosen his own favorite mares
from Pharaoh's stables and himself put into their mouths
the bronze bits finished in gold, put on the leather harness
and the lightest breastplates and cockades, making certain
the chariot was the lightest and strongest one the chariot-builders
had made. So these two appeared as the sun god Re

himself, blazing from his golden chariot in the guise of the Pharaoh,
with a driver of unearthly beauty. They were swiftly outrunning the goddess
Rumor from far downriver, so the people they were gracing with their brief light
greeted them and made much of them all on the way.
At last they turned to follow the ridges behind the bluffs
to my city. And here my own mother was serving in the palace
and she herself heard from Kamylos' lips and lyre
the sad song of that journey's end. For when they were crossing
great brown-swelling Aigyptos on the low-walled ferry,
Kamylos whispered his love to Janys. When at the start
of a moonless night they were lying down beside one another
for sleep to relax their limbs, Janys gave himself willingly
into Kamylos' arms. And this one was stunned with amazement
and afterward always sang with great tenderness of this moment.

   'For Janys was not the smooth-cheeked youth he had seemed, but a woman.
Smooth-limbed, small-waisted, sinewed as a driver of strong-surging horses
must be, but undeniably, to possessing hands, a woman,
reckless with desire. And after they had taken together full pleasure
in their lovemaking, hiding in the cool shadows of the endlessly restless
fronds of a date palm, she told him her story, saying:
"You are so gentle. I know I shall rue it whenever I lose you
as someday I must. For I never can rest – I have come now to know this.
So often I've wished to, from mountain to desert, but I have been hounded
to wander each time I have started to trust. I have driven for princes,
and driven for queens, but each time I settled to tether my dream
I was harried along. For I cannot be woman and horseman as well –
when someone comes close, I might have to tell what I am, how I came to it –
then I'd be tamed. I'd be penned in as woman, in harness, whipped, shamed.
But you are so gentle; and you have the touch of the consummate master –
whether lyre you play or my body, my heart wants to stay, wants to say to you,
Yes, I am woman, and yes, I'll be yours. . ." But she couldn't, of course.

   'For, as my mother heard the story, while the seasons were coming around
the two were making their ways separately to the palace. But here
the wrath of Pharaoh would catch them with its swiftly turning wheels.
The king of my country was pondering in his heart whether it was better
to refuse to send back so unsurpassed a charioteer,

risking warfare and bloodshed over him, or whether to give him up
into the hands of Pharaoh's heralds. In the end
the lovers were never to have their moment of parting
and Kamylos always after this wondered in his sad singing
whether she feared that to visit him could bring his destruction.
Or was she leaving him gaily, lighthearted as a sleek mare
tied to a hitching stone with braided silver when suddenly the ring
releases, the harness falls from her tossing head and she races
free with the wind across the meadow grasses and over the dune?

    'But none will go to war for a singer, and besides, our queen
had heard the lullaby that you and I know and would never
allow that singer go back to Pharaoh. So Kamylos stayed
in the palace to sing us his songs.' Mabantha wrapped me
in coarse linen and dried my body. She dressed me in a robe
of fine wool and caught it at my shoulders with ivory rings.

    And while we were busied in this way I spoke to her again, saying:
'Now you have answered a new question for me, but still
an older one that has been in my mind for many seasons
is yet unanswered. I would have you tell me rightly how
you came to leave your land and what you sought here, for I think
it was no caprice of the winds that set you in the well-benched
ship bound for Argos where Phemios encountered you and knew
your worth and threw his lot in with you, bringing you here.
And I would hear of your adventures before that happy meeting,
for although you dance with the grace of a goddess, you do not
resemble to me some mere wandering court dancer.
I question how, as a woman, you could have made your way
alone and without protection among the hardened seamen,
rough merchants and soldiers, and all the coarse rabble
that venture the treacherous sea ways until you encountered him.
I need to hear of such travels, for when I shall try them myself.
So you must tell me now, and give me an accurate account of it.'

    She looked straight into my face with those ebony eyes
and nodded gravely, as much to herself as to me, and spoke:
'Dear friend, it is as you are saying; it is time, and I can tell it.
Look, I will give you a full recounting and you shall know me.

64

I had one brother, older than I, and wise beyond the elders
who surrounded him and were teaching him all they could of what he was asking.
Oh, he was like a god, this brother, strong and fleet –
in the way he walked he was not unlike a king or warrior
although he never fought, so natural of grace he walked
unchallenged in our city. And to me he was friend, sharing all
his knowledge, all his hopes, and our spirits were as one.
But our city lies beyond – so far beyond – the barrier steeps
and lands that are more barren than your island, Asteris, where no water
slakes the thirst of lizard or locust and no palm
can pull shadow from the deeps of earth to cool the sand.
Yet always we were hearing from the traders with their laden beasts
and others who flee their homes for oblivion, such tales
of high citadels and journeying on the sea ways and marvelous mysteries
passing from tribe to tribe and country to country
that at last my brother, although we had pledged us never to part,
left me to go hunting for all he could bring down with the sharp arrows
of his mind. He had to. So he chose the time when I was apart
with the priestess several days for the monthly rite.

'When I returned to the household he was gone. I loved him
more than brother. I was straining to go after him or dash myself down
to the bottom of the well, but I was held, for weeks I think,
until no more was I weeping and railing, until the scratches on my breasts
were healed and I loved and pitied once again my aged father
and my mother, barren since my birth. Then I waited, certain
he would return to me if he could. Never would he be free
from me or our land; he would come back unless he lay deep
in the earth or unless some supernatural power restrained him.
But after seven years I came to search for him. I had to.
He was life itself to this Mabanda then: His name was Rbatha.
You named him Eurybates, your husband Odysseus' friend,
lost with all those dear companions he so lightly mourns.
And we were. . .'

                    Next she dropped her sleek head to her breast
and held still a moment. And I was stricken to silence
at how I might answer her. But then the close-fitting doors parted

65

and Aktoris came in to arrange my hair and to hand me my casket
of bronze inlaid with silver, with its jars and covered pots
and the flasks of swirled glass with perfumes for my morning ritual.
    For this reason Mabantha's tale was left unfinished.
It was days before I could implore her to resume the telling of it.
For in the days following each of us was busy with her tasks
preparing for our imminent journey in secret and without the concerns
of daily feasts for multitudes of men. For these had mostly
followed in Odysseus' service, with our son Telemachos, who was eager
to learn at the hero's heels. Others had left for their own holdings
to see to the young lambs and their fattening dams,
to clearing and piling up stones and planting their fields.
There was much for me to oversee also, laying up stores
for the household. The women were washing the new wool and combing it,
piling it in baskets for the expert spinners among them to take up
their distaffs and spin it into fine threads for our weaving. And again
I could savor the satisfaction I take from tasks
well accomplished, and feel at rest at the end of each day.
    And the days passed quickly, fading away like crocuses
when sky-blue hyacinths open, sweetening the air.
One day Laertes, Odysseus' stately father,
and patient father also to my daughters, came to me privately
as I walked among my beloved geese in the pebbled courtyard.
He caught me under the olive tree that casts a cloak
of cooling shade there by the spring, and spoke, saying:
'Dear daughter, Penelope, tell me how it is you have managed
to bear up under this new desertion. For although we both know
there was far more strength in you than even your own handmaidens
knew of, it is not only old age such as mine that wears down
patience and faithfulness in reaching a goal that is much desired.
You are still like one of the goddesses for beauty and stature.
    'My son trusts all too much in your steadfastness, or perhaps
in his fame among men who revere his manly powers
but do not know him as you and I do. Tell me then
so I will know it, that you have not quarreled and broken and I may still
hope to see my son united with his family and keeping

home from his wanderings before I die.' So saying
he held me to his breast, ever splendidly muscled and upright
despite his age, due to his constant labors in the orchards
and fields of his passion. I loved this man nearly as much
as I loved his son. Both had been seed to my green shoots.

　'Laertes, dear Father, how I've longed to speak to you
these last days. I know that our purpose could never
have been accomplished without you. Once again you came to my aid –
no, more than once, for when Odysseus was confounded
by the strangeness of us all, you led him into trust. I think
he would not have taken us to his breast had you not been there to guide him.'
I embraced him then. Taking his hand I led him
to the square-hewn outcrop of deep rock where two can sit to converse
in the dancing shade. I looked into his face and saw
his end descending steadily upon him from some crag
like the eagle that is sure to come for a slow-moving hare.

　'It is true that Odysseus was never minded to depart again
so suddenly. But men are always saying marriage is a painful matter.
I think that Odysseus has never had to learn it.
There is much that is changed here, much that he did not expect to find.
And I think it is hard to return to a wife no longer in the first
blush of her beauty and stature, especially after encounters
with nymphs and goddesses in shining garments.' I spoke lightheartedly
but Laertes knew the heart within me well. He took
my face in his hands and looked into my eyes, shaking
his head. 'You are so brave, but foolish also to think
I cannot see the turmoil that troubles you. You must tell me truthfully
how I can help you. For I love you as my own, my daughter, and I think
that I know your mind better than I know the mind of my son.
And I can persuade him, although I am old and past the age
of glorious deeds, for there is still spirit and resourcefulness within me.'

　'Father, what you say is true, and I have wronged you
by concealing from you all I must accomplish. See, I will tell you
the rest of my plan for our daughters. It was what angered
Odysseus, for it goes so much against custom and seemliness.
You already know of the goddess' will that our spirited pair

6 7

voyage from Ithaka to learn what she wishes them to do next.
But, dear Laertes, what you do not know, and I fear to tell
even you, is this: I am bound to go with them also.
I have given my pledge, and though it pains me to leave
three men I love, I am determined to accomplish it.
Now I fear you will think as Odysseus does,
and conspire with him to keep me from it. Then perhaps also
Nerianne and Ailanthis would never leave these rocky shores
on their own journeys, but rather would be given away like possessions
into the households of some kings from among the Argives.

    'But this is not what the gods meant for them, Laertes. You yourself
know this, for you have known Ailanthis' mind
and Nerianne's silver tones. And I must journey with them
like the goose when first her downy chicks gather at the lip
of the wind-whipped pond. They must see my wings unfold,
my webbing dip and shudder on the current like a sail
and make their first crossing in the lea of my passage.'
I spoke and the old man bowed his head. Tears
ran down his ruddy cheeks and spread a silver web
in the tracery of lines on his kindly face. I spoke again
saying: 'Do not cry, I beg you, Father. Tell me
it is not too great a sacrifice to ask of you who have succored
and supported me for so many years. For my breath will catch with pain
in my breast at every step I take away from your dream
if the postponement of it is too great for you.'

    Dear brave Laertes. He smiled at me then. He took my hand,
and drying his tears, he looked away from me a while, out
beyond the shade we were presently in to the bright courtyard
where the women of the household moved to and from the fountain
with the water jars, their children were tossing their little stones
among lines in the sand, and dogs were sleeping in the sun.
He was looking toward the gate of the palace, through the opening
where light shimmered, setting the groves and the peaks beyond them
quivering despite the midday lull. His hand tightened
on mine as if to still my speech, and even my thought
for a moment. Or many moments, perhaps, for when he turned

to me again his face was dry and smiling, full of resolve.
    'Do not fear for me, Penelope, for what you propose
is not altogether astounding since once my beloved Antikleia
hinted it to me before she left me and passed down
into Hades. But I never thought it would happen once Odysseus
returned. I looked to delight in your grace beside my son's
always until the end of my days. But no parent can sow
for his children as he wishes once he has set them in their own fields.
And since what you say is fair and orderly for such daughters
as these are, I know that you must guide them like the star
that points to the onrush of spring. And I think that my son will
let you go, although his heart will be against it. I see
that it is my task to persuade him to trust in your return.
I promise that I will do it if I can
before I die. But do not go too far nor stay too long,
for already the gods have conspired to set you hoeing separate
furrows for too many years. Now while the ships are high
on the pebbled shelf, and the jars are not yet filled nor the chests
carried on board, now it is time for our real good-bye.
Though you will not return *to* me, I beg you, oh lovely Penelope,
please return *for* me, and quickly, to him. Fare well.'
    So he spoke, and held my palm to those weathered lips
and kissed it, those wise yet lively eyes holding mine
in a tender look until he released my hand. I found it
moments – hours? – later resting hotly on my knee.
    It seemed there was never a time for me to rest again
until the tumultuous morning when a clamor arose in the courtyard.
Dogs yelped, women's voices rose, and shouts
mingled with the squeals of children and the slap of sandals beating
the smooth stones of the portico. Next I heard men
shouting and calling, laughing at the children squawking
and scattering like fowl before them and the dogs. They stamped
and grunted as they heaved weight from their shoulders to the ground
and let their bows and quivers clatter as they greeted the servants
who held out bowls of water for them to drink and pour
over their hot heads and shoulders, splashing in the bright halo

around my hero who stood barely contained within the door-posts
as I hurried to greet him in spite of myself. He looked,
in those awkward moments, just as I knew him in our choicest youth.
In a timeless time before he nodded, bronzed and burning
with vigor and pride as a warrior returned victorious from battle,
I knew we would greet each other again with a blush of recognition.

· IX ·

I COULD NOT keep my smile within me. So there we stood:
two victors flushed with success of the battle or the hunt
and smiling in triumph. But he saw my desire. He spoke to me,
saying: 'You are so strange. For when I came to you with shining treasure
and splendid garments, when I slaughtered the scores of your suitors
who had taunted and tormented you and piled them lifeless in the courtyard
for your glory you did not so readily greet me nor devour me with ravishing looks.
Yet here I am returned with simple sheep to replenish our sheepfolds,
and swine, and oxen and a few hares and succulent birds
from Mount Neritos' crags for our feasting, and your eyes burn fire
as for a hero returned. This is how it should have been then,
how I yearned for you greet me.'

                              I could not resist the flung challenge.
'Oh, but you are so different. The killing of beasts for our table is not
like the slaughter of glorious young men as a preface for lovemaking. Death
is always a painful matter to a woman. You forget

71

that there was much else then that weighed on my heart,
and which I longed to lift over my head like a heavy cloak
and lay across your knees. And besides, it was your property,
your serving people, and your great high-roofed house
you returned to possess. Now you have come back to me.'
I looked at him signifyingly and he laughed, all rancor gone.

    Now again the palace resounded with the bustle of men sacrificing
beasts, skinning and spitting them, piling up wood on the fires
and roasting meats while the polished chairs were drawn up to the tables
and other good things were brought in baskets and jars.
Old wine was opened and jars of water for the mixing bowls
and ewers for washing all set in place by the purposeful hands
of the maidservants. And when all had eaten and drunk their fill and the last
libation had been poured to the gods, Odysseus led me firmly
to our high bedchamber, and drew the bolt to. He turned to me
slowly and looked at me hard. 'My queen,' he began gently.
'Hush, my lord. Oh, be my lord now.' But he said:
'I dreamed it then? As a man in a fever of illness sees
the spirits of the dead rising to pull him from his corded bedstead
into the steaming pit of black ooze? You are mine
and will remain –' I stopped him then. I drew away
to stand by the smooth door-post of cypress wood and said to him:

    'Yes, my love, and no. Do not mistake me, Odysseus.
I am still the loving wife who waited years for you,
holding myself for you alone with your household and children,
refusing the raging suitors and keeping my purpose hidden.
My heart was filled with rejoicing at your return today.
O, most understanding of men, do not be hard with me.
For if you are, well then, I must endure it and wear
your harshness like a girdle on my journey, for it is decreed that I go.
And so it will constrict and sting my heart even
as I delight in shimmering Dawn, in the breezes of summer
or the brightest star of evening over sheer wine-blue waters.
I will feel the rub as I wonder at strange landfalls, heights
and plains and in the halls of high-roofed palaces where strangers
will greet me warily and inquire of you. And as I gaze

with wonder at the precincts of the oracle, or hear the next plan
for Ailanthis from the prophetess, as I listen again
to Nerianne's singing I may long to untie its bruising knot.
    'And yet I must go. But I will give you clear proofs
so that you may understand. Wise Antikleia, she who was your mother,
she who foresaw then raised our daughters for us,
called me to her, lying in piteous state as the spirit
of life was going from her. She spoke to me urgently, saying:
"Enduring one, my daughter, you and I are all too aware
of the strange talents of these daughters of yours
by my son, whom now I despair of seeing again
before I sink into dark Hades. It is hard for me to wonder
how they may come to their inheritance without their father to protect them.
I had hoped to greet him myself, to kiss his head
and eyes and give him counsel with you, as two women
together can have sway with men. But I can do this:
pledge to me your vow and swear by the golden wand of Athene,
who has ordered many things for us, even beyond the knowledge
of Zeus Father, that when these two have reached their maturity
you will send them on the journey we have long considered together.
And since eventually Zeus sees and governs everything,
so without his willing it these two cannot control
their destiny, and he is often capricious besides, pledge to me
by your woman's honor you will take them to their strongest godly defender,
pure Phoebus at Pytho, and hear whatever his priestess
prophesies for them. But remember this: whatever happens,
promise that you will make the journey also; nor do I think
that this will be a useless venture for you, even
should my dear sweet one, Odysseus, accomplish his homecoming first.
Fare well, Daughter. Sister, a woman's fare well."'
    There was silence then. I saw that his mother's words
worked powerfully on Odysseus' battered spirit, for he did not
question my accounting of it. But he warred within himself
and would not speak. If ever I wished for help it was then.
'O Goddess Atrytone, glorious Athene, help me I pray,'
came the words into my heart, unbidden, startling, as though

the goddess herself were with me, her lustral presence blending,
wavering on the flames in the lamps and cressets. Odysseus
busied himself with shedding his garments. He placed his sword
beside the great bed he himself had built. He bent long
over his sandals loosening the knots and cords
and unwound them turn by turn around his powerful ankles.
In this moment I appealed again to the goddess in my thoughts:
    'O shining divinity, hear me now. Give power
to my words in Odysseus' thoughts. And let this be accomplished soon,
for we have not enjoyed the years of our youth together, and now
we stand at the threshold of old age. We have too little time
to know each other on these shores. I make my journey
gladly, but eager to return to my heart's home again.'
    I felt myself relaxing then, loose-limbed
and warm as if on soft fleeces under thick coverlets.
And next my husband, who was standing deep in thought, immobile
beside the tall bedpost carved from the bole of the olive:
'O my queen, Penelope, who are you now? You are not
the loyal and heedful wife I left but held always
in my thoughts of homecoming from far across the raging seas.
I think that some god has helped you for you have a will
far surpassing any woman, like one of the goddesses.
And you have powerful help among men also. For there came to me
Mentor who spoke to me all unbidden of the strange talents
bestowed on our daughters and urged me to send them soon on their way
to the sacred oracle to hear what the gods would have them do next.
And besides this, prudent Mentor, though nearing the end
of his days and always loving the considered life and discourse
with men in the assembly halls of palace and city, offered
and argued persuasively to be sent along as guide and escort.
I think some god told him that you – but who are you now?'
He uttered this like a bull who senses malevolent purpose in the hearts
of serving men as they grasp his horns and hold him, preparing to sacrifice.
    I spoke to him gently: 'Odysseus, hear me. Do not let your grief
for what you left behind you blind you to what is at hand. I am
Penelope. I am your queen, the same faithful, patient

woman you sang of and whose echo you followed home. But also
I am not the same. As an echo is never the same
as the song's first utterance nor could the swiftest-footed singer
ever retrace the echo and capture it just as it was sung,
you will not find the Penelope you carried within you on your journeying.
Are you the same Odysseus of twenty years ago?
Did you not return from your journey changed? And should I not
have changed also, as though just because you could not hear my story
from across the seas it was not unwinding on the air?
I must still be allowed to accomplish the rest of my journey.
Do not forget that the goddess, Athene herself, ordained it.

'As for Mentor, I cannot know if he somehow has knowledge
of my purpose. Perhaps he has guessed it. I welcome his counsel, which would
surely be the best among men. For he has made this journey
with you and knows it already.' Odysseus started, saying:
'What you say, my wife, wounds me deeply. For what man
even so wise as Mentor can surpass me for knowledge
of the ways of the sea and the lands that encompass it? Yet I think
you did not consider that there is no man who is better
seasoned or could be a more fitting escort for such a journey.'
The heart within me stopped, for I never thought his mind
would devise this plan, nor his heart, so weary of journeying, so long
the plaything of the fiendish seas like an injured mouse to a cat,
would consent to be torn again from sea-girt Ithaka, once home.
But I held my surprise within me, and later I often wondered
whether the goddess herself had a hand in dismissing his thought.

There came noise and shouting and exchange of words in the hallway
beyond the compacted doors. And next Aktoris called
that we must come forth to hear news of Telemachos. He had not
returned with his father, but instead he had gone up the slopes
of leaf-shaking Neritos, taking with him his fleet-footed dogs
and his young companions. Now Odysseus sprang
to the doorway, loosed the thong from the door bar
and lifted it aside. I felt also the fear I saw written
in the jerking motions of his naked muscles, but I thought
to snatch up Arete's splendid mantle to lend him dignity

for hearing the messengers. When he had opened the doors and folded
them back inward against the high door-posts, Aktoris
was there, her face stricken with grief, and my heart
dropped. For I knew, as only another woman will know it
without any telling, that she loved Telemachos. But she would not, or could no
speak, but led us down the hallway as if crazed,
her torch weaving its wavering beam ahead and beside
and catching in lurid flashes face after face we passed
in shocked silence. In the hall was a knot of men –
none bore the face of my son, none even noticed when both
our daughters drew close beside me, clad only in loose
nightshifts. Nor would anyone speak until first my husband:
    'Speak, men, or are you still fit to be called boys only?
You Peraios, tell me your news, and tell it
fully, for although news brought at such an hour
with such gravity can bode only evils
you will see that I am not a king to punish the messenger
for his message. Where is my son, who went with you at the parting of our ways
lusting to hunt the great-bristled, wily old boar of Mount Neritos?'
Peraios swallowed. Then he drew himself firmly erect
following the example of his lordly ruler, and spoke, saying:
    'O great Odysseus, son of Laertes, pride of all Ithaka,
you give me courage. For although your counsel always has been called
great-hearted among those of the elders who knew you in the days
before you sailed to the glory of the Achaians in plundered Ilion,
I trembled to be the man to answer your question. But I will be truthful.
Telemachos, high-hearted friend since my earliest youth, leader
of all the best young men of Ithaka, is fallen.
He comes, borne on a litter corded with strong vines.
We lined it as we could with leaves from the copses and soft fleeces
to make his journey less painful since he is badly wounded.
    'It happened this way: all the day from shadowy Dawn
we followed the careless track of the great beast, deep
as furrows a mule plows in a field, through the lower groves,
but lost his spoor on rocky ground high up the slope.
There, as if some god put purpose and cunning in its mind,

it seemed to disappear. At last when the sun was dropping fast
behind towering Same, we cornered the shuffling monster
in a crag where many times before he had slipped
from our well-sprung trap. The night was clear and the moon
so bright that no one among us considered abandoning
the hunt. But then a strange mist, not
like a mist that comes from the great shoulders of the mountain
shaking off slumber in the dawn, nor even an evening mist
that comes after rains, but a sharp, cold cloud like a curtain
suddenly drifted from nowhere in that clear air
as if some god had devised it. We were all as if blinded and although
we were drawn in tightly like the mouth of a net, we were lost
to each other. And the fearsome beast turned at once
as if heeding a clear signal to ravage back. None
of us saw him, but we heard the heavy grunting and squealing.

'It seemed to slip past us all, but crashed directly for Telemachos
and tore a gash in his side below the furrowed ribs,
an ugly wound, neither deep nor jagged, but oozing still
dark blood although it is all day since the mist
was whisked away as quickly as it had fallen, and we hastened to attend
and carry your beloved son down from the wretched heights.'

Odysseus groaned and now Laertes clasped his shoulder.
We all hastened along the shadowed columns, lurid
with swerving torch lights, furiously coiling streams of smoke
behind them, and pale faces questioning as they parted
before our rush to the portico. Here the bearers were
just setting down a litter with our son lying upon it.
Our beautiful Telemachos lay twisted and white. His suffering
was piteous to see, but his rantings were more painful. His mind,
harrowed by wrenching pain, had abandoned him, and he shouted abuse
and senseless pleadings, writhed toward us, menacing, from his pallet
and had to be restrained by four of his companions. I called to him and named him
and tried to rush forward, but Laertes stopped me and Odysseus
held me fast while Telemachos screamed vile curses
at my name. My knees gave way, the breath leaped out of me
and my joints loosened. I was aware that they held me

and led me to a chair, drew up a footstool under my feet,
and wrapped me in my hero's sea-purple robe. They brought me wine
with few parts water, which made its way into my breast
like a spear plunged to its hand-hold.
                            I awoke to hear Laertes saying:
'But the healing-thyme was gone from the hills long ago.
I have not seen its strange green flower thrusting
from late winter snows in twenty years. I think some god has decreed
its disappearance from the Earth, for nowhere in the near-lying islands
is it seen any longer. There is nothing like it for curing such a wound.'
   Now I was fully restored to my senses, for Ailanthis issued
a blinding challenge. All who heard it were spellbound at its portent.
She spoke simply but with a quiet fire that seared our spirits:
'Then, dear Father, you must give me leave to go on my journey,
now, and my mother and sister with me. No, hear me,
majestic Father, and know my mind. The wound will heal
or it will not. How much better it will be if we start
at once to inquire in all the places men inhabit
along the sea-routes whether the herb is still known.
My mother, my sister and I are appointed by the goddess Athene
to make a journey. All the stores, the clothing and gifts
are readied and have only to be put in the hull of the ship
lying ready at anchor inside the breakwater. O glorious father,
the gods decreed our going. Surely they who have plans
for Nerianne and for me would not be found lacking in designs for our brother
in this hour of need? We shall question the prophetess at Pytho for Telemachos,
next about ourselves. First we shall do what she ordains for our brother,
even if we must return quickly. I think that this is best
and I am determined to do it, even if I slip away
to do it myself. For I think that not even Odysseus will detain
the daughter of a king who follows the gods' plan for her.
Only say you will sanction the journey and help us to depart
so in this way my hesitant mother and sister are persuaded.
For it is unthinkable that a daughter of Odysseus set out from her home alone.'

NERIANNE GASPED. We all were stricken to silence, for these
were bold words to fling against the will of a powerful father.
My heart was torn within me over what was best
for me to do, whether to stay at the side of my suffering son
to see if he would worsen and sink down to Hades.
If this was to be the way of it, then months could waste away,
and perhaps the seasons would come around full circle
more than once before we could leave on our journey. Or
we might never start. As I looked from face to face I pondered
which way to turn my shuttle knowing deep in my mind
that whichever I chose could alter the pattern of all
our lives. Laertes stepped forward then, but powerful Odysseus
raised his arm and held him back. He spoke, saying:
   'Dear family, none of us is unaccustomed to trials
and now we meet them together. For already much evil
has befallen us, and many hard hours, but even so,
by close counsel we have escaped squabbling and heedless rift.
Many things point to this journey and urge me on
to grant it. For even with all my courage I cannot defy
the goddess to whom I owe so many good things.
Perhaps this is the best way. The proud heart in me
is persuaded. Let us all be won over. But here
is my order: I will appoint it for the morning of the second day
so you may rest while the last of the provisions are stored away.
Now come, let us go in and pour libations to the gods
and then you may rest until Dawn comes in her misty cloak.'
So he spoke and again we stayed stricken to silence,
each searching his aching heart, her pounding breast
for what the sister Fates might be spinning for us next.
   However matters went now there was much to sorrow over,

much to fear. But my heart had chosen the journey
before my resilient husband spoke his astounding words.
My eyes misted over with tears, but first
I saw that Laertes was also shamelessly shedding tears.
Nerianne took hold of my hand, Odysseus pressed at my side
and Laertes laid his reassuring hands on both our shoulders. Ailanthis
leaned close and we clung together beside our Telemachos.
We did what we could for him, one of us beside him
with Aktoris through the long day, while the rest of us busied ourselves
toward our going and to prepare for feasting together.
I sent Eurykleia to Mabantha and Phemios, and asked Medon
to bring Mentor to us. And my maidservants came and went,
carrying bedding and bowls, sandals and wine strainers, incense burners
and bronze ladles to be packed away. And I wrapped
three silver bobbins to take away as talismans but left
my loom standing, fastened with the strong oxhide, there
to be a sign to Odysseus. Thoughtfully I filled the four compartments
of my silver unguent box with its golden studs and tied
the silver scoop in under the lid with a scarlet thread.
I looked around the great, high-roofed chamber
with its strongly-anchored bed built by my husband and bedecked
in cloths of my fondest weaving, and thought: *Fare well*.

    I went to take my place beside Telemachos.
Nerianne tended him ceaselessly. She bathed his forehead
and cooled him, squeezing water on his wrists and feet from a sponge.
His blued wrists were slack, the splendid calves wasting
and splayed in twitching sleep. She spoke as I entered.
'O, Mother, how relieved I am to see you. But see how he sickens.
Surely you can help me? For nothing now will take away
his pain. This morning he smiled at me. He took my wrist
to his lips for a time, shedding tears. He spoke to me saying
that I alone could cure him if I stay with him always. He bade me
swear I would not journey. But then he bent with a spasm
and from then he has had no sight, nor has he spoken plainly,
but only babbles senselessly. O tell me, what more can I do?'
She sank to my shoulder, overcome, worn out

from her sleepless vigil, perplexed by her brother's wild pleas.
I thought quickly which way was best to answer her:
'You must not feel useless, Nerianne, nor berate yourself
if you cannot help him. We are all doing the best that we can
and none is to be blamed if we cannot bring him back to us. See,
now that you have ceased to hold the cooling sponge to his forehead
he grows more restless, so I think that you must have been soothing him
greatly. No one could have cared for him better. But now
it is my turn, for I am rested and you are exhausted.'
Nerianne dried her tears and shook her head. She spoke saying:
'Mother, I cannot. My place is here with my brother,
who begged me never to leave. I cannot leave him now.'
        These words dashed on my ears like the gusts of a sudden
storm wind, but I hid my dismay within me to think on later.
For although I spoke sharp words to her she would not be persuaded.
I looked at her then in amazement and laid her replies
away in my spirit, for they were her first rebellion.
I knew our ways with each other were altered forever from this moment.
So we tended my son together, throwing on fleeces
and coverlets and taking them off again as he shivered and sweated,
cooling his hands and feet and wiping his brow. Soon
our eyes met and I put my arm around her shoulders and embraced her.
        Next came the last time I bathed my splendid Odysseus.
I filled the tub with hot water and cold just
as he likes it, and added to it the skins of green figs
and thyme. I dipped the water over his taut shoulders
and dried his back, his loins, the muscled thighs with the smooth
but unmistakable scar, and rubbed the gleaming oil all over him.
Afterward we took some leisure in our studded chairs with footstools
drawn up under our feet and then our daughters
and many people of the palace gathered to feast. But this
was a somber meal; there was no rejoicing, no storytelling,
nor any dancing on the dancing floor in the courtyard afterward.
We all put our hands to the good things before us, especially
as good Eurynome and Eurykleia were already close
to shedding tears and lamenting over us. But the truth of it was

that soon we had all eaten and drunk the little
we desired. Then Odysseus signaled and led us out
into the forecourt where the fires under the crusty iron-forged
spits were by now only darkening embers under
the stars. He took with him the golden libation bowl
worked in beechnuts and acorns with bees all among them. He poured
the libation himself and added a prayer to Goddess Athene
to forgive his past forgetfulness of all her guidance and to hold
us ever in her favor, standing beside us in the coming trials.

    At once a shower of sparks flew up from the pit, or so
it seemed, for then there was a raining of stars from the sky and wonder
seized us at the sight of it. Happy it was our eyes were turned skyward
for I could not hold my smile within me at this proof
that all that had been woven around us was according to the goddess' design.
I looked at Nerianne but still could not read on her features
the pattern of her purpose. Next Odysseus turned to face me
openly, with stars still falling around his shoulders.
He pressed the heavy cup into my hands, saying:
'Take this with you, my prized cup, sent by Agamemnon
from far Mykene when glorious Achilleus and Menelaos came
to urge me to sail with the Achaians in the bristling ships to Ilion.
It is sacred to Zeus Father and to glorious Athene,
Helen's goddess-sister. Keep it by you always,
so that they might grant that you stay clear of danger.
But store this deeply in your mind; use it if you must,
for it was never more precious than you are.'
My heart overflowed then and the lights danced and blurred
in my eyes, blinding me to all but his gentle reach across my breast
to wrap his great sea-purple mantle around my shoulder.
I felt his arm take me then, leading my steps
back through the portico, over the threshold, along the smooth stones
of the corridors, alone on the way to our own chamber.
There Odysseus closed the tight-fitting doors and undressed me
himself, and mounting our surpassingly beautiful bed, we turned
to each other one last time in our old ritual.

    The night shed a restless sleep over us. I awoke

early to await the dawn, and with a heavy spirit
and measured steps I turned from the smooth carved bedposts
and fine-woven coverlets to step through the doors of our bedchamber.
Fare well, and fare me well, was pulsing in my ears,
shall I behold this room again? as I moved down the passage
and across the hall to the room where Telemachos lay. Nerianne
was there before me, composed in her bearing, looking resolved.

    I could no longer hold my thoughts within me, but spoke to her,
saying: 'You are so calm. How I wish, though, that the goddess
had arranged everything so our journey could be as planned.
For you had dreamed to see so much in the wide world
across the seas. But since you are the one who must choose
what you wish to do with your life and your gifts, I will not urge you.
And store this away in your spirit. You owe nothing
to anyone but yourself in this matter. Fare well, my daughter.'
I turned to Telemachos. She came to me then and, taking my hand,
she spoke to me, tears spilling over her cheeks like the grains
of white barley from her tiny hands when she made her first offerings
to the goddess. She shook her head and spoke to me, saying:
'O, Mother, wait. Surely you do not think I stay?
I will journey with you, as we always planned it. See my bundles
there in the corner?' I answered her: 'But, Nerianne, how is this?
For only last night you spoke to me of promising
your brother you would stay by his side.' She shook her head.

    'O, Mother, it is true that my brother, delerious, asked me to vow it.
And I was pained to think how to answer. Never
was my mind in such a turmoil. Never, save only
when my father turned in horror from my song, was I so distressed.
For the truth of the matter is that it is hard to leave him.
But I knew I must go and stayed my tongue from promising.
And at once the storm of the fever took him over, and from then
he only babbled in its thrall and knew no more.
Is it not orderly to pursue the means of remedy, and to seek
to know the immortal's next devising for us?
For does it not seem that she has stood beside us in all these matters
and they have been ordered by her toward our intended journey?'

    Wonder took me then. I stroked my son's brow
with the gentlest touch of my fingers lest he awaken
and endure sharp pains upon our going. But he was bound
fast in sleep and did not stir. I kissed his eyes
and then hastened to greet Ailanthis as she entered purposefully.
    With nods and gestures we moved toward the gate of the palace.
And on our way we passed between throngs of those near to us
all our days: the serving women and men, my handmaidens,
gardeners, hersdsmen, Karymethe, expert in dying cloth,
Kitios, who watches my geese, Eurykleia and Eurynome.
And here Aktoris on her way to Telemachos' side,
Dolios with his sons and many of my son's young companions.
And all were amazed and stayed stricken to silence as we passed.
In the courtyard were Eumaios with Mabantha and Phemios, who spoke,
saying: 'Come, all of you. Let us carry the last provisions.
It is not an easy matter for a woman, even when she is a queen,
to leave her house and her husband to journey along the sea ways.
But see, Odysseus is gone before us to see to the fittings
but leaves behind this order for us. I am to play
the clear-sounding lyre so our footsteps will be light as we hasten down
to the laden ship. This way no rumor can go
abroad that Odysseus is unwilling for his women to make their journey.'
    So he spoke and led the way gaily, and the rest of us
followed in the singer's footsteps. As we walked down I could not
keep from casting my eyes over my beloved country –
the shallow bowl of the valley between the five peaks,
and three sea-views with the many islands drifting in them,
the little puffs of smoke from the steadings curling and clinging
in the hollows against the wooded slopes and among the outcrops,
and the lip over which the fields spilled green
down to the rich bottom lands close to the harbor. We descended through the town
looking for glimpses of the lovely ring of the bay with its cutwater,
the fringe of buildings and small boats drawn up on the sea-shelf.
As we passed through the port, still in the long shadow of Neritos
I delighted in the pebbles on the shore chinking under my feet.
I reached down as if to pull up a loose strap

on my sandal and quickly searched for a pebble to carry with me,
one small stone of Ithaka to remember her by.
I chose not a rounded one, such as the sea has held
and smoothed, but one more like Ithaka herself, rough
and pitted with a stain of the red earth running through it.
I kept this stone with me always on my journey and ever since.

    We came to the place where several small boats
were drawn together onto the shore. And Odysseus had gone before us
to urge the seamen to lay hold of the running gear and make everything
ready for our departure. And now my stately husband himself
rowed me to the great beaked hulk of a ship
lying at anchor. He handed me aboard and led me to my seat
in the stern of the ship. And after us came Mentor to sit
next to me. Then Odysseus led Nerianne and Medon brought
Ailanthis and they seated them with us also. And Phemios
set down his precious lyre and tenderly reached to Mabantha
to help her aboard. I turned to Odysseus next, with the mists
of morning casting an aura about him like that of a god.
And above him the swallows darted and a great white sea-bird
rose on an updraft, spiraling in ever-widening circles
until I looked away. Great-hearted Odysseus
spoke to me then a formal parting for all to hear:

    'Fare well, my queen. May Zeus Father grant you
a calm voyage with quiet seas and fair stern winds following.
Do not linger, but rather hasten your going and coming
with your spirited daughters. I with my son await you eagerly
for he has need of the medicine you seek. I cannot journey
again on the high seas for fear of the wrath of Poseidon,
Earth-Shaker, against me because I bested his son, but first
I must offer hecatombs to restore all the gods' favor.
Since it is your wish to go I do not stand in your way;
rather I send along as escort a second ship
named for my sister, *Ktimene*, with trusted henchmen aboard her.'

    He turned abruptly then, but I called to him softly, saying:
'O my king, fare well. You are so gallant. But store this in your mind
and make it your way of seeing also; they are *our* children.'

There was bustling then. A great clamor went up among the people
as the ship *Ktimene*, pulled up on shore, put out
into the harbor, oars singing in the oarlocks, white sail
lifting in the heartening gust of favoring wind just
as my Odysseus reached the curve of the beach and leaped ashore.
We too began to move as the anchor stone was lifted.
I watched my Odysseus stride up the beach. The men took
the oars, each at his oarlock, and dipped as one oar
into the green of the harbor waters. With even strokes they stitched
the sea-folds with a rhythm like the lift and fall of the bars
of my loom, like the beating of my heart pulsing with longing
for the faces on shore, which receded with the wild pennons
waving in the breeze. Finally even the outstanding form
of my hero disappeared into the brightness of white-shining walls
rising up the steep slope of the harbor approach.

Next I felt joy – release and delight such as
I last remembered when as a budding girl I shed my robes
on the hollow-sounding shale of a cove near my father's house.
There I walked till the warm stones gave way
to water deliciously cool like fine cloth on my toes,
ankles and forelegs; then it rose above my knees and thighs
to my virgin-zone and up my loins to the core of my belly.
It encircled my waist, lapped at my breasts and tickled my neck
as I gave myself up to float in the warmth pooled at the surface.
Now I delighted again as I gave myself over to the sea,
as I breathed in and felt its fresh tang in my nostrils.
And the running gear was loosened and the white sail spanked the wind
and, filling, lifted us easily on its billowing wings
and carried us, yielding, along. The skies were high and endless
with Helios rising, sea-birds dipping and calling, calling. . .

Soon we came to the headland. A conch sounded from land.
There, as we rounded the jut was proud Laertes, rod-straight,
gazing toward us over the lightening waters.
We drew closer and his stance softened. He raised his bent arm
as if to shield his eyes from Helios' rays,
but the god was behind him and behind the towering steeps above him,

which shadowed us still. I echoed his gesture, then stretched out
my other hand palm up. He answered with the same motion dropping
the staff he had lately adopted, and we stayed locked this way
in fare well until the sail swelled forward to pass
between us. When next I could see, the headland was far behind
with a mist of sea spray drawn low over the water
like a veil before it so it seemed to be floating from us.
    I do not know how long I stayed watching as Ithaka
glided by, looming steep over us and the luminous calm water,
which barely touched the hem of her skirts
along the reach, and Same shining opposite as Helios'
rays touched the rolling slopes, and the sea-mist rising.
We came to the last promontory, crossing the divide to the open water
and the sun broke over us, the sea shone white
like the face of an early-risen maiden in her polished mirror.
A playful breeze skittered around the hills and bays
between three points lying like geese with necks
outstretched upon the water, and soon the surface was covered as with stitches,
next with a weave of little ridges criss-crossing like rushes
in a basket. Soon the chop of little wavelets cast
a deep blue mantle over the sea all around us.
Already Same was sliding behind the mists and Ithaka's
hills were graying. I pondered deeply in my heart and this
seemed to me to be the best way to leave her: I nodded
my fare well then and turned my face ahead to the wide mouth
of the gulf between the islands and Elis, resolving
not to look back again at Ithaka nor to see her
ever disappear completely on the face of the sea, but rather
to keep her still visible in my mind as she was now.
    The sun lifted over the seas to run behind us
with the favoring stern wind so that our ship, the *Sea-Swift*,
and the *Ktimene* might run the whole of our course through the sea's waters.
And Mentor, who sat next to me, counseled me wisely and prophesied:
'My child, I think that your journey will be very different
from that of your long-absent husband, Odysseus. For he
went away with the Achaians to make war, to plunder and sack

the cities of men and to carry away their women and their treasures.
Poseidon, Earth-Shaker, was harshly angered and held it
against the seafaring men that they ranged across his domain
for violent pursuits. This was the reason why so many ships
of the Danaans were dashed to pieces far from home and loved ones.
Odysseus called down the god's vengeance when he blinded Polyphemos.
Yours is another quest; with its own kind of testing
for you and your splendid daughters. And I am here to help you.
But they, with their godlike talents, and you, with your own wits
and wisdom to guide you, will mostly find your own ways.'
    Now while we two were conversing thus the sailors
tended the running gear, the sails were filled with wind,
and the ship cut lightly through the curling froth
of the waves like the gulls that skimmed the spray to scoop up
silver morsels or rainbow-hued fishes that knifed
away from our dark prow. And often near us or beside us
dolphins, who are sometimes kindly toward men, leaped and plunged,
as comical as geese in a large flock arching their necks
and waddling toward the good things scattered below for them.
And soon we ran between Elis and the deceiving islands
at the near side of the long reach to Boeotia. Here
the waters shimmered so many shades of blue that I turned
often to my wide-eyed daughters and took their hands to squeeze them
hard in mine for joy, and they answered with delight
shining from their faces haloed with flowing hair. The helmsman,
fine-bearded and courteous, came to us often to show us
the nestled villages or sheer-walled promontories, asking us whether
we were comfortable, or lacking water, or desired good things to eat.
    And because we had twisted our veils behind our necks
to keep them from blowing into our faces, and since
the customs of men at sea are ordered differently from men
on the land so our spirits were loosened in us, he told me his name:
Apollytos from sea-faring Akaion on the western shores.
Before we reached the narrows where an arrow of land
menaces all who pass by, I called Mabantha to me.
And straight away Mentor made a place for her by my side.

· XI ·

EVEN WITH the ship rocking on the breeze-driven swell of the sea
Mabantha moved with a stately grace, the mantle that flowed
from her shoulders revealing a robe beneath it of strange colors
and startling design. But strangest of all was the pattern
of the weaving. It was alternately fine and coarse but warp and weft
were impossible for me to discern. It seemed to be woven in wondrous swirls
of changing slant that shimmered and faded from light
to dark on the restless colors of the pattern. I spoke to her saying:
'O my friend, word comes running with the wind that there is sickness
upon you. Surely after so much travel you cannot be sea-green?
You seem to be in splendid spirits now. But come,
answer me truly this thing that I ask you, and do not hold back:
how did you manage to range the seas by yourself in quest
of your brother? And how did you come to throw in your distaff with Phemios?
Where did you come upon cloth of such bold design? Nothing
can match it for color nor especially for the subtlety of the weave.

89

Never have I seen its like before, not among all the handicraft
of far-flung women traded on the shores of the harbor,
nor all the gifts from the suitors or voyagers, or my husband returning.
Come now, answer me fully so I may know the truth of it.'
   'O my lady, I answer. It is truth that sickness was coming upon me.
But always at the start of a voyage this happens. You are forgetting
I do not come from a seafaring people. In truth my people
are famous in all the land below Helios for weaving
since there is abundance of fiber growing in the high plain
of my country, and many good pastures for livestock. This robe
I wear I bring from my country. There women of inventive minds
craft looms more intricate than yours. But see,
I can show you how this is done if it pleases you well.
For you are expert in handicraft and delight in new ideas.'
'O my friend, why have you not shown me this garment before?
For this is the kind of fine handiwork women do
to place beside the fine crafted tools of men
in the giving of gifts, or trading for copper, gold or grain,
our perfumed oils or for spice. With a skill such as this
I, and the women of Ithaka also, could weave the most prized cloth
in all the seas, delighting men and their cities.'
'Penelope, my friend, I was not thinking of it for giving.
I was keeping it carefully stored away, to put on
for the matchless occasion when the word would come of homecoming,
to wear it to greet Eurybates, my brother, but he is lost.
   'You ask me how I have traveled far, a woman alone.
I will tell you truthfully so you will know it.
Many more women than you think journey on those ships. Wives
are voyaging with husbands, mothers and grandmothers are fleeing war
or crops failing, wives are traveling back to their fathers'
houses, widows with small ones dragging down their cloaks
are ferrying their produce or handicrafts to markets. I would sit among them.
There we women are safe from the grasp of any man.
But besides this I was moving always as if cloaked in some magical
robe. It was woven from my purpose, patterned of pained resolve,
colored with independent spirit. Yet always it was this robe.

I had patterned it to wear when I rejoin my family only.

'And then Phemios found me. He was not like the other men
in the ships. He would listen thoughtfully when people talked,
even we women. He would ask for our stories only,
moving among us with respect. Our ship was slow
and heavy in the waters, carrying oils and grain in great jars,
timbers from Syria, and baskets heaped with mountains
of shells to crush for purple dye and bound for Keftieu
which you name Krete. We were on that ship together to Ialysos,
Kamiros, Nisyros and Kos. Next, close-lying Naxos and Paros.
We were coming inside the breakwater of Naxos where men
were running down to the sand, and women and children with water
in jars and figs, and flocks, and geese flapping. Always
the coming and going of ships is exciting to me
and my spirit tells me it was so also for my brother. So always
I was looking at people in comings and goings, looking for him.

'Phemios was standing beside me. He notices things. He spoke to me
then, asking: "O dark one, you, who above all women
have intelligence and grace, are avid always to watch our landfalls.
Answer me this truly, so I may know it. Are you,
as it is said, only an itinerant dancer with no ties
to any city or people? Or is it true that you seek
someone secretly, and this is why you are drifting through seas
unfriendly even for men to cross, and treacherous to women?"

'This was a man not like other men and something,
some urging sent by the god was always drawing us together.
So with caution at first I told him – not the same way
I tell you, but this the storytellers do also.
I told Phemios how I bought my passage down
Aigyptos at fullest flood when none can catch up with any boat
ahead on the fast-moving swell. And when I came to the shore
of the great sea with the rolling surf, I trembled but never
thought to turn back. Ahead I knew not. Behind I knew
no good was coming, so next I chose a merchant ship
with grain and perfumed oils stored between the oarlocks
for trading with Syria. Some others were journeying also

aboard, returning home since Pharaoh had hurled the sea marauders
skulking back. I told Phemios of all
the many crossings I made on the balanced ships, always
searching. I told him: "Now I sail to the land of the Argives,
and here my story breaks off, for the next is yet to be told."
   'He was leaning his ear toward me thoughtfully as I spoke.
Then he looked at me gravely, in that way of his.
"Mabantha, I will name you, and this will be what all the Argives
will call you. I think that you will have your best chance of finding
your brother among them. For they are returned and returning from Ilion
by the wide ways across the seas, and have fought and sailed
with all peoples. Even among those who sailed from surf-fringed Ithaka
with godlike Odysseus there was one man, dark-skinned
like you, who went with them to punish Troy
for the name of Helen." At these words the heart within me
was leaping and I trembled with excitement. I spoke to say:
   ' "If what you are saying is true then this is a strange thing.
Even in all my journeying I have met few from my district
who wander far on the much-traveled sea routes.
Who was this man, and what country did he come from?
Has he returned from the fighting or is he still wandering the seas?"
Phemios answered me saying: "See, I will tell you all that you ask.
Eurybates was the name he had among the Ithakans. He was
dark-complexioned, curly-haired, loyal and agile.
Odysseus favored him above his other companions. They were kindred
in all their thoughts, so I think that even now he is making
his way homeward to sea-girt Ithaka with noble Odysseus.
He claims no other country along Helios' span."
   'But then the hot tears sprang from my eyes, and Phemios noticed
and understood. And nothing is better to urge on the releasing
of clenched tears than the proffered shoulder. Not yet
was Phemios my husband, nor had I lain beside him; yet something
was guiding his sympathy to me, and our thoughts were coming to be in harmony
I spoke then, saying; "You are so gentle. And besides,
unwitting, you are giving me the greatest note of hope I hear
around the whole of the wide sea. For my brother was named

Rbatha, and surely it is possible this is that same man."
And Phemios urged me to go with him back to Ithaka, saying:
"There you can wait for him, surely to return some moment soon
in the black ships with Odysseus. And I will call you wife
and keep you with me as mine, but lay no obligation
upon you." But, my friend, later, in that part of my story
you already know, this changed, taking us both with amazement.
I accepted and was grateful. For all those seasons I had accepted
no others. O, some would take me, in the way men will, but they
could not touch my spirit. I was bound to my brother. We were. . .'

But now Phemios came to us in our seats at the stern of the ship.
He pointed to the jutting coastline beside us and before us
and then to the towering peaks of lofty Parnassos lifting
higher and blazing white behind the scattered peaks.
For while Mabantha was telling me her astounding tale,
I was amazed and had noticed little of our journey.
But now we approached the harbor of Krisa at the head
of a deep bay. And Helios glided beside us, teasing
from behind the jumbled crags. The sails no longer billowed
full in the capricious breeze, so the oarsmen dipped their oars
in blue-green waters dappled with bright beams
from between the bluffs. Phemios held out his cloak, saying:
'Dear wife, it grows cool now that the land casts its shadows over us.
See how our queen is wrapping herself in Odysseus' splendid mantle.
I bring you mine to throw around your shoulders should you wish it.'

Mabantha roused herself also, startled to see how far
we had journeyed while in the thrall of her story. She smiled at him then,
but shook her head and lightly flicked her own cloak
across her proud bosom and shoulders. Glowing and windblown,
Ailanthis and Nerianne approached. I rose to stand with them,
arms about their shoulders. Theirs twined at my waist
and with avid eyes we scanned the quiet waters looking
always ahead toward the curve of the bay and our day's end.
In those clear waters skeins of tiny fishes
flashed and darkened skittering the bars of light like birds
quickly veering in flight. Now Mentor joined us,

yearning toward the broad green plain of the valleys that opened
away from rocky ledges that endure the sea's pounding.
    Soon the high peaks of Parnassos shone golden.
And now a current of activity stirred among the seamen.
While some still bent their oars in the sheers, others
leaned to the halyards to loosen the sails, and handling them easily
like sheer-woven linen they folded them and stored them away.
Next they took down the large mast tree, while beside us
the bustle aboard our companion ship *Ktimene* was matching ours,
throwing over the anchor stones to hold the ships.
Now we could see the steadings on the plain, the harbor
shining with Helios' last rays slanting from his couch
behind the cloud-boiling steeps. And now we could see
men moving about on the shore and the little breakwater
guarding a knot of small vessels gathered inside.
    I turned to my daughters' questioning faces, saying: 'My dears,
it is time to unwind our veils again and draw them
over our heads. We will not go among strangers unveiled,
for that may be considered immodest. But please, Mentor, answer me
this thing that I ask. For the mind within me is divided,
whether it is best that we all set foot on the shore at once
or whether first I should send you and some one
of the best men from our sister *Ktimene* to tell the uncles
of Odysseus we are here and to prepare a welcome for us. For we did not
dare to send word ahead that we were coming, never knowing
when our departure would be accomplished.' Mentor now
answered: 'What you say, Lady, is fair and orderly.
It is better to follow the people's customs outwardly in these lands.
Then they will not perceive your inward freedom from restraint
nor hate you for it, but receive you courteously as guest or suppliant.
But as for approaching these people, despite their blood ties
to your own husband, my mind urges caution.
For Rumor has circulated from here stories of lawless behavior
and insolence to travelers, defying Zeus who protects them.
I think that this is the best way; I shall put in
directly with several of the best men from sturdy *Ktimene*

and go straight to the sons of Autolykos, if they still live.
I will see what people these are, whether they are rude and savage
or just and hospitable to strangers, like Odysseus' godlike grandsire.'

    Apollytos commanded the seamen to lower the small craft
quickly for Mentor's passage to waiting *Ktimene*. Soon
other seamen were let down from the sister ship to go
with Mentor landward toward the rocky breakwater and its harbor.
Before he reached the opening to the harbor the day glow
faded to purple and the sea and the journeying ways were darkened,
even the gleaming tip of Parnassos, which was last to be dimmed.
Our good helmsman, Apollytos, made us comfortable, setting up
mixing bowls, filling them brimful with wine, and mixing the wine
himself. His men brought the bread and oil and other provisions
in their baskets. Eagerly we put forth our hands to the good things
before us, our bodies made hungry by high spirits,
by the wind and the sun and the ship's tossing, and by the glow
of the air in the rising moonlight. Indeed the thoughtful helmsman's
torches were scarcely needed, for all ate and drank quickly,
eager for slumber to relax all our joints within us.

    When Dawn rose again, pale and hesitant, from behind
Parnassos' broad shoulders, I arose and bound on
my sturdiest sandals. I climbed to the shadowed deck of the ship
and took my seat in the stern while the seamen scoured and mended,
trimmed and tested the running gear of the well-built vessel.
They did this daily, following the orders of their lord-like helmsman.
And presently the mists drew back, the waters gleamed
and the others who accompanied me appeared, two by two,
to greet the shining day. For some while no one
spoke, but all bathed in Parnassos' light with only
a sea-bird's calls, gentle lapping, the occasional hiss
of a swell on distant rocks or the thud of an oar echoing
faintly on our hull from far off. But then there was stirring
in the harbor inside the breakwater, and voices and scraping sounds
and oar thuds broke our reverie. Now came *Ktimene*'s
small boat swiftly toward us driving ahead of her
shuddering wavelets on the face of the water. The craft steered

straight toward us on the *Sea-Swift* and soon Mentor joined us,
his features stricken with outrage although his speech was measured:

    'O lady, circumspect Penelope, I think that these are not
a people for you to visit. Hard men, if men
they be, for they know not any graces of decent living.
There are no women among them, none with any pride
remaining nor any stature among the boisterous rabble
that surrounds them. Nor are any of the sons of Autolykos still
alive, for all have perished and gone down to Hades.

    'And this is the story as best I could glean it from the slavering lips
of underlings, leaning heavily over their battered cups
with ring upon ring of old wine crusted inside them:
of all the eight sons of glorious Autolykos, only
three returned from Ilion – Timenos, Anchises and Klostios
famed for his swift sword. And only Timenos' wife,
Kasti, came down to the harbor to greet them with wreaths
and white arms outstretched. The other two wives were weaker
by far, and each had lain with young men of the country
and taken up with them. These were taking their pleasure
even as their lords were homecoming. Roughly the brothers questioned
Kasti, saying: "Answer us, circumspect sister, you
who have come down alone to the sea's breakwater. Tell us the truth
so we may know it fully: where are our wives, your sisters?
Why have you not brought them down to the harbor with you
to greet us, as is proper for wives to do when their husbands return?"
But she was fearful to speak of her sisters' shameful acts, or perhaps
she pitied them and meant to shield them. None who knows the story
will say. Her Timenos had always been mightily favored by his father,
Autolykos, and these others were always envious of him, striving
to see him slain in battle, but never succeeding because
Apollo loved him and sprang their traps and shielded his back.

    'Now on the homeward-bound path the brothers grumbled
and glowered at the happy pair who would soon begin their lovemaking.
And when they were come into the disorderly palace and found
their guilty wives, they slew them on the spot, forcing
Kasti to watch them wreak unspeakable vengeance on the bodies.

Then they told her to . . . But there are things too horrible for your ears
or for your daughters and companions to hear, or my mouth
to utter. Their purpose was to provoke the envied Timenos,
and in this they succeeded, telling him harshly: "See, O favored one,
how treacherously your shameful wife has acted, provoking our just
wrath upon her. Surely it would be fair for her
to welcome us also with arms open for sweet
lovemaking as joyous homecoming has been denied us."
  'Timenos reached for his father's sword, but others of the party
held him at a signal from Klostios. They killed him outright, forgetting
even to prolong his dying and break the spirit within him,
so strong was the lust upon them to accomplish their ends
with Kasti. There followed an endless night of which no teller
I found had words to speak. But never since
has any woman suffered more, even now
when the depraved sons of these sons, sworn to consort with men
alone, allow only the most abject females to service them
like animals brought to slaughter. Their mothers' names were banished
from the lips of all and few know them. These men live
like beasts, knowing nothing of the graces of women nor fine handicraft.
I fear for you and your shining daughters, for it is told that they lie
in wait on the way to Pytho to manhandle any women who journey
as suppliants. I think that for men like these no ties of kinship
would avail a guest where there are no women of stature to mitigate.'
  At these words we all stayed stricken to silence.
We turned aside our faces so none might see our horror.

· XII ·

MENTOR BROKE the silence then, saying: 'Surely
there is little need for men to be conjuring sea monsters
to fear, seeing the way many a man among us
will prey upon others monstrously enough.
One night in that palace, if it ever happened, was surfeit
for me. No man from those halls will lift his head
high enough from his filthy table to think of me
or to question who I am and what my country is
today. But I left behind me men from *Ktimene* to say
I would be going down to my black ship to encourage
my companions since I am the elder among them. And I hurried down,
secretly watching for the path that would divert
away from their steading, but nowhere could I find it,
with only the deep chasm of Pleistos' stream below
where a vulture circled high and yet beneath me. My queen, here
is no more need of custom. You must go straight to The Pythia,
either praying to the gods that these brutes will remain slumped
in their stupor, or return by some other way, for this
was why you sailed on the open sea before the best season.
Or, rather, you might journey to Asklepios' seat, and there seek a cure.'
　　Now I could not keep my dismay within me and spoke,
saying: 'Mentor, how shall I change my design now,
how turn away elsewhere? It is here I was sent
and here I was destined to come with Ailanthis and Nerianne
on the divinity's purpose, long before Telemachos was stricken,
even before Odysseus returned to Ithaka. But how
shall I accomplish it if you urge me against it, and know of no way
to go there?' Next our helmsman, Apollytos, who was always at hand
seeing to all things on board his ship, came to us and spoke,

98

saying: 'O queen, hear me while I speak out. There is
another way. For many men journey on the suppliant's path
from far Helicon and Thebes by the Triple Ways
where monstrous Oidipodes slew his own father even as he recoiled
from the priestess' prophesy, and he married his mother, following it fatefully.
These pilgrims are eager, once they have heard The Pythia's verses,
to turn quickly homeward. And I think that this is the best plan;
I will send some of my best men to accompany
you and your daughters. You must leave at once, for all ways
are steep and rocky and you must return before nightfall.'

   He spoke steadily under our gaze and I knew his words
were well-founded. I looked from face to face
among my beloved companions, seeing there what I hoped they,
in turn, could read on my own features. We spoke together
saying: 'Yes. It is time. We will go at once.' And all
moved quickly to retrieve wallets, pouches, stout sandals,
veil or cap to shield their heads from the glare of the sun.
I thought of the snow gleam I had seen on mighty Parnassos' slopes
and stashed Odysseus' great sea-purple mantle
away in my bundle. Next I was handed with care
by Apollytos himself into *Ktimene*'s ready skiff
rocking beside the black hull, and the others followed
quickly in *Sea-Swift*'s boat. Our oarsmen pulled us swiftly
toward the inlet, around the breakwater, and up to the gleaming sand
of the shore. By now the people of the city were busy at their tasks.

   We soon obtained mules to carry us along the steep ways
to speed our journey. We started on the path from the green plain
that spread like a rippling mantle around the feet
of ancient white-haired Parnassos, with our strong-armed seamen
as escort, trudging the stony path in their thick oxhide sandals.
It was the time when the morning mists were steaming
from the valleys and deep ravines. As we climbed
they wreathed above us, unveiling in turn the rock-strewn slopes
that lifted from the plain, and then the ever-steeper
sides of the chasm of River Pleistos, still threading
the dry slash of the river bed down to the sea. And we climbed

and climbed, so that many times I thought my laboring mount
would lie down under me, or that surely our hardy men would call out
and throw themselves down upon some narrow verge to rest themselves.
    But we rose with Helios ever higher until we came
to the place where, looking back, we could see only a cleft
of sea. Around us was the high hush that sits suspended
over murmurs from below with the twittering of white-flashing swallows
and the hum of bees in the honeyed grasses. Soon only
the plod and scrabble of hoof and sole and the breathing of men
and beasts came to my ears for a time. Next a raucous screeching
assailed us from above. As we rounded a bluff an owl
spattered onto the air from a crusted tree. A murder
of crows wheeled and dove at it, croaking a wild chorus
that echoed from the crags and cliffs around. They rose higher
and plunged sharply back while our gazes were stopped at the sight
their battle heralded. For there on the brow of a steep slope
with deep blue behind it and the ever-sentinel cliffs, was the shrine
we sought, radiant Pytho, throne-seated in the distance,
the steps rising from terraces of huge stones, and beside
and below the earth falling away to the steeps of the gorge
beneath. And near us was the deep cleft with the hallowed spring
cascading. All feet had stopped. All labored breathing
ceased. For a time we imagined a peace that only
increased until it burned our eyes and melted our limbs.
    A hand reached then to touch my palm, which was resting
slack on my knee. It was Mentor, who spoke to rouse me, saying:
'Come, Lady, for although we are now nearly
within the sacred precincts, still in these crags the beast skulks
always nearby. It is better to seek to accomplish your designs
quickly and return to the safety of ships offshore
before he prowls the night.' We moved on. Yet in my heart
I lingered long in that wild place, with my first glimpse of the precinct
of The Pythia herself, whom we soon approached. We left Mabantha
and Phemios behind us in the town with the oarsmen, for Helios was now
high and the sweat was breaking out on all our sun-struck brows.
    But Mentor came with us to show the way. I and my daughters

were so giddy with joy and yearning for the coming encounter
that we would have climbed the heights of that sacred way
like young kids, over rocks worn soft by many sandals
and earth the color of a days-old piglet or a lightly baked bread loaf,
had we not felt Mentor toiling and short of breath
behind us. Up and up the path wound,
beside the jagged cliffs scored like ruined columns, the deep
gash where the sacred spring plunges to the chasm,
and among old olive trees where the grasses were splashed with the colors
of myriad wildflowers and smelled of earth and warm sun
on olive-stained rock and were alive with bees. We came to an olive
whose venerable bole had been cut in favor of an off-shoot which now
was thick as a girl's waist and cast its shade on the path.
      There Mentor came beside me and spoke to us, saying:
'Here I must stop and wait for you beneath the last olive tree.
I have to. For The Pythia herself once decreed it, saying:
"None shall walk the laureled pathway twice, but for last device."
Perhaps it could be said that I am no longer the same one
who journeyed in the region many years ago, since I
was only a youth when I came to accompany godlike Odysseus,
and he, as a young man, came at the urging of mighty Autolykos,
who was his grandfather, and who gave him his name.
For who, when he is old and the strength in him is gone and he has seen
the far places and many men, is the same one
who knew nothing when he walked in the careless grace of youth?
But the prophetess is never direct – each utterance is stranger
than the mind of the hearers can readily grasp, so the mind in me
is persuaded that this is the best way. Do not be concerned for me
but rather hasten with your daughters to your appointed journey's end.'
      'Dear Mentor, never shall I blame you because you do not
choose to trifle with the oracle's words. Already you have led us
far beyond the strength of most men of your years so that the mind
within me wonders at you. Rest well in this shade,
old man, and soon we will come back to lead you away homeward.'
We saw him comfortably settled and resumed our winding way.
Now there were stones expertly cut and close set

for our feet to walk on, and larger blocks for steps and the terraces
artfully fitting the contours of the slope and moving with it
to delight our eyes and draw our feet, as in winged sandals,
upward and around the curves. Then as we passed
the great ivy-grown boulder of the serpent, it burst before us – the sanctuary,
with columns stone-grown as if from the crevices behind them.

    As we moved closer it came forth from the cliff-folds and welcomed us,
tall against the immense blue, with purple-strewn steeps
a mantle shoulder-blown behind its crested diadem. Already
the great banded doors were opening and as we proceeded
up the steps to the portico, a breath from cool depths
between the columns enveloped us like an invisible veil. We smelled
the sweetness of the flowers wreathing the sacred Omphalos, which rose
majestic from the darkness as our eyes cleared. Nerianne took my free hand,
while on my other side Ailanthis held my shoulder
and together we stood amazed at what we saw and felt in this place.

    Soon the light entered also and showed us the way
to circle the Great Navel of the World, flower-decked and powerful.
Next we could see The Pythia herself below us, with stairs
rising on four sides. Her tripod rested on the bare slab
of the mountain. Through it ran that cleft
that winds to the bowels of the earth and from it writhed
the smoke-of-the-deeps so she seemed to dance before us
a weird dance to wavering notes we scarcely knew we heard,
wailing through the lofty columns. We stood close like sheep,
our shoulders pressed against each other's, and wondering so
we had no speech left. Next from some hidden place
a priest came out. He wound his way down the stair
with hypnotic slowness that confused our blinking eyes until all
stopped – the motion, music, smoke, the chanting that we noted
only in its abrupt ceasing. We saw nothing and everything,
until our sight was restored and our eyes fixed on the pillar
of the priest standing stiffly below us at the foot of the stair, arms
stretched up to pull us earthward into the endless well
where the oracle sat. As I stirred and took my daughters' hands
to begin our fearful descent the prophetess spoke, saying:

'Welcome, O artful Penelope, who comest to my beautiful house,
thou daughter of Aramantha and Ikarios, Queen of Ithaka.
Come and go. Go and come. I am the sum.'
    We descended into the pit, the white-bearded priest before us.
We had reached the last high step and my eyes were level
with his, which blazed from amid his unruly hair and brows.
Then he melted back and away. We stepped down
to the prophetess on her tripod and sat as suppliants before her.
    'I am the oracle, you at my feet – tell me what you seek.'
She pointed to Ailanthis, gazing at her. Ailanthis answered:
'O Prophetess of Pytho, you who see all, who know our hearts' devising
and the state of being of all things on earth,
we seek the healing herb that will restore our son and brother
to his mind and body. That which we know of, a wild thyme
of the mountains on our seagirt Ithaka, has fled. Rumor has whispered it
among the seamen that the weed is found no more upon the slopes
of Elis or the other mainland countries. Tell us this truthfully
so we may know it. Where does it grow and how shall we
reach it and return by the fastest way to ensure his cure?'
A twist of smoke issued from the dark crevice beneath her.
She threw her head back and rolled it from side to side,
keeping her eyes averted from us while she chanted:

> *'Three you come*
> *but two you leave*
> *to seek the far-flung*
> *queen all grieve.*
> *Together you*
> *may never see*
> *which two and one*
> *will someday be!'*

    As she spoke these last words it seemed that light flashed.
Certainly she was wreathed in a swirling cloud of foul-smelling smoke.
We choked and turned our faces away, gasping
and with tears streaming down. When we turned again to face her
the tripod was vacant. The pit was empty save for my daughters

and myself and the forbidding priest, he silent as the pillars
of stone. Terrifying though The Pythia had seemed with her ordered hair
coiled tightly, and wild patterns twining her clothing
and winding along her white arms onto her neck
and cheeks, her absence was a searing void. The steep steps
seemed to close in upon us from above and the priest
moved slowly toward us, who were turned to stone in awe.
I took my daughters' warm hands as he spoke to us, saying:
'Pythia is angered. You have not asked her what you truly
seek. Stay.' He slowly wound a way upward
and disappeared over the rim of the pit. We were alone
in a stillness as thick as wool until a shattering scream reached us.

  Our offering of a goat was meeting the knife. Entrails draped
on the Navel Stone would tell our fates. A silence held us
in the semi-gloom until we became aware of footsteps
returning. The priest appeared behind us, his hands covered
with the black blood. As he descended obliquely his footsteps
echoed in the deep mind-rending silence. We turned with him
as flowers turn to a sinking sun. The prophetess appeared
in smoke that cleared at once like the surface of a pond
when a fitful breeze dies and the depths shine. She was seated
on her tripod as though she had never left us and spoke, saying:
'I am the oracle, you at my feet. Tell me what you seek.'

  'O Prophetess of Pytho, you who see all, know our hearts' contriving
and the state of being of all things on earth,
we seek the return of my daughter's glowing voice in song.
She lost it singing too close to bone, too true to pain
for her father, Odysseus, returned to the home that was strange.'

> 'Three you came
> but two you leave
> to seek the far-flung
> queen all grieve.
> This can be done
> so you believe.
> Together you may never see

who two and one
will someday be.
This was not all!'

    Beside her feet was a box, ivory with strange designs
covering it. Rows of small carved markings descended
like steps down the sides between coils and circles. She picked it up,
lifted its top, and cast its contents, screeching mice,
onto the floor. At once we heard, from above us, a sound,
a whispering-sliding as of heavy fleeces dragged along the stones.
Over the rim of the pit narrow heads appeared.
Bodies followed. Serpents poured slowly over the edge
and rippled in rhythm over step after step
down toward the slab where the mice squeaked piteously, running
in circles. We looked to the prophetess, who smiled, bemused,
while around us the snakes wove and thrust as the mice leapt
and darted, seeking in vain to scale the first high step.

    We stirred ourselves now and as one we rose to step back and up,
thinking by this to escape the creatures' notice. But the priest
raised his arm toward us and we stopped there as if struck,
staring into the foul spectacle of beast devouring beast
before our eyes until the last small creature
trapped in a far corner behind the priest was gone.

    Ailanthis gasped. Above us slithered three more serpents.
They flowed down the steps in succession toward the three of us.
We forgot the carnage behind us and stared. A lyre sounded.
A voice sang out, clear and light. It gathered brightness
from the corners of that dim place and danced above the horror
we witnessed. It strengthened and soared while the loathsome serpents slowed.
They turned. Side by side like the streams of a river or threads
on my loom, they moved back up the stairs and away from us.
The voice was Nerianne's own. I threw my arms around her
and made much of her and Ailanthis embraced and held us both.
Nor could we keep our tears within us. They fell freely
until laughter took their place and even Nerianne's singing
bubbled into glee. But we had forgotten the oracle,
the beasts and the perplexing prophecy. We turned to stare again.

The pit was empty of serpents. The slab was clean
save for The Pythia on her tripod and the priest, who moved toward us.
Nerianne stepped forward now. An enchantment of grace
lifted in her voice so that she sang with the voice of a goddess.
'O prophetess, no words are adequate measure of my blessing.
Let me sing at your pleasure all my days.' The prophetess
looked at her long and seemed about to soften into a smile
but next her face turned furious and she again intoned her chant:

*'Three you come
but two you leave
to seek the far-flung
queen all grieve.
She will remain
who most receive.
Together you
may never see
how two and one
will someday be!'*

She rose abruptly. We stepped back one more step.
She turned and moved away, smoke hissing now
as it issued forth from the crevice: 'This was not all, this was not
all!' she chanted, filling the pit and the lofty space
above us up to the roof's joinery with fierce cries.
The priest cast us a dark glance from under his brows
and turned to follow her, who, seemingly without motion flowed
up the stairs and over the rim into the darkening air.
First to speak was Ailanthis, saying: 'Dear Mother,
what can this mean? Which two? Which one? What is to be done
for it grows late, and surely we cannot return to the ship tonight.'
And next Nerianne: 'And besides this we risk our cousins'
knowledge of our presence. And the mind within me fears also
that they may excuse themselves in anger that we have avoided their house,
spreading thoughts among the people that we have insulted them.'
I looked at my daughter in amazement then, and laid her thoughtful
words away in my spirit, for she was now a woman

and mistress of the situation. She whispered again, saying:
    'Dear Mother and Sister, the spirit within me tells me we must wait.
Though it seems to us quite the opposite, the prophetess herself
is kindly intending toward us. I heard a note of this
in her voice, despite its sharpness. The singer in her was singing.'
I was perplexed now and would have spoken, but Nerianne
put her fingers to her lips. Presently Ailanthis whispered: 'Listen.'
    Next I seemed to hear the cold of the place itself
creep over the sharp hewn stones and spill down
upon my shoulders. It swirled around my feet. I took
Odysseus' cloak from my bundle and threw it around my shoulders
while the sound grew like the sea's voice answering the assault
of an approaching storm. It became a scraping of stone on stone,
and now the stair we stood on moved beneath our feet
and we feared Poseidon, Earth-Shaker's, rumbling rage.
Each daughter grasped an arm and as one being
we stepped off that high step once more
onto the marled slab. A dark cone appeared
above where we stood and slowly widened as a section
of the stair ground back, receding into darkness,
grinding and shrilling as if bronze were striking bronze.
Then light – so bright we blinked; then The Pythia herself appeared
on our right from the bright opening behind and beckoned to us.
Nerianne straightened her graceful shoulders and turned smiling.
Ailanthis raised her eyebrows in her questioning glance.
    My spirit whispered that this was the moment for choosing
the path that the prophetess would have us follow. We entered that cone
of light and here were cressets flaming. A throng of chanting
women with clear brows and wearing robes of fine handiwork
drew us in and motioned us to follow in their winding procession
behind the prophetess. Some went before us
and others closed behind us as we passed between their two rows
lining the corridor, bright with their burning brands
and echoing with their unearthly singing. We moved at last
from the low passage into a high natural chamber.
Here the light was softer, now rosy as the gentlest approach

of lingering Dawn, but later tinged with the palest green
of early spring. It was warm without fire, cool without breeze
and the air was clear and dry. The Pythia took her seat
upon the smooth white stone there in place for her,
polished so it glistened like the surface of a calm sea.
The bevy of kindly women parted to lead us close to her.

· XIII ·

THEY SEATED US on polished stones with fleeces laid over them
and cloth in colors from dyestuffs unknown above those caverns.
Then most of them moved away, singing, to pursue
their own tasks. Many worked at looms, some at the vats
for dyeing, some washing or carding the fleece. Others
were grinding meal and forming loaves, some working
bronze, molding clay vessels, or twisting reeds into baskets.
Several were preparing various things to eat,
bringing in olives and figs, pouring oil
from tall jars standing on their bellies in the sandy floor
of one of the wide anterooms off the main vault.
They broke off their singing in laughter and amiable talk.
Then they pulled tables to us and brought pitchers
to pour water for us to wash over figured bowls.
They brought us bread in the sturdy baskets and nuts,

with fish from the sea and milk-curd at the last. And besides wine
in handled cups there were drinks of the juices
from fruits and barley water that delighted our parched tongues.
    But when we had put away our desire for eating and drinking
we spoke our amazement at the sights we saw around that chamber.
The Pythia spoke to us again, rousing us from our languor, saying:
'Now you must answer my question truthfully so I may help you.
Tell me what you seek.' She looked at me so I answered:
'O Prophetess of Pytho, I think that you already know the schemes
of Athene herself, daughter of Zeus Father. And she
is Tritogeneia, who helps the ones she loves, setting
them tasks and laying out the ways for them to follow. Was it not
she who years ago urged us to come for your counsel
to my daughters? What then is next to come to pass?'
    'Penelope, daughter, clever suckling of Queen Aramantha,
in spite of the many things I have told you yet you are impatient
for more, when in truth there is little more I will tell you. First,
release your mantle and let it fall around your chair,
for here I think you will find enough comfort without it.
Then think upon this; did I not say to you:
"Three you come and two you leave?" I think that the one
among you who will stay already knows it. And did I not say
"To seek the far-flung queen all grieve?" I think that among you
she who is to seek her already knows her. For each of us can only
start out, following her talents and desires, onto some pathway.
And soon she will come to a division in the path. Here she will choose
either the one way or the other and continue on.
Next will come another branching, and then another
and soon she must find she has chosen some direction she follows.
Already your daughters know their pathways, and are eager to tell them.'
    Ailanthis spoke to her saying: 'Prophetess, you speak the truth.
All this you say is true as I see it. I name the queen
all grieve as Helen – all the singers call her thus,
although I think that her part of the story is still to be known.
And she has subtle potions in her possessions, gifts
of Polydamna of Egypt, where many good medicines are known.

We will seek her.' Next Nerianne spoke to us saying:
'O Prophetess, yes. I understand you also. May I stay?'
Now I could not suppress a groan. The Pythia spoke:
'Penelope, O Daughter, Sister, Mother, you have given them the world.
I think you do not mean to hold them back from it now.'
Now I was silent for I had no words with which to answer.
Nerianne came and knelt on the folds of her father's robe.
She put her arms around me and laid her head on my breast.
'O Mother, do you not see? This is where I am meant
to be next. For a singer can sing different songs
and in various ways. And these can accomplish much or not as the gods
who can do anything decree and the passage of the seasons will prove.
Here is the division in my path. I choose this: to remain.'
    So she spoke and stirred the spirit within me. And also
all of the women were moved to murmur with delight
and approval. I was amazed and laid her confident manner
away deep within me, but I could not keep my fear
held back. I spoke then, naming them both and saying:
'All this is fair and orderly, my daughters, and I hear in your voices
the weft of truth. But tell me this, O prophetess,
so that I may know it. Is this a place unknown to men
or has some one of the gods cast a blinding aura
before them so they dare not defile the peace of this space?
For I myself am fearful of the designs of the men hereabouts
and wonder what to do next to resume my journey with Ailanthis,
if Nerianne stays, and how we can pass the marauding bands.
How much more dangerous for her who stays.' Pythia spoke,
saying: 'O sister, hear me and consider, for you are not thoughtless.
This life the gods have given us does not come with assurances
bound in the strong iron. There is no place in the world of men
where it is guaranteed that we may live in safety. Know
yourself and go in confidence. These are our weapons,
but unlike the shields and swords of men, they are designed
not to do battle with others but to find peace within ourselves.
Here your daughter is safe, for this is a sanctuary, hallowed
by the gods and by men also. But you are wise to think of the peril

that awaits you when you leave. For surely that is greater.
Even now you must make your peace and your good-byes,
for Dawn of the golden chariot is making her way up
toward the rim of night and you must be far away.'
    There was truth in her voice. Like the last notes of a bird trilling
at sunset, like the last beat of a drum beside the dancers, like the chord
of a well-tuned lyre at the end of a thrilling tale her words
played on in my mind as I kept my tears inside me and spoke:
'Dearest Nerianne, all that you have said seems well thought through.
But you must tell me this, and tell me truly, so I
can know it. You are too young to have concern for your life and your death,
thinking, as young people do, that you will live forever.
But there can be, in the world, worse things than death, and
life can be a painful matter. Tell me you have seen this,
tell me you have considered in your mind which way is best,
that you enter your life here with its risk of loathsome dangers
knowingly, in preference to a safer life. Then I can leave you
cheerfully, and never blame you or fear for you. For although we know not
the full design of our lives when we set the warp on the loom,
since forever the dyes are changing their hues and the yarn grows coarser
or finer with the seasons or sometimes burrs leave slubs
in the work, still it is sufficient to be thoughtful and choose. It must be.'
    Now Nerianne was silent. When she spoke she was grave.
'How is it, Mother dearest, you so often seem to know
my inmost thinking, as if we shared one mind
within us? I have thought of this in my own spirit, exactly
as you say it: I choose to live my life in this world,
dangerous though it is, rather than to accept a safer path
but not to live fully. For such a life would be hateful to me.
I find the words for my song and the chords to accompany it here.
Mother, Ailanthis, I am home, I am safe. Fare you both as well.
And to my father and brother, greetings and tears of parting.
Now the prophetess signals. It is time for you to be away.
I shall come with you to the brink of the rising dawn
at the cave's end. For parting is still a painful matter.'
And now there was a current of movement throughout the great chamber

as in a field of asphodel when a riffling breeze stirs it.
And the light changed again to rose from ambrosial green.
Many women came to attend to our needs, carrying
our bundles, spreading the cloak around my shoulders, wishing us
safe passage and pressing our hands in theirs in blessing.

Before us Pythia left the chamber ascending a passageway
swiftly, shawls fluttering behind her shapely arm,
which bore a torch high. With some of that kindly company
to help light our way we hurried up the spiraling slope.
Our thoughts seemed not to need any words
but flew between us – Nerianne pressed my hand in hers
and I knew that hers and Ailanthis', on her other side, were also
tightly entwined and speaking years and leagues of love.

The women's voices lowered as we climbed until there was only
the sound of our sandals and the women's feet on the smooth floor
of the passageway with its gentle echo. Near the end
Pythia turned and put her hand to her lips. As if
a babble had been with us, suddenly our climb was more hushed
and quickly we turned a sharp bend and there was the semblance
of light eking along the walls. Pythia slowed.
She snuffed her torch and motioned us on toward the gleam.
'Go, and know thyself, O Sister, Friend, Penelope.
But know thyself and go!' she hissed into my ears,
and then *she* was gone. Nerianne held both Ailanthis
and me in a warm embrace, the tears flowing freely
down our cheeks until I summoned to myself the strength
to press her one last time, to turn, and not look back.

Ailanthis following, I moved to the brazen glow
and just at the last bend I was rewarded with the welcome sight
of familiar shadows cast on the wall from inside its opening.
I hastened and came at last into the golden haze
of a new day and Mabantha waiting with Phemios.

I called to her and named her and fell into her arms. She was amazed.
Ailanthis joined us on the ledge. Now you, Phemios,
thought what to do next. You seized Ailanthis and drew her
deeper into the cave. Mabantha likewise put her hand

on my mouth and pulled me sharply back and shook her head
when I twisted to face her. I heard then the awful thudding
of blows on flesh, striking again and again, the gasps
for breath and groans of a creature suffering a beating, like the donkey
of a wine-sodden farmer plodding home late.
I drew breath sharply myself, but Mabantha pulled me
tightly to her so I stifled my cry. And then the shadow
of a man plummeted by on the wall of the cave and down
into silence. I looked at Ailanthis. We guessed it was Mentor, and wept
as our eyes met with those of our friends. They released us at once.

    Phemios motioned for silent mouthing and Mabantha whispered:
'O my friend, how are you here? We feared, nor we knew
you dead, or captive, led away. Since three days we have waited.
But then Mentor advised we must make our way to the ships
to escape – we must tell Odysseus the tale and bring him back
with ships and many men of your islands ready to do battle
to release you or avenge your fate. That was Mentor. They found him
on the pathway for he was too winded to climb down to this cave
which he had showed us, and he told us to seek our safety here
from the grim kinsmen.' I looked to you, Phemios, and whispered, saying:
'Tell me, Singer, how these things have happened. For surely
three days have not passed by for us. And what
of the oarsmen sent by our helmsman to guard us and to warn us of dangers?'

    'O my queen, I think that these were the first to taste the venom
of those pitiless men. For outside the town where you left us to await
your returning we came upon many corpses, horribly bloodied.
The vultures were gathered near them ready to tear the remaining
flesh from their bones, but the male parts were already torn from them
and dogs were slinking near, licking their jowls. Mentor
hurried us on, hoping to outpace the henchmen's frenzy,
but I think that he had decided already to distract and delay them.
And now he lies broken at the base of the sheer cliff, food
for vultures. But I think that not every one of the seamen
could have remained close-lipped and avoided revealing
your presence with your nubile daughters before their throats were severed.

Even now, I fear, the cruel curs are sniffing
for these morsels to work their evil delights and cravings upon,
and only I am left to shield you all and guide you
in the way that Mentor devised to return to the ships.' Mabantha
whispered next, gently reminding: 'And I was there also,
my husband, and together we listened to that man's thoughtful words.
But where is Nerianne, O my queen? It is not a moment
we can wait. For Mentor will be buying us only little time
by his design of turning back to ascend the path again.'
'My daughter has found her life and embraced it. We need
concern ourselves for her no longer. Let us go quickly.'

For now, outside the cave, the clamor of men and beasts
had moved away, and only the innocent calling of birds
sounded from side to side in the valley below, with the last hoot
of a homeward owl. Phemios led us straight down
the rugged steep. Stepping and sliding we grasped for handholds
of wild olive, with sharp rocks scraping our hands
and tearing at our robes. Down, though our sandals slipped on the scrabble
and it seemed we fell away from the face of the earth itself.
At last we gained the path turned back below the bend,
but soon, as we panted down, we heard men's shouting
from above. Boulders crashed sidelong across the path
ahead of me, behind me, so I dashed and dodged like a she-wolf pursued
by maddened shepherds, who close in on her with their slings and cudgels.
Above us where the path snaked back and forth across
the steep slope were men racing in howling packs.

We sprinted around a curve and down. Next we heard
the thunder of earth and bounding boulders. It roared across
the narrow way before us, and stopped us still. Among the cries
above and behind I heard a wail and turned. Mabantha
struggled, fallen. Ailanthis rushed to her. Mabantha screamed:
'Go on, my lady – take your daughter on.' You,
Phemios shouldered past, thrusting me roughly downward
and Ailanthis down also. You called to me saying: 'Follow
the sun – at every crossing turn to the light.' I met

Ailanthis' wild glance and pulled her, saying: 'Telemachos' life
hangs on our threads, daughter. Race for the light.'
      She nodded and grasped my bundle, making us a match,
older for younger, in strength for the climb now before us.
And we did as Medon planned it and Phemios instructed; we sped
like the runner in festival games who must never turn to look back
if he wishes to come to the mark ahead of the foes at his shoulder,
but keeps his head high like a fleet deer
and with his eyes on the purple ribbons streaming from the halberd
makes for it swiftly as an arrow on the wind. The clamor
behind us swelled and died away as we twisted and climbed
again on our race toward the sea, up to the low saddle
on a zigzag path worn by the feet of men and of goats
to iron-red rock. Always we took the path toward the sun,
which now had risen above us and glowered
hotly down on our tortured trail. We stopped by an outcrop,
confounded at last by a turning, so faint was the path toward the sun
that we looked at each other in puzzlement, pained at the choice and struck
with terror in our spirits to think we could lose our best chance
after all. For now we could see the sea, smooth
and sparkling as polished stone. Behind and above us we heard
baying as of fierce dogs, a din of scrabbling feet pounding
the pathway, rocks bounding and crashing, wild cries.
      My eyes were blinded with pulsing, but now Ailanthis
chose which way was best. She seized my hand and we plunged
onto the least trod way, uttering prayers to Athene
and Mentor that it be the right one, the light one.
And our prayers did not go unanswered, for soon it was plain that indeed
this was a pathway. It led easily downward along
the slippery, rock-strewn slope among low scrags
and blood-red soil to the sea-beach where we saw
no steading nor any men at their work by the sea, nor any traces
of people. We stopped in the shade of a wild olive
at the margin of the sand and I could no longer stand.
My knee joints were loosened. I fell to the ground and gasped

stinging sand. My chest burned, my eyes smarted,
my arms were scratched and sore and flies dove to bite
at the bloody clots. Nowhere was any help to be seen,
no ship, no fisherman's skiff, no women of the country who might take us
into their homes as suppliants fleeing marauding men.

· XIV ·

THEN AILANTHIS took my shoulder and turned my face
back toward the high headland beside us. There, rounding
the point, came two welcome ships. Swiftly like gannets
they skimmed the face of the water, making straight for the curve
of the beach before us. And quickly Ailanthis thought what to do next.
She seized Odysseus' mantle from the ground beside me
and running lightly as a doe to a stream bubbling through the meadow
she reached the edge of the surf and flourished the cloak, which rippled
above her on the wind. In answer the skiff came down
over the side of the *Sea-Swift*, swelling in close on the sage-blue
shallows of the cove like a swan swooping near her cygnets
as she gathers them closely together and paddles for safety. At once
there was a crashing in the scrub behind me. I turned, sure
of onrushing doom. But Phemios broke from the brush then,
Mabantha racing beside him. They reached me in two steps
and pulled me up. Their strength amazed me, as my own did next.
My legs donned wings and bore me forward
so I matched their pace, and when Mabantha stumbled,
I was the one who held her up and pulled her on
toward the nearing craft with skilled oarsmen already swinging
its stern wide to be close to our approach. Hands reached over.
Seamen alighted, splashing our faces and arms
with delicious cool spray. I felt myself lifted and set in place
beside Ailanthis and soon we were all borne over the water
as if on the smooth backs of gleaming dolphins. Next we were
handed up onto the planks of the ship and the oarsmen
quickly pulled up the small boat and lashed it down firmly.
    The seamen on board were already moving over the ship
adjusting the halyards, pulling the sheets to billow

the sails toward the open sea on a fresh breeze. Our helmsman
came forward. He took my hand in his hand and knelt
before us. We all looked at each other in amazement and stood
stricken to silence. Wonder and relief mingled in our hearts
with thankfulness and with grief for Mentor, no longer among men.
And soon a following wind lifted our spirits to billow
forward on the froth of the wave-tips with the fleeting vessels.
It cooled and refreshed us while Mabantha and I with Ailanthis
stepped behind draped cloths and to shed our ravaged robes
for fresh ones. Mabantha's ample body glowed darkly
beside my daughter's lithe form, both like goddesses
for beauty and stature, but in such differing guises.

    For Mabantha was thickened and billowed like the breast of a dove
in courting time. We spoke no words as we dried our bodies
and anointed each the other with oil. We reached
for our robes from the deep-stowed chests which Odysseus
himself saw lowered into the hollow ship's hull.
I undid the knot that he and I alone know
and took out a fresh robe of my own handiwork.
Mabantha was beside me and spoke as she took out
her wondrous robe again to put it on. 'See, my queen, here
on the inner side, how the pattern was twisting with the bobbins'
march in sequence across the warp of the fabric; two
across, one down, then one across alone.'

    I whispered to her then, since Ailanthis was already climbing
to the high stern: 'I see that from this moment you will never cross
the wide sea ways alone again.' She smiled with pride.
She took my hands in hers and spoke low, saying:
'Penelope, dear friend, what you are saying is true.
This is my almost last crossing, seeing you on your journey
around Myrsinos, past shining Elis
and Pherai, down to Krounoi into Pylos.
From there you are going to Sparta to visit peerless Helen.'

    I was amazed at her words and could not keep my wonder inside me:
'How is it my friend, that you know this thing you have told me. For none of us
planned farther ahead than to visit Pytho, since we were certain

that there we would find a source of healing for my son
in the course of my appointed journey with my daughters to consult the oracle
You were not with us when we heard the prophetess' braided words,
neither have we told you of them. Yet you seem to know, as we do,
where we must go next. Answer me truthfully so I may know it.'

'O Penelope, my friend, I cannot tell how this knowing
is coming to me, for it seems to me now we have known it always.
Must not we, each one of us, sometime be confronting this Helen
and have you not yourself foreseen it in your dreaming? And this
was not all. I saw Ailanthis was searching the pathside on our climb
to Pytho, never finding any leaf to pluck and place
in her bundle. But more than this, the spirit deep within me
was hearing a voice like one of the goddesses who spoke it to me
thrice. But I think our helmsman should not learn these things
nor even Phemios, my husband, although he is a singer and not
a thoughtless man. Now that Mentor is gone down to Hades
this helmsman will be following Phemios' commands
and he can persuade the *Ktimene* to turn toward Lakedaimon also.'
While we two were conversing in this way we put on our clothing
and ordered our hair with ivory combs and put on our sandals.

She nodded as our helmsman, Apollytos, approached. He spoke, saying:
'O my queen, do not suppose me a heedless man. I do not
wish to intrude upon your counsel, but I come to offer you my ship
and myself for conveyance to any far lands on the face
of the seas. While it is true that King Odysseus ordered me
to do it before you came down to the harbor, and Mentor also
left me his words to follow, I would never be the man
to let custom command me against the mind and the spirit within me.
You are the queen of this ship. I have no need of Phemios
or any other of your men to command me. Besides this, I
can give the order to *Ktimene* if you will ask me to do it.
I am senior on these waters and they will follow my commands.'

'O helmsman, what you say is orderly, and puts my mind at rest.
But I am not the only traveler on this journey, nor even the most purposeful
among us. Therefore let us rather discuss and consult
together among ourselves which way is best

whenever there are matters to decide. For this way seems best
now that Mentor has left us, for he was a man without equal
for advice.' So saying, I took my place at the stern of the ship
and called Mabantha to sit beside me, and with us was Ailanthis.
Together we decided, and Apollytos set our course toward Lakedaimon.

But now my body gave way at the joints and sweet sleep
drifted over me so that I knew no more of oars groaning and wavelets
slapping the purple cheeks of the hull, nor of Helios
settling on the lofty columns of the day, then sliding seaward
toward his couch while the oarsmen strained to round Challis and beat
a steady wind against us to make for Myrsinos' wide passage.
It was there we awoke with the day only a glow
on the rim of the sea beyond Ithaka – did she exist? – out there
in the mist. Strangely, I had felt no hunger all day since I was
satisfied from eating in that city of women. But hunger
claimed us all now. The seamen brought forth provisions
and we ate by the light of lamps and the night-pricking stars until
the moon rose. Now I was refreshed and considered all
that had happened. I turned to Mabantha and spoke to her saying:
'O my friend, you are so steadfast. In times of trial
you are always nearby with comfort and sure counsel. Even
Odysseus was never a closer friend to me than you are in this.
Still, I lack for the rest of your story. Tell it to me now
so that I may know it all, for nothing is more hateful than a story
that is thrilling and well told but forever left unfinished.'
Now Mabantha grew thoughtful. She turned her face away
and spoke to me, saying: 'But hear me, my friend, although it is pleasing,
never can you say that I am more steadfast a companion
than Odysseus. None will be more to you than he is. For despite the hardships
this one was suffering, and through the delights that were tempting,
he clung to you and kept his course for Ithaka. Not so
Rbatha, the one you call Eurybates, my brother, friend,
and my intended one – who was to share my people's ruling,
but preferred the company of men and sacking of cities to his life.
For willingly he stayed in rocky Ithaka and went with Odysseus
in the ships of the Achaians to be his herald before Ilion.

'We were lovers. This is the custom with my people, though I think
you do not know it here. We would marry when I came
with child. Even Phemios, good man that he is, he cannot
be for me as that loved brother was. And yet he. . .
Penelope, forgive me – even you are not more to me
than Phemios is since he is my partner in the deepest ways of living.
But I will tell you more also, since you have seen it. At last
I carry a child within me, long the hope of my people.
This child I too have hoped, but feared also.
Alone I was nothing to my people, but now – forgive this also,
my friend – I claim Aidamis, Queen of Aithiopia, as my
mother. The king is my father. Now nothing is withheld.'

    Now I could not hold my smile within me, for her words
seemed long understood deep in my spirit. I spoke to her, saying:
'Surely these are joyous tidings, such as a dear friend
counts as her own good fortune. And what you tell me
of your land and your parents rings true. I know it
for always I counted you close to the gods for poise and stature
and wise counsel. How many moons have filled since you conceived?
For surely your time for easy journeying is not long
and we must consider this well as we plan our journey to Sparta.
Now there are troubles among the cities of the Argives, a concern
to travelers by land, but with sea journeys there are always evils
to consider.' Mabantha answered me, saying: 'My friend, five
were the moons rising and waning on the seas near Ithaka. And now
it is coming heavy with me. For this we could flee only slowly
down Pleistos' gorge, and there was Mentor lost, who charged me
to save my fruit, and he set us free by his own dying.'

    Then we fell silent for a moment. Ailanthis approached with Phemios.
I looked from one to the other, questioning. Phemios spoke first:
'I see, O queen, that my wife has told you our glad tidings.
How I have longed to sing of this news.
But often what is closest to the singer's heart is the most difficult
to tune the lyre toward, and must be spoken simply.
I confess to you now that I fear for her safety and for the delivery
of our child. And so I would urge you to avoid harsh ground

under sandal and wheel, but to glide across the smooth surface
of the sea to Eurotas' green and reedy banks. And yet,
the sea-road is longer than the journeying ways, stony as those are,
and our helmsman may not be provisioned for it.' I answered him, saying:
'What you say is fair and orderly. But in this matter
time is our enemy, and speed must be chosen our chief.
And Nestor, who loved Odysseus best among the Achaians
when both were gone reluctantly to Ilion, will grant us conveyance
with the speed of his own horses and chariots and also protection.'
Ailanthis raised her brows toward me and spoke, saying:
'But remember, Mother dear, when Telemachos told us how
he had to avoid Nestor's halls on his return from Sparta?
I fear that if we too choose to beach our ships
at Pylos, and rely on the old king for protection and conveyance,
he may hold us for long in his brazen halls as guests.
This way we would lose all hope of saving my brother.'
I had no measured words to answer her, and pondered heavily.
At last this seemed to me the best way:
there was still one who had not spoken, and he had knowledge
and skill in the ways of traveling the width of the seas, and also
in other matters. And the spirit within me urged me to speak to him.

 I drew away from them, meaning to approach the helmsman Apollytos.
We had rounded Hyrmine and were gliding beside Elis,
shining in Helios' last rays from over Zachynthos,
lying on the Western seas. And the land was low-lying
and green, like the banks of a river plied with a following current
and a wind from Ithaka to the North. We seemed to skim the water
like a sea-bird just lifting for flight, outracing the driven
wavelets and bubbling foam to lift herself up and away.
And I remembered my dream of mounting the sky to ride on wings
and knew the journey well. For it is often this way with dreams;
they visit our spirits as familiar strangers, or clad in disguise
so that our halls are not quite our halls, and the dead speak with us
again as if living, yet we know even then they are gone to Hades.
And even our loves can appear in form unknown to us and desirable
for strangeness while yet urging our hearts toward delightful lovemaking.

Now Apollytos came down to meet me. I spoke to him,
saying: 'O helmsman, you who have knowledge of the sea's
wide ways, answer me this truthfully. Which
of the ways is best for Sparta on Eurotas' reedy banks:
to sail by the open seas, or to put in at sandy Pylos
where Nestor, renowned for welcome, might hold us within his halls
before he gives us conveyance and sends us along the journeying ways?'
    He was thoughtful a moment, then spoke to me, saying:
'O my queen, gladly will I tell you my plan.
While I would be ready to steer you around all three
of the rocky capes, even by treacherous Maleia itself
if you should ask it, there is advantage now to the land ways.
Warring has arisen along Eurotas' banks like flooding
since Menelaos was long away and younger men
are jealous of his return. Even so, I think that Nestor,
the Gerenian horseman, will not detain you long from your journeying.
The goddess Rumor has spread it far over the sea ways
that the glorious old man is sickened and is dying. Indeed
it may be that already he has gone to join his stricken son
Antilochos in Hades. Therefore I think that this way is best,
and I urge you to follow it: I will make for strong-founded Pylos
all night and into the dawn on this following wind
and tomorrow you will enter the courtyard of the hallowed old man.
    'There you will arrange for the next part of your journey. I myself
will see to it you are urged along, going with you to Nestor,
for I am not unknown in this quarter. And as I have sworn it in my oath
to Odysseus, but no less in my promise to you, I will wait for you
there, with *Ktimene* also. You, running swiftly over the ways
on the plains and through the cleft in the mountains, can then
return to me and I will convey you wherever it is
you must journey to next.' So he spoke and I was eased
in my mind about what was to come. But I was brimming with questions.
    'O helmsman, what you have devised seems wise,
and we shall see it accomplished as you suggest. But you
seem to know about many things beyond other men.'
He answered me, saying: 'O my queen, many are the ways

of the sea, and many the ways of men and of life in the cities of men.
How could I guide my ships and bring them safely to anchor
in the sparkling harbors or draw them smartly up on the break
of the sea beaches with all my men and the trading goods
to pile high before the merchants if I did not know
every feature of my sea-mistress, both her surface
and the inlets that frame her? When I see the sea weeds
stirring on the swell and the terns have all winged hard
toward the nearest rest, when great hooks of foam reach
to threaten my ship's hull, then I too must fold
my wings and beware the approaching storm. But when the sea-terns
in their spangled numbers tumble and soar joyfully, heedless
of formation, when the dolphins leap around the hull of the ship
in bubbling pairs on a gentle swell, when the sun's furious chariot
has dropped below the sea in a green flash
and the night is come and the stars swirl in a sky of a color
between purple and green, when the moon rises and a small cloud
or a halo or a light mist wraps itself around her while her arrows
of geese stream by from Aigyptos' shores to the North,
must I not be able to read all these as signs?
    'And how could I not, in my deepening knowledge, admire their beauty,
their symmetry and logic, or gaze wonderingly at some caprice?
O Lady, I cleave to them fiercely for what they offer me is life
beyond the fortunes of other men, whom they instruct me to observe.
And this I have done also, in all the cities where men
are hospitable to strangers and willingly show them their minds and customs.'
    'O helmsman, you are so different from most men, who are always
talking of war and death, and boast the swords at their thighs
and the bronze of their shields and their greaves. Answer me this, I ask you:
where do you come from? What is your country, and who are your people?
For I do not think you are from Krete, nor Achaia, nor Syria. Nor
are you Libyan or Egyptian, for they do not travel over the seas.'
He answered me, saying: 'I come from beyond all these –
from a place beyond Sikania which has no name to you.
We are sea-people who must harness the sea and ride her to reach
the exchanges of other men as those who live on land

harness oxen or mules to carry their oil or fleeces
to the city marketplaces. I come from a family of warriors, men
who even now are jealous of the greatest cities around the seas.
My father, King Akhior, was a harsh man, always
plotting the destruction of the lords in his halls who opposed him in anything.

 'It happened this way: Rumor spread all the way to our fortress
news of the Argives beached on the shores of the Troad, waging
endless war against Priam. The king, my father, said to me:
"You, Apollytos, breaker of men's wills, most devious
among all my henchmen, you will cut out of our numerous
well-manned ships three to join in the glorious fighting and earn
spoils of gold and bronze and women of surpassing handicraft.
See to it that these are comely and not too docile besides."
So I made ready to go, ordering many skins
of choice barley and handled jars of olive oil, water
and wine to be stored away in the hollow hulls. And the men
assembled to go on board with all their armor on them.

 'But next came into the harbor a ship with flashing oars
making straight for the port inside the breakwater. Rumor
traveled aboard her of marauding ships and men insatiable
with lust for killing and pillage, delighting in evil and disgusting practices
over captive women and children. I returned to my father,
although the libations had already steamed away in the fire,
and spoke to him: "O my King and father, here is a present danger
to our city coming in from the sea, and here we are,
our bronze buckled on us in perfect readiness to go meet them
and so to prevent them from ever feasting their eyes upon our harbor
or slavering over our terraced city or our lovely orchards,
our women or children. Put it in your orders then for me to steer
southward to meet them and show them that raiding is a painful matter."

 ' "Apollytos, you are a simple fool when you tell me to concern myself
with men such as these, for we are far better than they are.
I think rather that you only wish for glory close
to home to persuade the people to admire you and to hasten
the day you can push me aside from my throne. Or perhaps you plan
to avoid leaving the lovely wife you seem to be excessively

fond of, for a son of mine. Did you think I would not have her,
even with you here, if desire took me? Rather you had better
withdraw the ropes from the stone posts and cast off the stern cables
quickly for Troy and spoils of your own to enrich
your claims with me since your bitch has borne you no sons. Begone!"
So he spoke and I had no words to answer him then, for
always he goaded me in the halls of the palace and crushed my pride.

'I went away to follow his orders and prove myself to him
as never before, to bring home glory and piled-up spoils.
We sailed for Sikania, a following wind heaving us
into the churning seas. But we were heavily laden with men
and their battle armor and great stores of provisions,
so easily a fleet ship from my father's city caught us
in the next port with word that raiders had indeed overrun
the city. The messengers were men who cowered before the king
but wished to be rid of his tyrannical ways. I steered for home
at once, but the strong West winds were driving the seas
against us, so we came too late to prevent the destruction. We could
see it at once as we rounded the headland and put in
to the harbor. Death and desolation had raged through the streets
and everywhere the people stared dumbly at my well-fed
and hearty warriors. Along the ways from the harbor every house
was marked with stains from the spattered brains of babes
killed like puppies. Women turned their eyes from our glances
and children looked at us listlessly with eyes grown large
in their taut faces. Bodies stank on the cobbles and flies swarmed.
The brutes were gone – no fighting to be savored or vented in.
Each man ran to his own to tally his losses.

'I plied my way to my house near the palace like a skiff into the surf
of a storm, forcing my way ever higher over the crests
of fresh atrocities that lashed at my entrails and drowned my spirits.
When I crossed the threshold of my ruined house I knew that life
was gone. My wife, her chest bound where the lovely breasts
were severed, lay filthy and nearly mad with fever
and hideous remembrance. When she finally knew me, she spoke:

'"Husband? Come back then? Stay you from me, for I am fouled

and filthy from the bodies of those – but they're not men, not
like you – O tell me, husband, tell me you could never do such –
tell me on our daughter's life and maidenhead now torn and bloodied,
never – you have not seen her? Did you not pass through
that hall – yes there – O tell me does she live – O tell me
can she speak – O iris eyes, O hyacinthine curls. . ."
So saying she slipped back into fevered dreams,
but later she told me the horrid story of the deeds my dear ones
suffered under those men, my queen, a long doom over more
than one day, and again and again, many men in succession,
on my gentle wife and Athalia, my heart's tender flower.

  'She was not yet twelve but the bloom that was in her was budding.
I could not have treasured a son more or preferred him, despite
my father's raging for an heir. But during that accursed day
they fell on her one, then another, then another, then more, telling her
to say it was good, to ask them for more, forcing my wife
to listen to her screams and her to watch my wife while they cut
her with the knives. My dear one, my dove, my lily, my little girl. . .

  'I found her. She screamed at my beard and began a wild tossing.
She was smeared and wild-haired; the clothing still
upon her was stained and her face was old and narrow-eyed. I could not
bear the groaning that came from deep within her, fearing
we would all be maddened senseless from it so I shook her gently.
She stopped then. She looked at me, and knowing came into those eyes.
Next came a hard glaze of loathing. She cast me a look
so comprehending, so proud, so disdainful it could have come from one
as knowing as my wife, but in one so young it was fearful.
Then she relaxed and with effort and dignity worthy of a goddess
she turned to face the wall and never saw again.
She died and my wife, grieving and mad, followed her soon.'

  Now I was stricken to silence and had no words with which
to comfort him. But some impulse, whether from my own spirit
within me or from some goddess, put it into my mind
to press his arm. Later I learned to lament this heavily
because of the outcome. I questioned him, saying: 'You are so far
from home and I see that helmsman of a merchant ship forever

crossing the seas is not the pattern of the cloth you were woven to.
What of your father? Why did you leave when you were to rule?'

    'O my queen, it is hard for us ever to know
what it is the gods intended for us, unless it is by seeing
all that has been accomplished for us. My father the king prevailed.
He and his henchmen crowded about the palace like rats at the top
of a ship's mast pole as it sinks in deep water, and I think
he was not merely forgetful when he left my house unguarded,
just below his walls. From his stronghold he still held sway
over better men. And these, as often it is known, raised
their cups to him again, seeing they were better for it. My father
spoke to me with insults: "Boy, you shivering fish, see
how your bungling has cost you the spoils I sent you to win.
For neither will you bring back from Troy rich spoils
of gold and lovely women as prizes to beget sons
nor did you speed yourself homeward in time to prevent destruction.
A nit such as you is useless to me. Did you not
think to pursue the raiders at once? Of what good
are tears and lamenting to ones who are dead or dying? Revenge
is what I expected of you – swift and bloody. Minnow –
you have no home until Rumor hastens before you
or billows in your sails that you have punished them horribly."'

· XV ·

'So he spoke, but his words were strangely soothing to my spirit;
for something sundered, like the jesses that hold the falcon to the gauntlet,
or the purple thread on a maiden's pet dove when suddenly
the young bird, grown strong in the pride of its maturity,
breaks the sleek bonds that hold it in thralldom and takes
its delight in the winds that lift it close to the realm of the gods.
I feigned in turn contrition and shame, rage and vengefulness,
pleasing the brute and securing a sendoff free of suspicion.
I hastened down the steep steps past my house,
never stopping to look again upon my daughter
or my wife. I could not bear more. In this my father
was pleased, for he never knew it was weakness rather than strength.
But because of this I wander the seas in guilt and anguish
for their broken bodies, perhaps thrown on a dung heap to rot
without burial, though their lovely spirits were long gone down to Hades.
   'The men I had with me were all men I had chosen carefully –

loyal and honorable. Soon the best among them were
gathered with me on my ship, by far the largest. With us,
by contrivance, was all the men's bronze, the shields and greaves,
the merciless blades and helmets and many bronze cauldrons
and tripods. And when, in the group of islands that lies off Maleia,
the storm winds arose and the currents, fearful in those regions,
thrust us apart, I feigned a snapped halyard, letting
my sail dangle, helplessly flapping, and rode a strong current
away and was lost at sea to my companion ships. Straightaway
we traded that hateful cargo for timber to trade in.
　'Many years passed in trading oil and wines, pots
and jars from Achaia, grain and spices from Syria, perfumed oils
from Egypt, flax from Sidon and purple dye-shells
from Cyprus, before I would carry copper from Lydia, iron
or tin in my ship. I was free as a sea bird.
And freely, my queen, will I steer your ship for you wherever
you will it, and I will throw over the anchor stone at sacrosanct Pylos
for you to command me further. But here is an end to it. It is useless
to babble on when a story has been told.' He bowed abruptly
and turned away. And the ship ran on through the night
and the stars and the sea's singing and into the dawn on her journeying.
　As Helios was rising, we came near Pylos, Nestor's splendid
stronghold. We steered into the great harbor between the islands,
admiring the town on the curve of the shelf with the distant citadel
high against the misty hills in the early light. We put straight in
and the seamen expertly released the anchor stones.
They let down the sails and the mast and stowed away all
the gear while we stepped out of the ship to land in the skiffs.
Apollytos spoke to a man he knew on the shore. He returned
quickly and spoke to me, saying: 'Here, my queen, is no need
at all for dissembling to speed you on your way. For the breaker of horses
languishes, and none in his glorious palace is eager in his spirit
for feasting or holding strangers in the shadowy halls.'
He led the way with Ailanthis. I followed with Phemios
and Mabantha; just as I had dreamed it, we left the sand of the shore
and climbed to the citadel, roofs blazing in Helios' rays.

We came to the Pylians gathered in assembly. Here was no cheerful
discussion that accompanies everyday feasting and sacrifices,
but a low murmuring of voices from clusters of men. Then
a beautiful youth approached us and gave us greeting with his hands.
He welcomed us and led us through the fabled Sphinx gate
across the courtyard with its portico and into the hall.
The throne was empty but he bade us sit beside the hearth
and he himself sat down before the long wall
with striding gryphons and lions painted on it, guarding him.

    He spoke to us saying: 'My guests, make your prayer to the gods,
especially Asklepios who heals the sick and eases suffering.
For we need him now in this house where my father suffers the pains
of old age and is near dying. But you would be dismayed
at coming here if you did not receive a show of hospitality
according to custom. And I would never be the one to deny it
to a woman of your beauty and stature O queen. And my eyes
tell me that you must be the lady Penelope, guardian of home fires
and mother of Telemachos, my friend because of our fathers' bonds,
and because of the journey your son and I made together.
Therefore I give you the golden goblet first, but this one
must also sit in a place of honor since she is no ordinary handmaiden,
but has the air of a goddess about her as well.'

    I was pleased to find him as gracious as his regal father.
For the young nowadays are not always so thoughtful, but arrogant
like my suitors. I saw much to admire in Nestor's brilliant hall
with even its great hearth painted in wine-dark colors.
We feasted well on the many good things his servants,
generous with their provisions, brought to us. When
we had put aside our desire for eating and drinking, I spoke
first, saying: 'Since you claim to be Telemachos' friend
and journeying companion, you must be the hero Peisistratos.

    'O son of Nestor and Eurydike, as I see by your looks
and your gracious manner, I am indeed Penelope of Ithaka.
I announce that my companion is my daughter Ailanthis, second daughter
of Odysseus, my lately returned husband. She was born
twinned with Nerianne who is now apprenticed at The Pythia's shrine.

They are sisters to Telemachos, but never known to men, save
Odysseus' illustrious parents, until their father's homecoming. Even
Telemachos never knew of them. For how could I expect
that he could withhold them from the overbearing suitors before
the time he came to strong-founded Pylos and journeyed
to Lakedaimon with you? But I have this to tell you also; all
goes badly with my son – at this moment I do not know if he lives
or is dead. For while he hunted on Neritos' slopes some god,
jealous of great Odysseus' prowess, or of his homecoming,
drifted a mist over him and sent a supernatural beast
to gouge him deeply with its cruel tusk. He lies, sickened
and feverish, beyond reason. The heal-all, that alone could save him,
is gone from our land and also from the mainland, men here tell us.
Therefore we seek Helen's gift of healing, which Telemachos
spoke of and you yourself witnessed with him in Lakedaimon.
We came here hoping to travel by land to her in Sparta,
but I think that no one will escort us since your father –
sadness takes me when I think of him –
is old and ill and needs his sons to attend him to his death.'
   'Never, O queen, would I be the one to refuse succor
to a guest who asked it of me. Nor would my father wish it.
For should he hear of such a misdeed in his house, he would call me
to him and rebuke me, saying: "Send them now with horses
and chariots and you yourself be at the reins as their escort.
For there are plenty here who can help me totter in my dotage
on the way to Hades, enough for me to provide entertainment."
Such is the mockery a man makes who has avoided death
in battle among his companions, and these will raise no mound for him
but gently he declines on his couch of soft fleeces and in comfort.
And here is another point on the matter. It is no mean thing
for a youth such as I am to sit at the knees of glorious heroes
and learn from them all we can. Gladly would I have returned
to Lakedaimon, since Menelaos asked me. And my father urged me to do it.
But I was unwilling to leave him while his troubles besieged him.
Now I think the gods have arranged it so I have a purpose
that is just and urgent, and I will fulfill it, carrying Nestor's greetings,

to powerful Menelaos and Helen of the shining robes.'
I would have spoken to dissuade him, but Ailanthis spoke next, saying:
    'O Mother dear, see how all he has said is right
and sensible. We know majestic Nestor well from Telemachos'
story, from Odysseus' and the singers' tales, which have circled the seas
in the years since the Troad was plundered. I feel his son's
strong compulsion to make this journey. For he also loves
Telemachos. And as for Helen, skilled as the gods with potions,
she will also do what she can for his father; I know it.'
    I saw how he looked at her then. His dark eyes blazed
with admiration for her measured words. Apollytos spoke next:
'It seems, O my queen, that what you now require is provided,
so if your host will grant me leave, I will return to the harbor.'
Peisistratos spoke to him saying: 'Helmsman, I, for my part,
will never detain you if this lady is content that you go.
It bends the bonds of friendship to hold a guest who hastens to leave.
Yet stay, O Penelope, you and your well-spoken daughter, until
I can prepare the chariots and suitable gifts. I must take leave
of my father, if he still knows me. It will be better,
with so much traveling and such a distance to cover, to rest the night
and set off early as Dawn rises from her golden couch.
And besides this, it would be churlish in me not to hear
the visiting singer, Phemios, tune his lyre and sing
his divine tales after our feasting, according to custom.'
    Then Phemios spoke to him in answer, saying: 'Gladly,
O prince, will I sing for you in your household. How I wish
that you would send me also into the inner chamber
where your ailing father lies. For music is a soother of spirits
whether they languish or are whole, and a story well sung can stir
the heart of a dying man and light his journey even
into Hades. For this Antikleia, Odysseus' mother, called me
to her when she was dying, but I came too late to cheer her.'
Peisistratos answered him saying: 'What you suggest is fair.
If only I could leave you here in my palace, so you could sustain
his spirit. Then I could find him still among the living to welcome me
back from my journey to Lakedaimon.' I spoke to them next, saying:

'O Peisistratos, since you ask it this can be easily accomplished.
For all know how men can be roused to new distraction
even if they are old and feeble. And besides,
this singer's wife, my handmaiden, carries a child. It is better
for them to remain at your pleasure here in your palace, attending
your father and your brothers' wives while we make the teeth-rattling journey
by chariot across the plains. With you and your henchmen we will need
no retainers, for you are the son of Nestor, friend
to my husband and yourself host-friend to my son, and godlike besides.'
    'This is well-reasoned, O queen. I appoint it all as you say,
and our departure for tomorrow. But first we shall have our feasting and songs
to joy in on our way.' He told the serving maids to lead me
with Ailanthis also to the high bedchamber of his sister,
Polykaste, who kept a vigil night and day by her father's
couch. Then Ailanthis spoke to me wonderingly, leaning
her head close to mine so none could hear: 'Mother,
just look at the beautiful paintings all along the hallways.
Even the floors are covered with lively patterns and there is color
everywhere. Surely none around the seas can love
life better than these who bring their birds and beasts
of earth and sky so brilliantly alive inside their halls.'
    The servants bathed us and anointed us with perfumed oils and arranged
our hair with silver combs and ivory according to their custom.
We put on our finest robes of our own handiwork, took
from our chests the bracelets of lustrous beads and put on our veils.
    Then we walked through the striped columns into the courtyard.
Already Helios leaned toward far Ithaka. The men
were busy preparing the beasts for sacrificing, heaping the fires
and spitting all for roasting. Polykaste came to us now
and took us by the hands and led us to the high-roofed hall, saying:
'Never would I linger even at the couch of my father but I would greet
Telemachos' mother and sister and call them my friends.
And my mother said to me: "Go now, Polykaste, greet Penelope
the steadfast for me, for you knew her thoughtful son, Telemachos,
come in search of his father, and you yourself bathed him."'
    She seated us before the splendid wall with the towering gryphon.

She drew silver-studded chairs and tables before us.
Her handmaidens poured water from a golden pitcher to wash in.
Peisistratos himself mixed the wine in a worked bowl and poured
it into the footed gold cup with doves on the handles.
We put our hands to the good things to eat, abundant and zestily
seasoned with strange spices. Peisistratos spoke to Phemios, saying:
'Now, singer from afar, take up your hallowed lyre.
Beguile us with your singing, for now it is not yet time
for the last libations, but neither is there desire in anyone's heart
for dancing within the palace. But all of us long always
to hear new tales sung by a divine singer
for they can lift us out of the cares that are ever with us.'

So you, Phemios, began the singing and we listened
again to Odysseus' many hardships wandering the raging seas
driven by Poseidon, while hordes of boorish men
besieged me in my own house calling themselves suitors.
And you did not forget to sing them my story as you knew it,
how I bore my daughters to Odysseus in secret and how with Laertes
and Antikleia I raised them to lovely maturity.

And while they were listening rapt, I called Mabantha to my side,
She spoke, saying, 'My Lady, I would journey with you,
but gratefully I am staying in the ease of this house that puts me
to thinking of splendid Thebes. Phemios was fearful for me also.
No longer am I young, to be carrying this child lightly.
But my friend, I could be easier far in my mind
had you not called me friend, and raised me above the other women
of your house, had you not often lain your head
on my breast to weep and told me the deepest scourges of your heart.
Yet I think that now Ailanthis is becoming the friend you raised her to be,
and in this was wisdom. I will be thinking of your ways
as I raise this girl-child to be, always aiming for her friendship.'

'Mabantha, dear friend, it is difficult to leave you behind
for even this short journey, for you have been kindred to my soul.
But I will think of you and store up all that I see to recount to you
when we return, and soon, for we will make our way quickly.'

Then Mabantha had no more words for an answer but took
my hand in her two hands and held them.

　　While we two were speaking, handsome Peisistratos
leaned his head close to Ailanthis and these two were conversing.
And always his dark eyes blazed as they looked upon her
and my spirit stirred within me for Odysseus' youth and mine,
forever lost to jealous gods. Ailanthis spoke of him
later in our high bedchamber, saying: 'O Mother, here
is a man who matches my brother for thoughtfulness and purpose.
For he was already mindful of Helen's skill with potions,
and considered whether to journey again to Lakedaimon to learn it
and gain good reputation and counsel for his people. He confirms
that the healing-thyme is gone also from the slopes
of Parrhasia and the passes of lofty Taÿgetos. He questioned me
intently about Telemachos' wound and there is much wisdom in him.

　　'He spoke to me saying: "Already you are dear to me as my sister,
for Telemachos and I are brothers more than friends, such
is the feeling we have for each other. I would love you anywhere
for him, for there is no mistaking how you are like him in looks
and bearing, except for your eyes, for his are dark like your mother's."
And, Mother, it put me in mind of Telemachos and how the hours
of his life are fleeting like our ship before the wind.' At last
we thought of going to bed, and accepted the gift of slumber.

　　As Dawn glimmered in the mists we took our clothing from the pegs
and dressed, binding on our sandals. We gathered our bundles
and went on our way from our chamber and down the halls to the courtyard.
Peisistratos with Echios, his guest-friend from Elis,
harnessed the splendid horses and we mounted the chariots
of gleaming bronze. We drove clattering out of the gate
and the echoing portico. The men's hands whipped the horses
to run and they seemed to wing their way along the gorges
with an eager spirit, leaving Pylos behind, bright in the sun.
All day the horses shook the yokes they bore on their shoulders.
Ailanthis and I signaled each other between the chariots,
wondering at the wide-stretching plains abundant with streams.

And the sun set toward Ithaka and the journeying ways darkened.
We came to Pherai and reached the house of my sister, Iphthime,
and Eumelos. We slept the night and they gave us hospitality
after tireless Peisistratos handed us down,
eyes kindling as Ailanthis praised his skillful driving.

    Later Ailanthis spoke to me of Peisistratos, saying:
'But Mother, do not look at me with such show of delight
in his words to me. While it is true that he questioned me, "Must you be always
with your mother on your journey, or could we two make some detour together?
I spoke to him saying: "O Peisistratos, friend of my brother,
you know I have serious business that I must accomplish
besides my brother's healing. It is this that I must be about
before I can think of dallying." And, Mother, my spirit delights
in this journey we are making together.' We shared a heartfelt moment
before sleep drifted over us, relaxing our limbs.

    When the young Dawn showed in her lovely robes
the two men yoked the horses anew and we mounted
the cars behind them. They whipped the prancers lightly, and soon
we were out in the plain beside black-shrouded Taÿgetos.
All day we sped along the byway where the wheat bends,
while Zeus rumbled along the peaks and sent his thunderbolts
down the valleys beside us. More than once cold rain
lashed our faces and whipped the horses to break
for the dry margins beyond the bellowing clouds. When
we had rounded the end of the range and were turned again toward Sparta
we followed the greening banks of Eurotas down to the cavernous hollow
of Lakedaimon where Sparta of the two hills
lifted before us. But towering above the city loomed
steeply forbidding Taÿgetos. Now the mountain was white-clad,
with clouds writhing and streaming off like steam from a cauldron
or the manes of horses driven wild by the reek of a lion.
I drew in my breath, stunned by our narrow escape.
As night came on and the ways were darkened we approached
the city, drove through it, and made our way to the house of Helen.

    From the moment the chariots clattered through the high gate crowned
with gryphons and into the wide forecourt, I marveled at how

this palace was the place of the journey in my dream. For singers have sung
of its brazen beauty, and Telemachos too had told me the details
I longed to hear. But often it happens that when a sleeper dreams
of a house she knows, yet it is not the house as she knows it.
Now I saw that this was indeed a palace I knew
and I entered it, confident. We walked as if in dream between columns,
through the portico and into the great hall, all blazing
with bands of cobalt and bright carnelian around the walls
and under the high eaves. Birds in flight and sea-creatures
adorned the walls. Some excellent painter had arranged them,
brilliant and playful and delightful to the eye, so even I
wondered how Helen was ever persuaded to forsake it for Paris.
Peisistratos was beside me, but when we entered the hall
he never needed to speak, for Helen knew me at once.

SHE ROSE from her beautiful throne, letting her handiwork fall
into her silver basket. She came to me herself with measured stateliness
yet with the lightness of step that spoke of youthful spirits.
The women of her household followed. Manservants turned from their tasks.
    'Welcome, Penelope, queen among women. A queen's greeting.
You honor my house, downfallen as I was, yet still I give you honor
as much as I can, though my husband is away, for he too would wish it.
I know you well, and Nestor's glorious son Peisistratos
who came to us some time past with Telemachos, your son.
But who is this lovely girl with you, in stature and poise
so like a goddess or a young god to whom the singers have yet
to give voice around the seas? Can I be wrong or has she too
a likeness to your son, though her eyes are gray. I look at her in wonder.'
    'O Helen, gracious queen, I thank you for your greeting.
Next I thank you from my heart for receiving my son with hospitality.
Your fame for this reached all in Ithaka, even Odysseus,
returned at last to his waiting family, his homeland and his people.
Here is Ailanthis, my daughter of Odysseus and sister to Telemachos.
Her twin, Nerianne, is now apprenticed at The Pythia's feet.
Their birth was unknown to all save Odysseus' parents
until the day of his homecoming. Even Telemachos never knew
of it then, for I could not imagine that even he could withhold them
against the arrogant suitors, stripling that he was until the time
he journeyed to Lakedaimon and came to maturity at your knees.
Nor could the singers tell of it, for it was not a part of their stories.'
    'What you have said is fair and orderly. Wonder takes me
when I think of it. How you must have suffered for fear that someone
would guess it. It was enough for thoughtful persons, knowing
how you stayed alone at the head of your household raising your son

and keeping your people and possessions together for Odysseus' homecoming.
I know also how, lately, your house was besieged
by those insolent young men – how well I know the difficulty
of resisting such advances – and these laid burdens upon you.
But you shall tell me more of this later. In my delight to greet you
I forget the customs of men, who sometimes have the best ideas.
Come now, let my women bathe you and dress you in fine linen
of my own handiwork. Then we shall feast and know
the purpose of your visit. Afterward we two can enjoy
the delicious exchange of all the details of our long stories.'

She took me by the hands and led us to her own bedchamber
at the top of a doubled stair. I was amazed to behold the walls
and ceiling of this room. And Ailanthis nodded to me with her brows and leaned
her head close to mine so that Helen, bustling happily,
might not hear us wondering. But Helen saw and heard her
and spoke to us both, saying: 'Dear friends, it is plain
that you take pleasure in the world around us as I do also.
And wonder takes me when I see how sharp-eyed and quick-minded
is this young woman, your daughter. May you always be blessed
in the friendship I see you have with each other, unlike me
who for years was far from my Hermione, in the bloom of her maturing,
and now she is given to Neptolemos and dwells in far Phthia.
But come to my lovely bath. Adreste will attend Ailanthis.'

They bathed us in the silver bathtubs Polybos of Thebes gave Menelaos.
When they had dried us they anointed us with perfumed oil from flasks
of swirling glass given by Alkandre, wife of Polybos.
Helen went to her storage boxes where she kept her most elaborate robes
and lifted out two of them, lovely in design
and finely woven. One she draped around me expertly and tenderly,
fastening the shoulder pins and drawing the girdle down
over all. The other she gave to Adreste who put it on Ailanthis.
Next Adreste and Phylo ordered our hair in the silver combs
and fixed in our ears our pendants of beaded gold.
While we two were relaxing thus, radiant Helen
questioned us eagerly about Ithaka, our house, and our customs.
We exchanged our ways and spun strong bonds of friendship.

Next we descended the doubled staircase to the hall.
Wood was heaped on the fire and the cressets and oil lamps burned.
Handsome Peisistratos was there, bathed and dressed
in fresh linen also. He resembled a young god
beside Ailanthis, herself nearly as lovely as Helen.
The servants brought in rich fare, with honeyed drink
from the mixing bowl in well-wrought goblets.

     Helen and I conversed, and Peisistratos with Ailanthis,
his head close to hers so that none of the company might hear them.
But when we had put away our desire for eating and drinking
with light chatter, then at last Helen questioned me:
'Penelope, my friend, it is little known for a woman of your stature
to travel far without her husband or a father
or watchful brothers, even when she serves as guardian to her daughter.
And what of that other daughter you mentioned? Whence have you come
since you left your hearth and on what avowed intent?'

     'O Helen, what woman hearing your beauty sung by the poets
and men alike – of armies of men and fleets of ships
hurled to destruction against a mighty city in a war
like none other for your sake – which one, even
if she be a queen, does not seek you out and come to question you
in her own mind? But I come on an urgent errand,
for you have knowledge and possession of subtle medicines from Egypt
where the greatest number of herbs grows. Telemachos told me
this when he returned from these halls. But now I have this to tell you:
all goes badly with my son – at this moment I do not know
if he lives or is dead. For while he was hunting in the mists of night
some god sent a wily beast to gouge his body,
slipping under his guard, and he lies feverish, beyond reason.

     'No more does the healing thyme grow on our slopes, nor
on any shore between here and The Pythia's sacred shrine. For we journeyed
to Pytho first, as the dream urged it. And there Nerianne
resides and seeks her way, she of the silver voice,
skilled in the singing of tales with the lyre. The Pythia sent me to you
in her verses. And with me, to seek her own way,
is this daughter, Ailanthis, whose mind has become as astute

about growing plants as learned Laertes himself, Odysseus' father.
She would learn from you all she can to apply your potions
to Telemachos' wound, if he still lives, and if you will teach her.'

   Helen answered me, saying: 'Penelope, my friend, how cruel
the gods are, toying with you and yours once more
after years of hardship and outrage. All the world knows
your patience; the singers tell of it everywhere. There is no understanding
the designs of the gods. See, here I am returned to my home
and Menelaos stays by my side, except when unruly upstarts
throng against him, while you are driven to wander from Odysseus.
Yet we are not without resources to help one another.
Gladly I will show you what I brought from Polydamna, wife of Thon,
on my sojourn in Egypt. And tomorrow I will show you the plants
that grow lush in my gardens by the river and these you shall take also.'

   I had no words for an answer, for in my mind I pondered
two ways, whether to press on toward my son
at once or to remain in delightful companionship one more day,
for there were many questions I still would put to Helen herself.
Next Ailanthis spoke, saying: 'O gracious queen,
we would gladly remain here with you in your splendid palace,
visiting your gardens and delighting in your matchless hospitality.
But truly, my brother's life, if he still lives, gutters low,
and we must return to him quickly.' Helen spoke, saying:

   'Dear child, what you say is sensible enough. But consider this:
the most powerful medicine I have grows nearly to ripeness just now.
I think you will no longer wish to hurry away when I tell you
of its powers. But you are of an age to be impulsive, as I know well.
Only wait through tomorrow and you will be glad you did.'
'O gracious Helen, already you teach me my first lesson,
and I will learn it well. Willingly I stay at your knees.'
'And willingly will I share with you all the secrets taught to me
in the land of the followers of Païeon. But I wish that you
yourself could journey to Egypt and bring back even more
of the subtle arts in healing, for I see you are a woman of talent.'

   Now Ailanthis could not withhold a glow from her cheeks.
Peisistratos admired her, leaning closer. Helen smiled

and arched her brows to me saying: 'I appoint a visit to my gardens
for tomorrow, and I think we shall find the healing greens ready.'
We parted for sleep. Ailanthis and I lay under the fine coverlets,
our bodies still pulsing with the chariots' sway
until sleep drifted over us, unstringing our limbs.

    As Dawn tinted the sky in yet another strange city,
we arose and took our garments from their pegs to dress
and put on our sandals. We bound up our hair in the golden circlets
and went on our way from our bedchamber out through the halls to the courtyard.
Peisistratos harnessed the horses to the chariots and checked the fittings.
And next smiling Helen, restless and impetuous as always,
mounted her elaborate chariot with the golden swan encircled
by rings of cobalt, and silver mountings on the bronze traces.
She reached down to hand me up, laughing gaily
as a young girl who trips with her sister from their steading to wash
clothing in a stream, knowing they can bathe there because it is hidden.
She urged on the horses with a golden whip and they dashed unreluctant
out of the gate and down through the city to the river.
Peisistratos followed, Ailanthis mounted beside him in the car.

    Soon we came to a stream of the river. There it bends
like the curve of a bow into the sheltering bluffs of the hills
below treacherous Taÿgetos. The slopes face Helios'
life-giving rays and are sheltered from the cold North winds.
Here Helen's garden was laid out, like none I had seen
on Ithaka nor in the lands of my parents when I was little.
Here were rolling orchards with trees in rows, heavy
with ripening fruits, and bedded plantings, all well ordered,
with pathways to walk between them. Figs grew here
in abundance, and pomegranates. Farther on toward the stream
were flourishing plants that like to grow near the flowing waters
of rivers, and these she had carried with her from fertile Aigyptos.
She took Ailanthis' hand and led her along the pathways,
pointing here to a flower, here to a stippled leaf, there
to the bark on the stem of a low bush or tree, instructing.

    'And always when the merchants come to Esopus' banks with their tin
and grain and purple dyes I send them next to bring me

the prized growing things of every people around the known
seas for my garden, and with them some knowledge of their uses.
And here is a place with its own seasons, and in it I can grow
juniper and papyrus alike – the one on the higher slopes
and the other along the banks of the stream, just as I found it
on Aigyptos' banks. And here is a naba tree, and a persea,
both already growing well. Here coriander, parsley.
These are my charges, now that my only child, Hermione,
is far away and the gods granted me no more children.
But you, Ailanthis, come with me farther, for you are the one
to handle the weed. And I will instruct you carefully in this medicine,
malignant or good in mixture according to how we prepare it.
What I will show you is implausible, but whoever drinks it down
once it has been mixed in an iron bowl can be restored to strength.'
She touched Ailanthis' shoulder and led her away down a path,
and next they were out of our sight in a grove of tamarisk.

    I remained silent with Peisistratos as we watched them recede
in the pathway. We wandered with our eyes along the gentle slopes
of orchards and fields with the patterns of growing things
in their various hues, textured as a cloth of many weaves.
And I could not keep from noticing how his eyes
followed them openly down the way. All at once he turned
and caught my eyes resting upon him. He straightened. Then
he seemed to me taller and thicker, with a grace about his wide
shoulders and splendid limbs. His eyes kindled again.
Now we two stayed speechless as we walked down
the orderly rows toward a spreading tree, fruit-bearing
and casting a leafy shade on an outcrop beside the path.

    Some things that pass between people must never be spoken.
For impassioned words, once they have passed the lips,
are like the breeze that comes to riffle the branches of the pear tree
in full blossom and shudders them suddenly bare, spoiling
their glory. At last we managed to converse carelessly –
wondering at the riches of the house of Helen and Menelaos.

    The circle of shade crept along the ground before us,
a breeze unfurled and the day was cooling when Helen returned.

She led us to the gate of the enclosure where we all mounted the chariots
and the horses sped us on the way back to the city
and the palace over the river's plain. Touching the horses
only lightly with her restless lash, and driving into
the evening's warm glow and the glittering stars' rising,
Helen spoke to me again, questioning me carefully, saying:

   'How I wish that Paris had yearned for my dear Hermione
instead of lusting after foolish me. Then I could have enjoyed
his flashing glances safely and from a distance,
still kindled toward my wedded husband, and given Hermione to Paris.
Never, then, would countless Achaians have lost their lives,
with their wives left weeping in their houses and struggling alone
to bring children to their maturity. O, bitter
the day Menelaos went roaming in his thoughtless way,
and I tried to confront the disturbing presence of Paris.
As when too much barley is added to a steaming cauldron
and it froths and rises boiling, and each ingredient added
to tame the mix raises it higher until it bubbles over,
so my words and entreaties were useless to dampen
the fires that burned in us both; we had passed the barrier that held back
the rush of recognition in us. And next Paris took me.

   'He forced me on board and the oarsmen dipped their oars
into my husband's unguarded harbor and set the mast pole for Ilion.

   'All the rest you know, at least what the singers tell.
And you as a woman may also know what all women must know
or discover to their sorrow. It is a difficult thing for a woman
to hate a captor when he has her completely in his power. I came
to cling to him, forsaking my husband's image in my spirit, believing
I would never again return to my homeland. In truth, since in those days
I was chattel both there and here, it seemed to matter
little whose wife I was or where. I made my way
into my new life as the mind within me thought best.
I was like unsung women before me and captives ever since.
They take us from our cities like so many sheep or cattle,
like cauldrons of shining bronze or hammered golden cups.
Nor did it matter where I was, or whose; the war

was fated, chosen, imminent, and I was but the guise.
But you, Penelope, whose fame goes up into the heavens as circumspect
and blameless, how would you know of such a fate? Tell me
this thing that I ask, and tell me truly, how did you manage to
prevail in that degrading household of arrogant men?
What strange persuasion led you to journey alone with your daughters,
away from your husband, newly restored to you after twenty
years of separation, and he is a man who lacks no endowment
of strength or cunning? Some one of the gods must have helped you.'

   'O Helen, sister, I too have known the deliciousness
of young men's looks, and desire. For what woman
of beauty and stature is not often bothered by men
who set upon her in their minds when they look at her? Still, not many
men are the likes of Odysseus, and I had my children to provide for,
especially my daughters. But I had, at least, the help
of Antikleia and Laertes. They forsook the stately palace
to live on the estates, and there I bore my daughters in secret.
They were always well instructed and inclined toward the designs
Athene herself has woven for them. But I was anxious
for their father to return. For how could I wrest us all
from the claims of overbearing suitors without their father's protection?
And as for this journey, the goddess herself, Athene of the Aegis,
decreed it for them, a journey to The Pythia at Pytho
to question her as to what to do next. And also for me, so that I
could be a shining example to them on their way besides.

   'And Antikleia urged me to it; she persuaded me to swear an oath
that I would do it. I had to, even when my longed-for husband
was just restored to the country of his parents, his halls and his family.
And never did I know how to accomplish it except in dreams
since Odysseus himself opposed it. But then Telemachos was injured
and Ailanthis announced she would leave to search for the healing plants.
In the end my husband was gracious, almost the longed-for Odysseus
whom the gods, in jealousy that we two, always together,
should enjoy our youth, bore away in the black ships,
never to restore him as I remembered him and longed for him to be.

   'How could I know, how could I ever guess he'd return

to me in guises so estranged from all I had awaited –
first a shriven scrawn in rags, filthy and foul-smelling,
then erect as a god, his hair gray-shocked but his beard nearly
as brown, his mouth as full as I always remembered it? No,
I couldn't accept or open myself readily to either
apparition. As always I needed the talk first,
the drawing near in spirit that disarms me and infects me with desire.

 'Tell me this, Helen – how is it to journey yourself
and return to the same dear husband you knew once,
and yet he has taken a different journey, separate from yours?
And no longer is he the young man with slim loins
and thoughtful glances, attentive to you and keen in discourse.
How it is for you when you sit in your halls entertaining the important men
of the country with feasting, and how when you two
lie together in love in your beautiful carven bed?'

 'O Penelope, my sister, how is it *you* are questioning *me*
in these matters? Have you not also journeyed as I have?
For did I not know you at once when you slipped between the columns
of the high portico? That was no dream but a shared vision.
And you in your life were journeying even as Odysseus was journeying.

 'But put in your mind also this thing that I tell you. Never
in this life is the journeying done. Even once returned, still
we are accomplishing it separately and yet we journey together besides.
And this is hardest of all. But you are like a goddess for wiles
and good sense, and Odysseus is not lacking in thoughtfulness.'
We two went on conversing thus, through the forecourt,
in the hall at the feasting, and later in the upper chambers
of the palace until the lamps burned low and paled.

 'O Penelope, Dawn is rising to her golden throne.
My heart is reluctant to part with you so soon, for we
are kindred spirits. I wish you would stay; I wish I could set you
beside me at my loom. We two would take up the glorious weaving
and together we could accomplish a singular pattern,
recording the struggles of women around the wide seas
and the men who say they love us but ignore our wisdom.
But I will not keep you longer lest the fear of your son's life

ebbing out of him take you over. Rather I will send you
on your way, rejoicing in gifts to remember me by, so that
on every occasion we will be close in spirit, whether in suffering
or delight, since the goddess bestows all upon us in life.'

    Helen called Ailanthis to her, and led us into the chamber
where her treasures were stored. She stood by the storing boxes and lifted out
three elaborate robes, woven and dyed in shades
of sea-purple, wondrous to behold. For in them she had worked
the siege of fallen Troy. Here were the black ships
of the Achaians in the darkest hue, the decks bristling
with men eager for blood. Here were horses straining
toward the walls, men riding lightly in their chariots despite
ponderous armor, gripping the railings and flourishing their weapons.
Here were vultures and dogs circling the mounds of the dead
and the gods clustered in their appalling ranks, watching the show.

    'But here, too, were the far-off homelands, the strong-founded houses
and rude hearths of the leather-bearing heroes, with patient wives
and sweethearts, mothers and children carrying on their living.
These threaded their looms, herded geese to a reedy pond,
gathered in branches for the weariless fires, heaped
millet into great skin bags and attended the sick,
the old men. And toward the last of the supple folds,
a boy with a little girl, their fingers sweetly twined,
looked up at a pigeon tumbling straight on toward the great gate
of Ilion with the huge horse drawn up close
and a hawk perched on the stone lintel, terribly tensed.

    All this was worked exactly the same on each
of two robes that Helen held out for us. She spoke thoughtfully:
'Here are gifts from Helen's heart but accomplished with her hands.
Always, even if I were to weave this story for every woman
to wear pinned above her breastbone, still would
my fingers go on tirelessly spinning it out.
For all my sorrows are in it, stitched among all our lives.
I would pass these down through the houses of women to come.
And here is a third for the lovely day when your singer returns
to her homeland. Until that time let it lie away in your chamber,

and with it a woman's greeting.' She spoke to Ailanthis, saying:
    'Dear child, already I have stored away in the chariots'
carrying baskets all the clay-stopped jars and flasks
of potions from Polydamna and many growing things besides.
These are yours to hand down through women. But one day,
when you make your journey to Aigyptos' banks, you may return
some one of them to Polydamna herself as a gift from Helen.
But also I give you this bowl carven from fiery carnelian
to mix things in, and my spoon with the curved neck
and swan's head for a handle, to apportion the grave liquors and salves.
The antidote I send in the open amphora with sustaining waters,
and I pray you return to your homeland in time to restore your brother.'
    She turned to me next and took my hand in hers.
She drew me away to her own upper room and spoke to me,
saying: 'Here is the possession I prize above all others.
Take it as a gift from Helen and work with it wondrous stuffs
to be seedbed without mire, story without singing or lyre,
light unto the gentle souls who live around the seas.'
Behind the pillar stood an elaborate loom, wondrous
to look on. The frames were ebony, studded with silver nails,
and the fastenings were thin strips of well-tanned oxhide
dyed sea-purple and twisted to fine cord. The shuttles
were carved of ebony with a curved-horn deer and wing-borne geese
in the hollows and the weights were of gold and silver, one side
showing Nereids riding on the backs of dolphins, with rosettes on their reverse
    Helen continued, saying: 'Here also is a robe for Arete.
It may be that on your journey homeward some
one of the gods may stir up the storm winds against you –
and who ever knows where journeying may take her besides?
I would have you take it with you in case, and with it
a woman's greeting.' I spoke to her in answer, saying:
    'Daughter of Leda, listening to your sayings I feel a strange mixture
of pleasure and dread, but still I am restless to be going.
How I wish it would please you to let the gift you give me be something
I can carry away easily stored in my chest
with a strong knot. I cannot take the loom to Ithaka, but leave it

here for your designing, since no high-wheeled wagon,
mule-drawn, could keep pace with chariots behind Nestor's
horses around the clefts and pinnacles. And I would give you
presents also, since you have been more than host or friend.
Rather you are like the sister I see only in my dreams,
and dearer than she is.' I pulled from my bundle one silver bobbin,
of the three I took with me. I gave her also the pride of my loom,
the loveliest robe I had ever woven, as sheer as the webs
of spiders in the dawn mists. It was fashioned from the lustrous threads
carried from beyond Phoenicia that a steersman once gave
to Mabantha. I had Mentor build me a lighter loom for it,
plane it smooth to a chalk-line, and fastened it myself with thin strips
of oxhide dyed purple. I had woven the robe
all over with lovely designs in the pattern of earth-spirals and sea waves
mingled with spring flowers in waving grasses. It shone
like the haze around the moon before rain. Helen delighted in it.

    Impetuous as always, she seized a bronze knife inlaid
with gold and began to cut away the weights from the edges
of the cloth still hanging from the loom. These clattered and rang out
as they rolled and spun to the far corners of the room dancing
in the glow from Dawn of the saffron robes peering
through the deep-shuttered window. I would have spoken, but Helen
spoke to me, saying: 'You are so sensible, dear friend.
Happily will I change my gift to you since I am able to,
for the one I prize the most among all those given me
by Polydamna. It is my golden distaff fashioned in Thebes
with a bee on the hollow end. I would give it to you for a present
to remember me by as each of us works at her own loom.
And take these weights from Clytemnestra, my sister, dead in Mykene.
I will not detain you further but speed you on since you wish it.
I hope you come back rejoicing to your own household, but if
you first come to Arete, give her my woman's greeting.'
I spoke to her in answer: 'May Athene so appoint it. Fare well.'

    Ailanthis and I climbed into ready chariots. Peisistratos
and Echios took up the reins and shook them. They laid their lashes
hard on the horses and with eager spirit these dashed

through the city to the plain. But Helen's chariot stood by also,
its horses harnessed and stamping with impatience to carry her with us.
And she, laughing like a young girl, sprang lightly
into her car and winged her way beside us along the riverbank.

But Peisistratos, a horseman nearly as godlike as his father,
whipped his team to a pace unmatchable by merely skilled mortals
and soon he and Ailanthis were far in the lead.
Helen stayed beside me while Echios drove me
along the sandy shallows of Eurotas' stream. At last
we came to where the mountains bow to the plain. There Helen
turned to race homeward on the wind, flourishing her golden whip
like a standard high above the waving grain.
Now we thought to see Peisistratos' chariot before us
between the shimmering plain and the green foothills,
but we could see them nowhere. Echios, my steady driver,
pointed then to a column of dust like a whirlstorm blowing
toward us across the grainfields. He called to the horses and reined
them in while we waited for Peisistratos' chariot to appear beside us.

We heard strange cries then, and our beasts twitched
their ears and pranced in their traces, straining to turn toward them.

• XVII •

THE DUST-CLOUD veered to speed ahead of us while still
some distance away, and we saw it was the length of two ships.
The feet of many horses pounding the thrashing wheat to earth
flashed swiftly beyond us toward the narrow pass through the foothills
where our paths would converge. My driver bellowed and brandished
the whip. At once the horses were beating the earth with their hooves.
We raced so that stones in the pathway flew to meet us
but even so the dust cloud boiled closer, ever ahead,
until it seemed to stop around the bend before us,
swirling in place as if a fiery chimera were crouched
on its haunches waiting to snare us at the turning point.

     Echios called and tried to slow the horses, to pull them
aside and turn our chariot back toward whence we came,
but the creatures were wild and unheeding. They raced the faster for his efforts,
drawn by some command we could not hear or understand.
Suddenly the whirlstorm moved closer. It gaped wide

before us through wildly flailing grain. Our team halted,
quivering. Echios stared. A tall figure swung down
off the bare back of a carriageless horse from among
a throng of mounted riders and ran to our horses' heads.
They quieted at once while my own senses reeled.

    For that herald was a woman, and all the riders now wheeling
and drawing close around us were women, iron-eyed,
erect and purposeful as a pack of wild dogs tracking
a lonely shepherd on the hills. The herald turned to Echios:
'Speak, poor male, and tell me, where is that other who journeyed
beside you all morning? For our business is with her
not with the likes of shivering you.' I spoke to her, saying:
'Here, maiden, you have done this man discourtesy.
He is not some ordinary driver of horses but the son
of a king among the Epeians and friend of Peisistratos,
Nestor's noble heir. As for that woman who drove beside us,
long ago she turned her horses back
toward her city and her people. You will never be able
to catch her now, for her coursers were sired by mounts
taken in Ilion from Penthesilea, Queen of the Amazons,
breeders of horses fit for the gods. And they are warriors
as you are, so I think that you must be of them also.'

    'This was well reasoned, O queen that I see you are.
My queen will be well pleased to question you herself
to learn who you are, where are your hearth and your people,
and where it is you traveled, with Helen of the far-flung journeys
riding along beside you. Come to our queen now.'
'O sister, friend, although I would gladly go with you to greet
your queen, yet I cannot delay my journey, which is homeward.
An urgent matter calls me there with my heart's prompting
and many are those who await my return and count on it.'

    The herald tossed her head and, laughing, she spoke again:
'O woman, do not speak of what you cannot do.
For we know that better than you, who cannot go where we
do not will it. You will find that your horses obey us.
Your man can do nothing with them and already he has seen it.

You will come with us, just as I order it and I will lead you.'

 It was true. Echios raised his shoulders and held up
his hands. Our horses wanted no guidance from us.
Eagerly they followed the striding woman, pacing
behind her horse as she mounted and led the way onward.
But mindful of our stature in the eyes of all, Echios held
the reins with poise, and so we made a show of dignity.

 A storm was raging inside my breast. What of my daughter,
my dearest Ailanthis, and Peisistratos? Were they far ahead?
Had they stopped for dalliance, to lie in love
along the grassy banks of Eurotas' stream among the blood-red
and plum-blue wildflowers the wind set quivering there?
Or had they thought to go on to Pylos to carry the heal-all
straight to Ithaka, mindful of Telemachos' dimming spirit?
Would they come back after us and blunder into the swarm
that surrounded us now, or were they beyond the pass
to Pherai, all unknowing that, returning to find us, they too
could be taken? I spoke to Echios, close to his ear, and said to him:

 'O prince, be mindful that you never betray my daughter's nearness
nor that of your friend. For if these warriors do not know of them
perhaps Ailanthis with Peisistratos can journey on to Pylos
and somehow we can make our way homeward later.'

 Just then our captors turned from the well-worn byway
to a narrow track. We passed between ranks of thorny scrub,
past outcroppings of rock and stunted trees
up toward the mountains we had driven all morning
to pass around. The trail was narrow and rocky. Our chariot
lurched and grated so against roots and boulders
that I soon stepped down to walk behind it. Our guide
never noticed me walking, so for many strides I pushed myself
to keep pace with the horses although the dust choked me
and my feet were quickly raw from the rubbing of my sandals, and stones
cut them till they bled. Bronze squealed on bronze. We came to a place
where the path became merely a thread through the tangle.
Our horses stopped at last. The herald turned and quickly
loosed the traces, secreting my chariot deep in the hollow

of an outcrop. She led the horses on. I took my bundles
with Odysseus' dear mantle and Helen's gifts.
    Not heeding my feet, I turned to fall in again
behind the insolent herald. She turned to Echios, saying:
'You, male cur, are no longer needed here.
Hold him, warriors. See that he stays to the rear.'
Distasteful as it was to ask for any boon, I spoke:
'O maiden, he is my driver and since we set out with no retainers
he also serves me as herald. I would have him beside me.'
    But this she would not grant and Echios was shuffled like chattel
back through the muscled ranks and out of my view. I drew myself up
with all the bow-taut dignity I learned in those years
of enduring the arrogance of men far more nefarious
than this she-wolf. I bore the rest of the day in silence,
sitting apart at the two springs where we stopped for water,
since Echios was held away from me. Helios had leaned
far toward Pylos when at last we came to a wide ridge top
that looked out over the plains and foothills on three sides.
    Here were tents with fires blazing before them, horses
standing in grassy shade and women busy between the encampment
and several caves that opened in the face of a cliff.
Golden-haired girls carried water, piled firewood,
tended the horses and stirred the cauldrons alongside women.
All wore mannish tunics girt up at the hip and covering
only one breast. They wore colored fillets in their hair
and had bows and quivers slung on their backs at the ready.
Some of the children stared and pointed as we marched to a pavilion
next to the cliff face. It was the largest tent of all,
with crocus-yellow pennons waving at the entry-pole.
    A tall figure, long-legged and goddess-like in stature
came out. Her corselet and the fillet in her flowing hair were rainbow-hued.
She looked me full in the face, smiling at first.
Next her brow furrowed in question as I held her eyes
with mine till she turned to the maiden, my captor, and spoke to her, saying:
'Ho, Celendre, here is no Helen – not she I met
and lost my youth and reputation fighting for, long

ago in Troyland. Speak, O guest, for I see that you
are brave and intelligent. This I admire in other women.
I am Penthesilea, leader of this band and of all
the golden Amazons. Tell me who you are and whence you journey.'

'I am Penelope, Queen of Ithaka and all her white-hemmed islands.
I come from a long line of strong women.
Yet never did I know of a woman or a man who was strong enough
to endure death and walk again among the living,
except for my husband Odysseus. But that was a goddess' doing.
So I think that, although for poise and stature you could be that queen
whom all the Trojans and even the Achaians mourned
when Achilleus slew her, you must be some other one. The mind
within me tells me you seek to test me in speaking thus.'

'Do my ears hear rightly? Penelope? Of all the women
who are sung in lands around the seas for holding their households
together when their men had sailed for illusive glory
in Ilion, you are the one most praised by the singers
for your steadfastness. Rumor has whispered even to us,
that you have vanquished many men. If you are Penelope,
I, Penthesilea, give you welcome as a sister.'

She crushed me to her half-bared bosom in embrace. Then she whistled
shrilly like a hawk. A small figure stepped from the tent
and hobbled to her. Not only was the child dark-haired
among all this golden company, but I could see clearly
in his frame and limbs the body of a young boy. He was beautiful,
his eyes black and quick, with only a hint of sadness
about them for the misshapen left leg that made his walk
a lurching gait. He limped to the queen, who flung a hand
in my direction and spoke to him crisply saying:

'See to our guest, boy. Take her bundles and mind
you let nothing fall from them as you go. Make up a couch
in my own tent with the best skins and finest linens.
And place a purple ribbon over the door, for here
is a sister worthy of honors. Bathe, guest, for I see
you are grimy with dust and sweat from the journey, although
you refuse to give in to your own discomfort. The boy will attend

to your needs. That male who was with you will be elsewhere.'
    She strode away abruptly as I turned at the light touch
of a hand on my arm. Her slave took my bundles and led me
quickly to the raised flap of that large pavilion. At once
the shade bathed my spirit in such cool relief
that I sank to the floor and sat for moments breathing it in.
My poor servant crouched beside me, tender concern
in those dark eyes. He moistened a cloth in a water jar
and wiped my brow and cheeks. After a questioning look
and my nod for an answer, he cooled my neck and reddened arms
with the touch of one expert in soothing ways. He brought me
wine mixed with many parts water and placed figs
beside me in a basket and a cushion on the skins of the floor.
At first I could not bear to watch him twisting to and fro
as he moved to bring water for my bathing.
But by the time the shallow tub was half filled
and he signaled me to shed my filthy clothing and step in
I could see in his movements an unaffected grace. His hands were sure
as he helped me to undress, and I gave myself over easily to his touch
as he bathed and dried me and anointed me with fragrant oil.
    At first the spirit within me was too exhausted for speaking.
But then, as my sinews loosened and my limbs relaxed, my mind
could once again take hold of thought, as a sparrow
blown about by a stormwind finally alights on a tree branch
and grasps it, gathers herself together and smooths her feathers.
I spoke to him saying: 'Tell me your name, child.
Is it the one your parents gave you? Who and where are they?'
    He turned his face away and answered softly, wringing
the linen in his hands: 'Leus is the name I go by; none
can say why. They say I came from far away
even from my queen's city, some months' journey from here.
They say I was found in a basket by a river one day.
The queen has been decent to me. She teaches me all I need to know
as you will see. Now let me show you how she wishes you
to wear the robe she gives you. It is one I wove myself.'
    He brought me a tunic of fine stuff, expertly crafted.

'But, child. . .' I saw how he drew himself up, stung. ' 'Leus, then,
you are a boy. All around the seas
the weaving of cloth is women's business.' He smiled
and answered me, saying: 'Not when you ride with the Amazons, O queen.
With us, the bridle-boys who serve them, it's the one art
allowed us, the best part of our service. We pride ourselves
on handiwork well woven as any from the best of women weavers
in all Phrygia. My mistress takes pride in my skill.'

  He arranged the robe over my left breast and under
the right one, leaving it free as all the women did.
His manner left me no room to consider adjusting
the drape of it. Besides, it is best for a guest to accept the hospitality
of a kind host with an open spirit. And at once I felt
a delicious freedom on the side that was no longer swathed
in folds of cloth. While I fastened up my hair in a fillet,
he rubbed soothing ointment over the raw places
on my feet and gently tied on fur-turned sandals.
'How soft these are, 'Leus. And how your gentle touch
helps to restore my strength. Fortunate your mistress
for your skills, and I to be her guest also. I thank you.'

  He grinned. Then as a shadow crossed the doorway he blushed
and turned away quickly, saying: 'Go now, lady. She
awaits you outside.' I left that cool haven,
stepping out into the glow of Helios, beaming low.
The Amazon queen stood before me, frankly appraising.

  'You wear the tunic well, O guest. After this
no one will know you from the rest of the Amazons' pride.
And I myself will teach you how to ride and shoot
and wield the double-headed axe if you so choose.
But now, come. Eat with me, and drink, to stoke your strength,
for you have traveled hard.' She led the way to the edge
of the plateau where a grove of trees cast a pleasing shade
and we could see the hills and valleys spread below us
all around. Here skins were spread, with cushions
for our ease and here we ate fruits and warm bread
with curd both strange and sweet while the child shuffled near

to bring us all that was needed. Penthesilea began
our discourse saying: 'Never did I think I would know you,
famed Penelope. O, I had met Helen, that one
who traveled with you, long ago in the Troad, and I
have business still to see to – promises to fulfill to her.

   'And she is one who never could amaze me by recklessly
dashing along the byways in her chariot alone. But you
are renowned for prudence, for staying close to home. Yet
you are not as I thought of you – pale, white-armed and unfit
for venturing out into the world of men.' I laughed
and answered in turn: 'Neither are you as I thought,
gone down to Hades in your youth, slain by Achilleus,
and thrown by his thralls into Scamander's stream.
Wonder takes me to speak with you now, if truly
you are the same Penthesilea the poets sing of.'

   'Those men could not kill me. They who scrabble and vaunt themselves
to gain their pitiful glory down the generations
always assume too much regarding their prowess
in battle. Of course they misjudged my resilience and, truly, I let them
think I was dying. Brute strength alone is only
for bullies. There are other ways a warrior can prevail
as you know, O crafty wife of Odysseus.
They tossed me into the bloody stream and presumed the rest.
But allies pulled me from the flow and slowly I recovered strength,
too late to rejoin the battle. Before I could rise
from my bed of fleeces the thing was over – Troy in flames,
blood drying in the streets, on walls, on broken altars.
Helen was taken. At first the goddess Rumor told that he killed her –
Menelaos, *him*, her next captor. But we learned that she lives,
and I set forth to redeem my pledge. You seem surprised?'

   'Twice now you have spoken of Helen. What do you know of her,
and what is this matter of a pledge you must redeem? For I
am come from Lakedaimon, as your herald must have told you,
and would bring you her woman's greeting if she knew we were to meet.'

   'She knew it not. Years passed while Rumor never
whispered her fate, if she lived or whether Menelaos killed her

after taking her off, for he gave an oath
to do it. Seven years passed after his ships
were split from the fleet on the journey home. Some said
Menelaos was living in Egypt where the King gave him hospitality.
But none told that Helen was with him until they returned
to Sparta. At last Rumor brought us news that she lived.
At once I chose the best women among us to come
to this hateful land where twice my foremothers rode
to no avail. This journey will redeem a flood of oaths
and rub out all the stains of missions failed. Tell me
of Helen. Does that cur humiliate her still?'

    I hastened to answer her: 'Indeed he no longer holds her
guilty and in thrall. Rather she is free again to follow
where her spirit leads, and it leads her in these days. . .'

    The herald striding toward us caught my host's glance.
She turned abruptly toward her and they spoke in a strange tongue.
Penthesilea's face told many tales in a quick sequence
of expressions, like the face of a babe asleep. A sly look
winced about her eyes, soon replaced by a guilelessness
before her minion turned to walk away. She echoed
my last words, saying: 'It leads her in these days to ride
unescorted on the plains to see her friends on their way
homeward. Tell me now, where you came from before
you arrived in Lakedaimon, what you were seeking and also
what you found.' So I told her then all that my mind
had been thinking of, without revealing that I had journeyed
this far always in the company of others. She listened
openly, her face in sympathy with every twist of my well-crafted
story. When I finished she shook her head. 'Truly
you are as devious as that husband of yours, ever-scheming Odysseus,
and here is the measure of it. All through your tale
I listened for the place where something you said might reveal a flaw
in the telling and betray a thing left out. Your telling was seamless.

    'But I know what it is you were hiding. Even now my warriors
are hunting those two who traveled with you on your way
to Pylos, and they will be brought here soon.' With stopped breath

I lifted my cup to my lips and looked into its dark ripples
while I thought of how to answer. I felt the queen's eyes
watching. My hand shook. 'Do not try
to deceive me on this, O devious queen. I have it
from between the teeth of your craven driver. Readily he told us
all we asked, thinking we would grant him . . . certain favors
and set him on his way. He told us of your spirited daughter,
who travels with Nestor's son, and that one whispered to Echios
of plans to dally along the way. Echios told us
all too eagerly of rich presents you carry from Helen,
thinking that these would interest us.' Now I shook in anger.

    I spoke to her, saying: 'How I wish you would cast him out.
For the sight of him will now be hateful to me, and never
shall I wish to exchange words with one so treacherous.'
'O, we shall let him go, but first we shall teach him the lesson
we reserve for those who grovel in weakness. We shall torture him
first – such sweet, stirring torture as will make him writhe
like the child who has been stung unawares and soon the swelling
itches terribly even as it aches and he is hard pressed
to keep from clawing at his own flesh to stop it.'

    'And what evil thing will you do to me for my deceiving?'
She leaned closer and spoke to me as to a friend: 'Do not think
that I hold your dissembling ways in my spirit with anger,
for yours was an honorable guile, to protect friend and kin.
Rather, I admire the mind and will within you, worthy of the best
of my warriors. And here is what I would have *you* consider. Come,
ride with me. Join the Amazons and fight glorious battles
beside me. Already you have bested many men.
Up then. You and your daughter will do us honor to join us.'

    'O sister, I might be happy indeed to join you and ride
free with the wind, free of men's often overbearing company.
But although you yourself have never raised a family,
never known the heartrush and agony a mother
suffers for her children, surely something plucks at that fibre
of womanhood still within you in sympathy with a mother's wish
to save her son. And this is what I would have you consider;

keep me here, and I will agree to stay as you wish.
But let my daughter and her escort journey on,
and she can take healing to my stricken son.' Penthesilea
tossed her mane and spoke: 'I would be a fool indeed
to allow a daughter of Penelope and Odysseus to slip by my lance
without conscripting her. And as to your offer to stay,
you will see that you have little say in the matter.

   'But I am not heartless, as you may believe, nor am I childless.
I have many daughters among this company, and a son.
For he who waits on you is mine, and although I must not show it
before the rest, I care for him just as you care
for your broken son. Yes, 'Leus is mine. I see
that you too are smitten with his beauty and his winning ways.
He is the one prize granted me on Ilion's plain.
His father, Achilleus, he who all the Achaians thought
had slain me, pierced my armor otherwise. It was he
who sent henchmen to pull me from the river's stream and carry me
gently to a hidden place where they sheltered me. And he himself
came to me there, where later we lay together in love.

   'He filled me with his strength and daring and helped me heal.
How we laughed when Priam erected my funeral pyre under the corpse
of some wretched camp follower! But then I had to endure
watching Achilleus' pyre. I grieved as I never had
for any man. And I bore his son despite my wounds
and grief and the harsh journey homeward. And, as you see,
I keep him by me.' I remembered then the way
her eyes lingered on his face and on his retreating form
each time he came to serve us, and her hand stroking
that misshapen leg.

                        'But you keep him as a servant. He's no better
than a slave.' She looked at me, surprised. 'Of course,' she said,
'he is my slave. There is no other way for a man
to live among the Amazons – or even a boy. For only
once a year, this by accord, do we consort with men,
to replenish our ranks. How gladly those studs reclaim the boys
born to Amazons, and few are those we deign to keep.'

163

Anger pricked at my eyes. 'But this is cruelty! It is unseemly
for so great a hero's son not to know his father,
or his mother, although he sleeps by her side each night
and tends her fire by day. What are these hateful ways
of yours meant to accomplish?'

           'Freedom – the liberty to live
as we choose, away from thralldom. Think again, my friend, on what
you judge so cruel. Would it be kindness to tell the boy,
pitiful as he now appears, that his father was the greatest warrior
of all the Achaians? Would he be stronger or merely
a whinnying colt, coming to me for every scrape
of his knee or scathing remark from some slip of a girl,
had he been told to call me "Mother?" And what of my tribe?
How could I lead them boldly if I let myself be mastered
by my boy? No, my friend, far better for me
are my own ways, and they are not thoughtless. Do not weep,
for he is content. But now I see I shall meet at last
the worthiest issue of Odysseus, and know her for your child.'

∘ XVIII ∘

INDEED, there was now a stir throughout the camp. Horses
whinnied, small bodies darted and a general clamor
of calls and greetings reached our ears from mingling figures.
In the midst of the throng I saw the strong brow and oiled head
of Peisistratos. The crowd approached. The foremost
fell away and I saw Ailanthis next to him, pillar-straight
and glowing defiance. She proved herself resourceful
then, betraying no sign she knew me. Nor
did her worthy companion. I disarmed them, saying:
'Here, O Queen of the Amazons, I would have you greet my daughter,
Ailanthis, and she will call you "friend." This hero himself
will tell you his name, his parents and the country he came from.'
    But Penthesilea stepped between us and spoke first:
'A warrior's greeting to you, daughter of Penelope, who is no less
a warrior than Odysseus. And also to you, O handsome one.
Your fame precedes you and makes you welcome,
even among the Amazons, who have little to do with men.'
    The queen looked on both with appraising eyes that saw
Ailanthis relax as I stepped forward to kiss her eyes
and to take Peisistratos' hand. We turned as one then,
as if we had planned and practiced it, to face our captor.
    'What do you intend for us now, O queen? We would have you
tell us at once so we can know the measure of it.'
This was Ailanthis speaking, nor did Peisistratos flinch from talking:
'If indeed you are the queen whom long ago the Argives praised,
I would not know it. For in appearance you still
resemble some nymph or a goddess herself. But here
you are far from your Amazon homeland. Surely some portent
has drawn you so deep into the land of the Achaians,

165

and I would learn of it. Or are you here to storm
some unfortunate city, bent on vengeance for ancient losses?'
    Penthesilea stepped back and smiled up frankly
into his eyes. I saw how she admired him. For a moment
she did not speak. Then: 'This was well spoken,
prince, and well considered. We are come to release
the woman all men conspire to hold. I vowed
to Helen, should Priam's Troy hold fast against the Argives,
she could come with us to be free of men at last.
She had tired of all and wished no more husbands
who would take her as a prize and vaunt her like one more
colt-giving mare, or golden cup, or fine-weaving concubine. With us
she will be free to choose her lovers, as I would choose you
for your godlike form and prowess. You are better by far
than that dog, Echios, who betrayed you while you called him friend.
Now Helen is captive to Menelaos, who valued her little
when he had her before. Even she, like a golden ball tossed
between lusty dancers, deserves some days at rest,
hidden among reeds by the edge of the dancing-ground.
She will welcome deliverance at last, and hearten my whole tribe.'
    Ailanthis spoke to her, saying: 'All of this, O queen,
is as she would have received you, were she still a woman
unmolded, as she was before. But since she sojourned with Polydamna
and Alkandre in Egypt, where the fertile earth produces
the greatest number of medicines, she has more understanding of plants,
medicines and potions than men and women elsewhere.
This she puts to good use, tending her garden and calling
for plants to be sent from around the seas. She is content.'
    The queen was struck speechless. She looked to me
in a show of disbelief. I spoke to her, saying: 'O queen, our host,
my daughter speaks to you all too truthfully,
I would tell you even more strongly that Helen is at last
a woman fulfilled. Even Menelaos admires her skill
and praises her for it. Besides she has regained his trust.
Surely you would never be the one to wrest her from a life
of purpose, now that you know of it.' The queen looked down

and scuffed at the rocks with her sandal. Abruptly she paced
toward the plateau's edge. Then she turned and whistled.
    Peisistratos spoke next, in words of blandishment, saying:
'I see, O queen, that you are not the one to betray
a friend, nor are you known to be harsh to those who are not
your foes. Shall we remain your unwilling captives, always
looking for ways to escape so that never again can your women
take their sleep in peace?' Ailanthis spoke, saying:
'And if you keep us, you will feel forever the wrath
and vengeance of Ithaka and Pylos and all the Achaians. Together
they will hound your troops once more from shore to shore.'
    Penthesilea gazed at Ailanthis and answered her, saying:
'O do not think, my young friend, that you will remain unwilling
to join our ranks after you see more
of the way we live, any more than this hero will remain unwilling
to be taken by the Amazon. For I know that you are searching
for the way that will be your life. Shrewd as you are,
you will see that ours is the best way, and the freest.
But do not think to answer me now. I will hear
no more speech this night.' She turned to approaching Celendre
and 'Leus, who shuffled close, and spoke to them in their alien tongue.
Then she spoke again in ours: 'Take these two guests
to separate tents. The hero I will show
to another place, where he will find himself willing to share
the queen's fire.' She gestured to 'Leus, who took Ailanthis'
bundle and led her away. Stiffly Peisistratos submitted
to the massed ranks of tall women who stepped between him
and us, casting long shadows from the leaping tongues
of the fire. Celendre led me back to the queen's large tent
where she laced the doorflap with ceremony and lay
across it all night. I scarcely noticed until morning,
for as soon as I entered exhaustion loosened my limbs
and I slept until well into the light of day.
                              I awoke to the thudding
of many horses' hooves on rocky ground and the sounds
of whoops and whistles thinning on a light wind. One side

of the tent was bright where the sun struck it fully,
and it billowed and swayed as the breezes played it like a maiden's veil.
I could hear the calls of birds in the trees, the snorts
and tail-swooshing of nearby horses. I smelled the kindled fires
and milk puddings cooking over them, and now and then
I heard the high thin shriek of a hawk in the cliffs.
I could have lain there in thrall to the myriad pleasures
of that sheltered spot had the spirit within me not been urgent
to hurry outside and learn what the Amazon planned for us next.
My guardian, keenly watchful, loosened the flap at once
as I rose from my bed of scraped skins. She slipped outside,
leaving me alone to dress and arrange my hair. How welcome
those moments of solitude would have been, with no servant
to chatter beside me, none to ask me for instructions nor favors
and no one to question the thoughts that roamed free with the tides
of sound and scent around me. But eagerly I pressed to finish
my dressing, wondering whether I would soon meet with my daughter
and together we might find a way to resume our journey.
For always the thought of Telemachos' desperate state pulled
my thoughts toward home, like a rough strand in the warp
that will always show up in the weaving even through dye-stuff.

    But as I entered the light and caressing air, my breath
caught in my throat. A golden splendor suffused everything around me,
and a mist shrouded all but the tops of the mountains.
I knew I was seeing the earth with the eyes of a goddess
on Olympus. While all around was sound, like the constant sea-swell
echoing even far inland on Ithaka, here also
was a silence below sound that kept me from speech for a time.

    As Celendre led me to the tree-shade to give me breakfast
I guessed that Ailanthis was gone. I turned to her, then saying:
'Tell me this truly, herald, where is my daughter,
and where is your queen? When shall I speak with her again?'

    'Our queen rode out with your daughter at dawn. They will spend
this day on the plains and I think you will find your daughter changed
in her spirit toward us as I was, when once, long ago,
Penthesilea rode near the hovel I tended

for my loutish husband. She came beside me, leaned down
from astride her steed, and pulled me up to ride me away
from misery, her bronzed arm around my waist, my legs
warm against her thighs in their unwavering grip
on the horse's flanks. And I am the one to show you
many things about our life and our ways. Come.'
    All day we walked through the camp or sat conversing.
Around us women and lusty girl warriors flowed
between their tasks and laughter with an easy rhythm, seemingly free
of constraint or hierarchy. The women sang as they tended the horses.
The girls laughed and clapped their hands with abandon as they practiced
shooting their arrows at a bladder set in a tree. All day
they would run and climb and shout, seemingly at play
but honing skills they seemed to relish. At mid-day
they gathered under the trees in the shade of tents
around some older warrior to fashion arrows and shields
or watch her sharpen her double-bladed axe or tip
her arrows with gum. All day they would mount the horses,
seemingly free to go and come with whoops of joy.
At last, as Helios leaned far toward Ithaka, the clatter of hooves
and a piercing whistle announced the return of the queen.
    With her rode Ailanthis. Glowing and windblown she swayed in front
of the queen on her great horse. Ailanthis' tunic was draped
below her right breast. She held a bow in one hand
and the mane of the beast in the other. Penthesilea held her
around her waist and on the queen's left arm perched
a falcon with rippling plumage. Penthesilea swung down
first. Ailanthis stayed mounted, beaming in triumph.
    'See, Mother, truly this is the way of life
for women who wish to be free. Now that I have ridden with the Amazons
I know it is so.' She slid down easily, ran over
and embraced me, saying: 'Tell me, Mother, that just
as you released my sister to live the life she chose,
so you will bless my joining the Queen of the Amazons.
O, do not be so troubled, Mother, for you can return
to Ithaka bearing the jar of healing balm from Helen.

There you can see to my brother. The queen will grant you
passage and I can easily instruct you in all that Helen
taught me.' Penthesilea stood behind her, proud
and fierce in victory, the skin of a leopard at her waist, her hawk
preening its feathers. Ailanthis led me away to the queen's pavilion.

    'O my daughter, tell me how it is
this woman has beguiled you. Are you sure that this is the path
your life is meant to take? What of your gift of healing?
Shall you forget the lessons learned at your grandfather's side?
What shall I tell Laertes?' Ailanthis laughed. 'Tell him,
Mother, the best thing he ever showed me was the leaf
that is balm for sandals' chafe. To be sure, some other parts of me
would be sore, did I not know it.' She raised her brows
in that look of hers. We laughed, easing the tension between us.

    'Think, Mother, how many lands, what various cities
I shall see as I ride beside the Amazon queen.'
I leaned closer then and spoke low so none
might hear us. 'This queen you admire so, was it not
she who threatened to take your lover from you with ease?'
Ailanthis stiffened then. Next she stunned me, saying:

    'He is already taken, and she has told me how readily
it was accomplished. If such a man can be won over
to lie in love with many women, much as a bull
is always able to mount a new heifer brought
to his enclosure although he has already spilled his seed, of what use
to eat my heart out in constancy? Shall I not be
as free and as skilled in the mastery of men as this queen
and shall I not have the delight of taking the man
who pleases me as my own desires urge me to it?

    'My mother, there are more ways of living than we knew of
and this is the way for me.' We continued conversing while Ailanthis
told me of Helen's instructions, my mind now spinning
with thoughts of how to try to retrieve this impulsive daughter.
Was this not the same excessive zeal I saw
kindle her spirit so often since she was but a girl?
But was it not important that she learn to cool her ardor

before choosing her way herself? Soon Celendre darkened
the door-flap and called to us, saying: 'The queen will have you go to her
now, for it is time to deal with that low, babbling male
who betrayed you so readily. Surely you wish to confront him
and have a say in his punishment.' Straightaway we rose to follow her
out and among the shadowy tents toward the light
of the queen's leaping fire near the edge of the plateau.

    There Peisistratos sat next to the queen. Ailanthis scarcely
looked his way, nor did he seem to see her. Ailanthis
spoke to Penthesilea, saying: 'Here comes Echios,
a pitiful man. Will you tear off his private parts
to feed them to the dogs, or have you some subtler means
to teach him more honorable ways?' Penthesilea rose
and pulled her double-edged axe from her belt. Echios
stumbled as warriors on either side thrust him forward.

    His arms were bound, with his hands behind his back. No
clothing was upon him so he burned with shame, ruddier by far
than the glow of the setting sun or leaping flames. He sank
to his knees: 'O lady, Penelope, if only I could clasp your knees
as a suppliant. . .'

    The queen turned her axe in her hands. She spoke to him,
saying: 'Do not think to appeal to any one here.
All of us know you for a traitorous dog, a weakling pup
at that.' She turned to Ailanthis. 'As for his meager stones,
already he has found them a painful matter. For what little
they gain him he may keep them. Soon wild beasts
may taste them and certainly the thorns all down the hillsides
will tear at them as he makes his way back to the world of loathsome men.

    'And do not think to use the pathways, O unworthy.
My warriors will be on watch to set dogs upon you
then, or if you approach our stronghold again. So
unless someone here will speak to persuade me against it,
this shall be the outcome.' I looked to Ailanthis. We both turned
toward Peisistratos, for he was Echios' host, and the one
who had the most right. Peisistratos looked away
and did not speak. Again I looked at Ailanthis, and saw

her eyelids lift slightly. The Amazons pulled Echios
to his feet and pushed him to the edge of the clearing at a steep place
till he fell forward. He rolled in the brush among the rocks
while women and girls shouted from the camp and dogs
bayed and snapped in excitement. He struggled to stand. Dropping
his head he lurched into the darkness and the unforgiving briars.

    'Now, Celendre, bring us a supper. Penelope, my friend,
Ailanthis, daughter, now I would have you tell me more
of Helen. For I have pondered what you told me. If she is
truly content, then I must know it and decide
what to do next.' So I told her all that befell us
in Lakedaimon, of Helen's long wanderings homeward,
the wisdom gained in Egypt, her meaningful pursuits and delight
in them, her husband's new respect. As I spoke of the rewards
few youths can perceive in the graying marriage bonds,
the queen caught Ailanthis' eyes. She turned to her, saying:
'Speak, O young one. If she is fulfilled so that I must not
re-enter her life and care for it, you will say it also.
Then I must withdraw and lead my band homeward
to Themiscyra, for I would never be the one to wrest a woman
from her chosen life to impose some other, as men do.'

    'Nor will my mother, O queen, as you will see. For I
shall ride with you in place of Helen and together
we shall defend the Amazon lands and rebuild your queendom.'

    Now Peisistratos, who had not spoken, nor had he seemed
to notice our presence, moved closer to Penthesilea.
He pressed his hands to her flanks and stroked her languidly,
She tossed her head and smiled in indulgence.
'It is settled. Worthy indeed is the addition of a lusty warrior.
And what of your life's course, Penelope?
Would you not share the road from here with us,
serving as a beacon to those of my women whose spirits flag?'

    'Penthesilea, truly I am swayed by the life you lead,
the freedom of it, the shared tasks, the space of it. But still
I am drawn steadily homeward by the weight of my son's suffering.
You will understand this, you the mother of a suffering son

yourself.' She snorted: 'Do not invoke your mothering talk
with me. For I am a warrior queen, and just as I broke
the leg of Achilleus' son to keep him with me, likewise
will I break the bones of the child I shall bear from Peisistratos
if it should not be a daughter. So will Ailanthis, once
she has killed in battle so again she may lie with a mate.'

The heart within me prompted me to speak out:
'O my host, can this be so? I thought that 'Leus
was injured while still in your womb because of your wounds
and the hardships of wandering over the plains.' She shook her head.
'You need not think that ours is too harsh a life.
Still, there are rigors we must endure to secure it.'

Peisistratos spoke to the queen, low and thick-voiced,
clasping her wrist. Ailanthis started. Now she, too,
had guessed the contrivance behind his addled behavior.

Penthesilea rose and said: 'I see, Penelope,
that you are not one to be persuaded. It is time to end
this talking and send you to your tent. Do not be concerned.
This handsome one will be ready to drive you on
in your chariot at dawn tomorrow. But for now. . .' She whistled.
Quickly 'Leus appeared with Celendre. Ailanthis embraced me
and turned toward her tent. As my guardian led me
away I caught the sweet boy's eyes on mine.
His smile was eager as he jerked away to follow Ailanthis.
I pondered all these things in my spirit as I walked to my tent.

Surely Ailanthis understood the subtle means the queen had devised
to take Peisistratos against his leanings. My daughter –
would she journey through life on such a course? But again
I resolved that no longer was I the one to guide her path.
Bats swooped among the flickering shadows and a wind
rose from the valleys to rattle the dry scrub. It chilled me,
still clad in the queen's short tunic. I lifted its folds
to cover my breast, and entered the tent composed.

In the night – did it really happen? – I awoke to a hand
pressed on my mouth, hot breath in my ear. 'O lady,
Penelope, do not be startled, please. I am 'Leus.

I come from your girl-child, as she urged me to it.
She tells you that she will not stay with the Amazons. She begs you
to forgive her impulsive thoughts and to help her hold firm
against the queen's persuading.' I hugged the child then.

How I had longed to take this sweet boy to my breast
and fill him with healing love. He clung to me as a child will.
I spoke in a whisper, saying: 'O my child, what good words
you bring me. Take these in turn to my daughter. I never
in my mind heaped blame upon her or questioned her right.
But I will hold the queen to her words to win back my daughter's life.'
He answered: 'How I wished, O mother, for you
to remain with us, for your ways are so gentle.
And my mother's are so hard. Yes, O queen, I heard
her tell you of it, but I think I knew it long ago.
Always I have dreamed that one day she would hold me to her
in a sweet embrace and call me "child" as you do.
But she is a good master and sometimes she will even touch
my twisted knee with tenderness.' I was stricken to silence
and held his head to my breast, his tense little body close.

Now I remembered the time when my own dear son
was very young and would come to me for comfort, letting me
hold him as this boy did now, and I felt how hard
the queen's life must be. As I thought of Telemachos my heart
tightened within my breast, but I knew how things would go
with Penthesilea. At last the child's joints loosened
and he stirred. I whispered in his ear: 'Here is one thing
you must remember always, 'Leus. While her ways
are not my ways, they are better for the world
you both live in. She keeps you with her, and she does love you.
Now return to your post and hearten my daughter. Go.'

He slipped away with less murmur than a mouse makes
creeping over a polished stone floor, less
than a nestling dove under the eaves when its mother
has tensed to a falcon's whistle. I thought I never slept,
but soon awoke to sounds of morning stirrings. I washed
with water and put my own clean clothing upon me,

but tied on the wondrously soft sandals with horsehide
turned in. Stony Celendre led me to Penthesilea's seat
at the edge of camp. Here my daughter was standing
straight as a column, dressed in her own silver-threaded robe
from Helen. As I approached I heard an uproar
from the part of the camp nearest the sheer cliff face, a bellowing
like that of a bull brought in for slaughter or a lion driven
from his kill by furious goatherds. Penthesilea stood
tall and imposing as Ailanthis spoke to her, saying:
     'Tell me, O queen, where is the glory of conquest in this –
this shameful taking of one reft of his senses and will
by the use of potions? Where is the honor in such trickery?
Never was the reputation of the Amazons sung for this,
and I would not be the one to live by such a code.'
     Penthesilea tossed her head and answered in turn:
'Such squeamishness suits you ill, my young cohort.
Can it be you harbor desire or that you are still
in love with your companion despite the claims you made me?
Are you as crippled as any one of our slave-boys by girlish yearnings
for tender coupling such as I'm told the poets
sing endlessly into the minds of foolish young women?
Such mating is always fleeting as spring's fever
in a splendid stallion. Surely you are better than a whinnying mare.'
     With shouts and cries a scuffling throng approached us now.
Peisistratos heaved and swayed at its center and only by force
of many hands pinning his bound arms, holding him upright
and dragging him on did he come again into the queen's presence.
'Ho, Queen of the Amazons, will you then
drug me again to unman me and make me compliant beside you?
You will have to force me now, for I will eat
nothing more of your bread or meat. Nor shall wine
or sweet mare's milk pass my lips unless by force.
And troublesome baggage will I make to slow your journeying and hamper
your fighting. . .' He stopped as Ailanthis stepped near,
and red shame lit his body and face. A pained
look flickered briefly there, but then he straightened.

· XIX ·

Peisistratos stood erect and proud, but he spoke in blandishment:
'Never, O queen, should you have doubted your power to sway
both women and men. For even without the use of strong potions
you are akin to one of the goddesses for beauty and stature,
and I have never been the one to refuse a lusty challenge.
But you are no longer the same fearless warrior
mighty Achilleus mourned and my lovely companion, Ailanthis,
still takes you for, since she has abandoned all else
to follow you.' Ailanthis spoke in answer:
   'You speak of one who follows her no longer. Here
is shameful business, and I am as one who emerges from a dust cloud
to see the roadway clearing straight ahead. As for loving,
O queen, always it is better when two hold
to each other freely; this way both can give as they take.'
   Penthesilea dropped her hands from her hips and stroked
the handle of her axe. She spoke slowly: 'I see. Ailanthis,

you speak to one who always listens to her warriors' thoughts.
And you are such a one as even I can admire
and hear in counsel. Therefore I ordain it that you alone
will not have to wait until you have killed in battle to take partners
in our yearly love-rites. In this I honor you particularly.'
    Ailanthis shook her head and answered her, speaking carefully:
'Perhaps, O queen, you did not understand me just now
when I spoke as one who has stepped from a maelstrom into calm.
For it happens that again my pathway urges me on toward Ithaka,
to return to my father and care for my dear brother. Then
only can I strike out to care for my own life.'
    The queen turned and strode away some distance,
her palm outstretched behind her. She shook her head and wheeled
toward us again, fury on her features. Ailanthis spoke to her:
'Our host, may a woman's knowing guide you, a woman's oath
bind your honor. For remember the words you yourself
spoke when last we met – never would you be the one
to wrest a woman out of her chosen life and impose
some other, as men do. And this is the code of the Amazons.
It is what sets you apart from all the cities of men
and will compel the singers to take up their lyres
to sing your fame endlessly around the seas. Surely
you would not diminish the tribe's honor and your reputation
by keeping me with you, either by force or by use
of potions.' The queen's eyes were wide with amazement
and perhaps a glint of admiration. I was the next to speak:
    'And this is what I would have you consider besides, my host.
Since my daughter also knows your inmost secret, the one
you did not wish to reveal to him who is closest you,
never can you rest with her among your tents, for someday
she will fill his ears with the words you do not wish him to hear.
She has sworn me an oath – you will not avoid it.'
Penthesilea stepped back and looked at me wonderingly.
Her eyes narrowed. Then her mouth turned down in mockery.
    'How is it, Penelope, circumspect as always you have been,
that now you are ready to bruise one who did you no harm

in your eagerness to aid your own child. Or are these merely
bold words spoken craftily because you know
that the one you would whisper secrets to now knows
he is my child, so your telling could not hurt him. I see
in you a spirit that begins to fear nothing. The bold woman
proves the better for every occasion in the end.

    'But there is still one secret I would never wish
my son to know. I do not doubt this true Amazon,
your daughter, would someday use her knowledge of it to confound me.
How I hoped that a woman's trust could bind us together.
I never thought, O impulsive Ailanthis, that you were as skittish
as a colt when, bounding down a hillside she comes to a turning
where water flows abundant on one side, but the smell
of wild oats swaying on their tawny stalks reaches
her nostrils from lower down and she kicks and plunges
in sweet indecision.
                'Never yet have the Amazons forced
a conscript, and all our tribe believe in the path of choice.
Shall I be less than the least of my followers, or far less
than their queen? It is not our way; I will never do it.
Be restored to your mother now, daughter, and go.
Take your own way. I and my band will return
to our city on Lake Meotis' shores, for it seems our Achaian sisters
weave their own designs.' So saying Penthesilea
whistled. Swiftly she gave the orders for her women to lead us
back down the mountain. She strode beside us
to the edge of the camp. She nodded to me and again she spoke
to Ailanthis: 'An Amazon's greeting to you always, my child.
Remember me sometimes when you are back at home.'
She turned to stroke Peisistratos' shoulder. 'You, handsome hero,
I will remember you always – how only through guile
and the strongest of my potions could I take you. I will tell
your Amazon daughter – for the divinity decrees our child
will be female – of her father's strength and prowess. And she will match it.'

    We started down the slope. Next 'Leus shuffled
from a knot of children standing there and came to me.

He took my hand and held it briefly. Then he kissed my wrist
in the formal way of courteous men and released me
to follow my companions. We descended a pathway that seemed
far shorter on returning, like all ways, once traveled.
Quickly we retrieved the chariots, yoked the horses again,
and mounted the cars, Ailanthis to drive the splendid team
of Peisistratos, and he taking Echios' place beside me.
They laid their lashes on the horses, and we set off
urgently again and journeyed along the plain to Pherai.
Later the sun set and the journeying ways were darkened.
We came to Pherai and stayed the night with Narcethe and Diokles.
But we had resolved on the way that we would tell no one
about the Amazons' presence among them, and so it was
they escaped incurring the wrath and indignation of the Argives.

　　When the bee-rousing Dawn appeared again, Peisistratos
took Ailanthis out and they yoked the horses. Never did she tell me
what kind of words passed between them. We mounted the chariots
and sped out of the courtyard and through the front gate.
The drivers whipped their teams to a run and they paced their way
across the plain and on toward the high stronghold of Pylos.
But as we approached the splendid dwelling of Nestor, a clamor
of wailing reached us. Euridike, Nestor's grave wife,
was raising the outcry since the life breath was gone from Nestor,
her venerable husband, breaker of horses, a man
of much wise counsel who best advised younger kings
in the time when all were gathered by the gates of hateful Troy.
We drew up to the narrow close and stopped before the great gate.
Manservants ran to the heads of the foam-mouthed horses
and took their reins and held them, spent and shuddering. We
were dazed and stricken to silence in the whirlstorm of dirges playing
and the smoke from the torches of countless men shifting about
in lurid firelight. We made our way toward the gate
led by solemn Peisistratos, and the people fell back
and gave us passage to the great pyre where Nestor was lying.

　　Beating her breasts, Eurydike led the shrieking of her daughters
and daughters-in-law before the high tower. His sons

and sons-in-law stood by in their gleaming armor, each holding
one of the king's favorite horses, and these quivered,
sensing their imminent doom. Phemios with his lyre
was prominent among the singers moaning the awful dirge,
but although I searched the many worn and drawn faces
I could not spy out Mabantha, and the spirit went out of me. But next
Polykaste came to me and leaned her head close to mine
so that none of the others might hear us. She spoke to me saying: 'Daughter
of Aramantha, mother, friend, I see that your eyes are troubled
as they flit among the faces of the people about the courtyard.
I think it must be that you search for your maidservant, Mabantha,
who is gravely afflicted and lies on her couch within the palace.
She would not have me tell you this now, but urged me to wait
until all was accomplished before I lead you to her. But never
would I be the one to refuse comfort to a guest. Come.'

My heart was troubled then and I wondered whether to go to her
or to honor Nestor, lest any person in the family hold it
against me for slighting such a man. I answered her, saying:
'Dear child, never could I say that I or any of mine
has received less than the most loving treatment at Pylos.
It is not an easy matter for you to leave your dear father's pyre
to conduct me through your house to my friend's couch.
But let us make our way quickly;
I would not keep you long away from your rightful place.'

We went through the palace, weaving behind the needle of her torch
like bright thread through a maze of dark purple cloth,
to a chamber deep in the queen's wing of the palace where Mabantha
lay, disheveled. She was overcome at the sight of me
and spoke to me, saying: 'O my dear friend, surely
some goddess has made you even more knowing
and thoughtful than you were before. For despite the words
I sent your way by Polykaste's lips, still I was longing
to see you sooner. How this old body is protesting
its late burden. But tell me this truth,
so I will know it: does far-roving Helen send you returning
with those things you were seeking, or are you coming with hands

empty and some further journeying uppermost in your mind?'
    'O sister, friend, Mabantha, how I hate to see
that you suffer, to know that I have not been near to comfort you
as a friend should. All we hoped for is now accomplished,
for the horses drove us easily to Sparta. It was Helen
who received us in Menelaos' absence. Our spirits were easy with each other
and she took us to the place where her strongest herbs grew.
She sent us on our way laden with thoughtful words and gifts.
    'But still I have not questioned you about your troubles.
Tell me, is the child in your womb still living? How diminished
is your strength, and how long must you rest before you dare
to journey again on the seas?' She told me in answer:
'Thanks to the goddess, my child still moves inside me.
My friend, how I am wishing that I could be
as strong as you when, bereft in that palace, you were carrying
two babes within you. And you hid it from all within the city,
looking after your household and your husband's possessions.
This was your character as men sing it. My spirit is telling me
Helen spoke words to you of this and about your own quest
as well. I see this in your eyes and your bearing.' I answered her, saying:
'Helen has indeed spoken heartening words to me.
But now my thoughts turn toward our journey homeward
and clearly, in my mind, you are not now able to travel.'
    'O Penelope, my friend, never did I wish to hold you back
from what you must be doing. And since you must make your way quickly
homeward, leave me here in Pylos where they give me
hospitality. Take Phemios, my husband, since Odysseus has commanded him
with Mentor that always one of them would stand at your shoulder and never
leave you alone journeying the seas.' I could not answer her,
but taking her hands I held them in mine. While we were conversing,
glorious Nestor's monstrous pyre burned to ashes
with only his blackened bones, flanked by those of his steed
and six of his favorite mane-tossing horses left in the sifting.
    Then Polykaste brought Ailanthis to us, and Ailanthis knew
what to do next. She greeted Mabantha first,
then spoke to us both saying: 'Mother, dear, and Mabantha,

our host Peisistratos sends word; though deep in his spirit
he grieves for his illustrious father, still he is able to be mindful
of his guests. I asked him to receive you in the hall
of the palace, and now he will hear our plans for returning homeward
and appoint it all to be accomplished exactly as you wish for it.'
I had to take leave of Mabantha, telling her I would arrange
matters the best way. Her limbs were unstrung and she lay back
on her couch for sweet rest to overtake her. We wove our way
behind the torches of maidservants among the beautiful columns
to the threshold of the shadowy hall. Peisistratos gazed at us
with imperious eyes as we entered and walked by the hearth in the center
of the floor to join Phemios and the helmsman Apollytos. The helmsman
took my hand at the wrist and held it. Peisistratos spoke first:
    'O queen, many would say that some one of the gods
does not will it that you should make your way quickly
homeward, since he sends down many events that would hold
you lingering about the precincts of this household. But yours
is a grave mission, and never would I try to keep you against
your wishes or those of your daughter, although I might desire to.
And I will help you continue on your way to Telemachos,
as I helped him also. What have you thought of?' Relieved, I replied,
'Son of Nestor, will you accept what I say and bring it to pass?
My handmaid and friend lies piteously weak on her couch.
I cannot think of leaving her; yet my adored son –
if he still lives – also lies sickened with his wound.
Ailanthis has Helen's skill for healing my son, but I
must stay to care for this loyal friend, who has tended me.
    'Let it be accomplished this way. Give my daughter
conveyance at once, with Helen's plants and potions.
Let her make her way quickly to the great vessel
of helmsman Apollytos so he can carry her swiftly to Ithaka,
if only he will do this thing that I ask. For although,
helmsman, it is the custom always to send retainers
to walk at the side of a young girl as she goes about,
yet I will put her into your care. I see
there is nobility in you. Will you now think of your solemn oath,

and fulfill it, only conveying my daughter in my place,
who, with my son and Nerianne is more precious to me
than I am to myself?' But next Phemios spoke to us saying:
'Hear me, my queen, I too am at your bidding. Respect what I say;
you will be glad if you listen to the singer and follow his words.
For although this helmsman is worthy and can be entrusted with whatever
you wish for him to accomplish, I am the man whose duty
it is to see to this matter. For long have I been the singer
in the household of Odysseus. And the king has inspired in me
fierce loyalty, since once he listened to my winged words in supplication
and spared my life in that time when he thrashed the suitors all
about the palace and slaughtered them mercilessly to the last churl.
I leave my dear wife with you unreluctantly, for here
a guest is given surpassing hospitality, and you will care for her.
I will be the escort for Ailanthis, my queen. The duty is mine.'
    At this Apollytos stepped forward and spoke to us, saying:
'O queen, this strikes my mind also as the best plan.
And here is another matter to consider; my vessel
is larger than most. I had it built straight to a chalk line
and curved to the trough of the sea swells myself, for my own comfort
since forever I would ply the seas aboard her, and she would be my home.
Ktimene is lighter and faster by far in cutting through
the wave-crests against the Western winds. Since Phemios is willing
to accompany your daughter, let him do it, and aboard the fleetest
among the ships in Pylos' harbor. I myself
will remain inside the island that shelters the harbor to await
your passage, and convey you wherever you will journey next.
Nor will your host detain your daughter. He is far too thoughtful.'
    I turned to proud Peisistratos. I named him and spoke to him, saying:
'All this that he says makes sense. Son of Nestor,
would you accept for your house what these men suggest
and bring it to pass? For you have avowed yourself Telemachos'
friend forever and yours is the power to help him live.'
I spoke this way in supplication for although he had solemnly vowed
to arrange for us to make our way as quickly as we wished,
all of us assembled could see in his face the youthful fire

of his passion and feared he might keep Ailanthis here longer
than we wished. For his was now the power in this hall, a heady state
and always dangerous for a young man unseasoned to it.
But Ailanthis told me later she had seen it already
and had spoken to him saying: 'I must go back to Ithaka.
Nor is it possible for me to think of dallying now.
For I must take care of my own life, and marriage would be
a painful matter. This I have told you since we met.
It is useless to speak of what is settled between us.'

    And now Peisistratos, true son of his noble father,
did not flinch from his duties as host, but turned his gaze
upon me with my loyal companions. He spoke to us manfully, saying:
'O queen, circumspect Penelope, the spirit within me
tells me also that this is the best and only way.
All that is fitting for a host to send away with his guests
your daughter shall have, whatever is in my power to give.
And to you also I will give what help I can.
As for conveyance, I appoint it for tomorrow. Urge your companions
to go now in haste and make everything ready. Now you may rest,
giving way to slumber, for I know this thing well in my heart,
how weary you both must be, and anxious at the hour of parting.'
Ailanthis answered him next, saying: 'Good-bye, O prince.
I will think of you often when I am back at home, and will tell
my brother how you are one to whom he owes his life,
if he is restored.' We walked out over the threshold
and climbed the stairs to our beautiful chamber. There
we spent the last third of the night exchanging our thoughts.
It was as if we knew that years would pass with their seasons turning,
rather than days only, before we would meet again.

    When Dawn with her gold-tipped fingers came whispering we arose.
Ailanthis fastened on her sandals and took up her veil.
She put on her robe with three flounces and the seal ring
of carven amethyst that Peisistratos gave her. And Polykaste
was there and bound up her hair in the woven band and circlet.
Ailanthis took Odysseus' great mantle, which I gave to her,
saying: 'Dear daughter, here is your father's purple mantle.

Take it with you as protection in case of storm winds
blowing up unruly seas. Or if you step out
on land in some strange country they will know
you are a powerful king's daughter and give you hospitable treatment.
Tell Odysseus I intend to follow you homeward soon.
Kiss your brother for me and do for him all
that is in your power to do. There is none better than you.'
    Then Ailanthis hurried down to the beach with Phemios
and took sail for home while I remained in Pylos
beside Mabantha, who was resting and gaining in strength.
And she and I had loving treatment from our hosts also.
The women gave me relief from watching by her couch.
They brought us herbs and berries from far inland. They mixed
wine and fruit juices for us with cool spring water
they carried to us themselves. In days she was stronger. Then
one day, while we two were walking, she spoke to me, saying:
    'Penelope, my friend, I give you thanks from deep in my breast.
For while I always thought you were that friend who would stay
beside me in time of trouble, yet still I was pondering whether
you could do it. But there is a thing dividing the spirit within me.
This way seems best to me – to tell you all
I am planning so you will know it. And then perhaps you can forgive
my shameless scheming. You cannot be forgetting the many years
I plied the seas alone since escaping down
Aigyptos' swell from mighty Thebes, always searching
for my brother Rbatha, always hoping to persuade him to return
to our country and our parents, to secure our line and our inheritance,
and to care for our kingdom. This child within me was long the hope
of my people, though better if she were my brother's child also.
And now that I know he is gone to the kingdom of the pale ones
I know also that I am the only one to carry
words to my parents, if they are still living, and to take to my kingdom
the just and hospitable ways of seafaring peoples.
This I must do, but Phemios refuses. Never
will the heart in him be persuaded to leave the house of Odysseus;
he is far too loyal, and also he loves the lands around the seas

where the stories of men spread wide upon the lift
and swell of the sails. Lately I questioned him saying:
  ' "Phemios, my husband, would you not go down
with me into the country of the plain in the hills, into the heart
of the great heartland, and carry your singing to parched ears
and reign with me over all the dark tribes?" He answered me:
  ' "Never, my wife, can I leave the house of Odysseus. For he,
like the god, had mercy on me when I caught his knees in supplication,
and inspires me in every kind of song-way. I gave him my word on it.
But do not grieve for your far-off country and the people who may
or may not still be living there. There is abundance and esteem
to enjoy in serving in the palace of Odysseus and Penelope,
and she gives you loving treatment and friendship above all women.
Our child will be honored by gods and men alike for the songs we can teach him
Our fame will go down among the generations for singing
Ithaka's story. For who can know whether Nerianne,
if she still lives, will return to hear and sing it?
No. I would be sorry in time to come if I did this." '

° XX °

'BUT, PENELOPE, my sister, you are mother also to a child
with possessions and inheritance you struggled to protect;
you will understand these things I am saying and the course I am planning
to follow. I must make my way homeward.
I will cross again the deeps where the fish swarm,
passing up the river of Aigyptos to the crimson cliffs
and climbing the twisting ways to the plain on the black hills.
I am going with this girl-child inside me, to take her home.
For this I urged my husband to leave, then sent him away.'
Now I was amazed and spoke to her saying: 'But my friend, how can you
even consider this journey? For surely, though the spirit within you
wishes it, your body is no longer that of a young girl
who can carry a child in her womb as easily as a bitch or hare
or fleet-footed deer carries her young. You are just regaining
your strength after sickness. You could not ever do it.'
   'My friend, as for my sickness, it was not as it seemed even
to you, knowing me so deeply I feared I would never
get past you in contriving. For deceiving you I am sorry.
But this was my devising: to give way to my body, unstrung,
and stay groaning on my couch. Since always you were
a steadfast friend, the kind who would surely stay beside me
giving me care, I urged Phemios to leave with Ailanthis.
Now I am free to return to my people if only you will grant me
my homecoming, and see it accomplished.' So she spoke and my knees
gave way and the heart within my breast also. I stayed speechless,
my eyes filling with tears. Next she spoke further, cajoling me:
'How I wish that you could be coming with me to the high plains.
There my people have some ways different from you and the cities
around the seas. But much there is beautiful, living

is freer and happier than here. Women are admired
for their skills and wisdom and people will listen to us both. There
we can both be queens, both reigning together. There,
my friend, I can show you all the patterns of the weaving
my women are using, and the rich brown dyes I never
see among peoples by the seas. Fast ships are lying
dragged up on the sandy beach of Pylos' harbor.
Penelope, my friend, will you come?' At last I found words
to answer her saying: 'O my friend, these are unthinkable things
you speak of and yet I listen to you with strange excitement.

    'My heart flutters in the cage of my breast like a dove. I could be
well satisfied to journey with you to that fortunate country
and to sit beside you for some time. I was held back so long
against my desires for adventure by custom and necessity. And by love.
My life was ordered by these as a chariot is pulled and guided
in its traces and harness while I longed for Odysseus' return
to take care of my life and share the driving with me.
But now he has returned to take the reins from my callused hands.
No longer must I bear the endless straining and pulling
of the mane-tossing horses alone. Now the plain spreads
before me, the rippling grain threaded with many ways,
all delightful, so I might let the reins go slack, giving
the horses their heads to prance and taste the wild galingale
beside the winding streams. But Odysseus would seize
the reins and check them, turn me back toward the iron gate
and the narrow courtyard. And this both pleases and weighs
on my spirit so that there is division in it. But also I am mindful
of your own thoughtful words when once you admonished me:
"Never can you say that I am more steadfast companion
than Odysseus. For none can be more things to you than he is.
Even you are not more to me than Phemios, since my husband
is my partner in all ways of living." How is it that now you urge
me to leave my life behind and to journey with you
to life in a strange land, leaving the husband I am bound to,
and how is it that now you can flee your faithful partner?

    'Or do you think that by urging this thing for me also

I will forget that you are bound not only
to Phemios as wife but to me as handmaiden of the house of Odysseus?
You cannot leave our service.' Now Mabantha stayed
a long time without a word, the voice stilled
within her. At last she made an answer: 'O my lady, Penelope,
what are these words you are saying to me, this talk
of bindings to custom and show of things? I was not expecting
you to speak such words, but rather your inner heart's
answer. Yet although they are seeming haughty there is longing
in them, and longing is a ram of many fleeces. I am doing
this thing because my real life is elsewhere.
Now I am accepting this, no bounds
can stop my journeying. You are forgetting – always in my mind
that Janys races free across the meadows.
But also I am sad; I am leaving not one but two I love
since you are not one who will take this journey with me.
For I leave you as a dear friend leaves another, tenderly.'

'O my friend, forgive those hateful words, for never
would I choose to hold you with any bonds except for those
your heart urges. There is truth in what you say. My anger
was truly the cloak of fear and longing that seized my heart
at the thought of losing you near to me always in friendship.
How I wish that you could return to sunny Ithaka,
and together you and I, with Odysseus and Phemios, would live out
our days, forever weaving at our looms our stories for posterity.
Now the heart and mind within me are torn, for my spirit
inclines strongly also toward this journey. But then
I would not know whether my son lives or dies
or if my daughters continue to unwind the spools
of their own lives so their accomplishments go down
among the generations of women and of men.
What is the pattern of my life now – which thread
should I pick up? My mind reels with confusion.'

Now we two were silent for a long time and stayed
looking down at the dusky harbor ringed with lights
from the fires of seamen beside black hulks, the dark shield

of the barrier island and the flickering torches on two
ships at anchor between them. I was the next to speak:
'Now let us go to bed and pray for the gift of slumber.
I will set loose the running mares of my desires so my spirit
can choose the best way, the one I can follow most easily.
I will tell you in the coming dawn which way my spirit inclines.'
　　While we continued conversing we wound our way
back into the shadowy palace to our chamber. We took off our veils,
our robes and ornaments. We loosed our hair from the bands,
bound up our bundles, filled my chest and sank onto the beds.
A deep sleep came over me then and held me.
When Dawn of the fleecy heels crept over the sky's threshold
still I slept, the division in my mind holding my eyes
fast against the painful choice. From behind my eyelids
I sensed the bustling all about the palace. The serving maids
flitted through the halls as birds whirled from their nests in the eaves.
I heard soft rustlings in the inner chambers as doors opened
and closed. Water trickled from pitchers as they clanked against bowls
for washing. At last the division of my spirit was resolved. Decision
lightened the heart in my breast so I could lie no longer
but arose eagerly to share my true mind with my friend.
　　At once Polykaste came to me, her brow furrowed in concern.
Mabantha's nearby couch was empty, the coverlet thrown
carelessly back, and the linen cloths hardly impressed.
All her jewelry was taken up from the polished table,
as were the comb and her bottles of swirled glass with intricate
stoppers of carven stone, which I saw her stroking thoughtfully
before putting out the burning lamp the night before.
I fastened up my hair, Polykaste helping, and put on
my robe and skirt. She led me from the chamber down the stairs
and out through the columned forecourt to the portico overlooking
the harbor. There were ships resting on the pale shallows
and men mingled and moved along the shore. But in the blue
of the deeper part, near the passage that leads to the sea
only one ship pulled at her anchor cable, Apollytos' large one.
Nor could I be certain, through the tears that filled my eyes,

whether there was a speck of a ship on the thread of the horizon
like the slub on a strand of spun yarn. How I wished
that I were aboard that ship, her white sails raised
like wings to carry me swiftly with my Mabantha to visit
the splendid cities along the Aigyptos river, and to journey
to my friend's fabled kingdom where only gods had been invited
as guests. But there was no time for tears or lamenting.
    I knew what to do next. I spoke to Polykaste craftily:
'Dear child, do not think that I hold either you
or your household to blame for this, nor do I bear ill will
toward any. My friend wished only to spare me the pains of parting.
These I would gladly have borne if only I could have clasped
her one last time and sent with her one token
of a woman's greeting to keep beside her always, and received
some one from her. But for me, since my dear friend
who was ill is recovered and since the spirit within me is eager
for my homecoming, will you not urge that conveyance be given quickly
to that great hollow ship that will take me home to Ithaka?'
'O lady, yes. I will send an attendant quickly
to the port to tell your helmsman to make your ship ready.
And with you I will send many good things which are stored
away in our storerooms, and white barley to lay in a basket.
Together we will pray to Atrytone to grant you a safe journey
homeward and a swift one, and the gift of healing to your beautiful son,
the one I bathed here in the spiraled tub with these hands.
If only he had returned to the palace, but he also
was eager to make his way homeward quickly. How I wish
I could see that place you call Ithaka. Surely
it must be a lovely land, since you yearn for it just as he did.
When you see him, ask if he remembers his sojourn at Pylos
and urge him to think of me sometimes since I was the one who bathed him.'
    So we two conversed as we turned back to the palace.
I gathered my mirror and remaining jars to store them away
in the polished chest with my own knot. Serving women
came to carry it down to the sea-beach. Next came Polykaste.
We prayed to Athene, but deep in my breast I prayed

for an unsuspected outcome, far from the one her words bespoke.
I made my way quickly from the splendid dwelling place
down to the harbor and there my attentive helmsman waited
with a small craft to convey me swiftly over the shallows to his vessel
that strained on her anchor cable like a reined-in horse.

    Apollytos spoke to me first, saying: 'O Queen Penelope,
word has come that your attendant rose from her couch and fled.
That high-riding ship which lay beside mine on the breast of the water
pulled up her anchor in the darkest watch of the night so quietly
I doubted what my ears heard as I lay tossing on my bed.
If only I had known that she bore away your maidservant
I would have roused my shipmates and urged my oarsmen to stop her
before she could leave us far behind. But listen to this
I say to you now. Still, if you wish it, I can order
my men to make our way out of the harbor quickly with their oars
and then to raise the great square of our sail and chase her
down. For you have heard me promise to carry you wherever
you wish to be carried, and now I am eager to make good that oath.'

    'O helmsman, how I also wish you had held her back.
But I think that the thing I wish for next will amaze you. What
I would urge you to do if I thought it could ever be accomplished will stun
you to silence, since it goes against the customs of women and my life.
I wish that after you had stayed my friend from making her way
without me, you had then carried me with her to her far-off country.
For to me she was a friend; how could I hold such a one
in servitude as men do? She urged me to go there with her.
Now the spirit within me urges me to do it, though not
to bring her back as you suggest. Rather I would ask you to carry
us both to the mouth of river Aigyptos. From there
we would make our way through Aigyptos' cities to my friend's kingdom
of the high plain where she is held in favor.
One thing only speaks against it; I know that this ship is unsurpassed
for comfortable living, since you yourself fashioned it.
But it is slower than lighter ships like that one
which looked so small floating alongside yours before this.
Since I do not think that a ship such as this one can

easily overtake that other, my heart grows heavy in my breast.'

We pulled alongside the *Sea-Swift*, which leaned with men
brimming toward action, ready to obey Apollytos' orders,
as he seemed eager to act on mine. He spoke, saying:
'My queen, you must not suppose that size alone orders
the speed of ships on the sea; neither does it predict
the fortunes of men in battle nor the contests where most men strive.
Ships, like men, have their subtle ways, and there is craft in seafaring.
There are winds and currents such a ship as that one cannot
meet head on, nor can she make much headway stitching
the seas piling up from the South. I will set the *Sea-Swift* against her
gladly, since it is you who ask me, and my skill besides.'

While we two were conversing, the men of his crew
were pulling the little skiff onto the deck of the *Sea-Swift*.
They fastened it down with twisted ropes and each man
made his way quickly to his bench while others pulled
on the stout anchor cable. All was accomplished so that soon
we were surging over the gentle swell of the harbor.
As we rounded the sheltering island I gazed at Pylos, high
in the green bluffs overlooking the harbor. Now at a cry
the well-drilled oarsmen put aside their oars as one.
They swarmed over the deck of the ship to the halyards and stays,
the mast pole and crossbeams as if taking part in an intricate dance.
And the ship shuddered lightly to the rhythm of their practiced feet
while I gazed on their taut shoulders, their nimble hands and their bodies
bronzed and supple like young men in the first of their youth.
The sails lifted like shining wings and I felt the *Sea-Swift*
lean forward and steadied myself as if for flight.

Now we raced the running sea foam that tipped the crests
of the swells while sea-birds dipped and flared beside us
against the glare of the sun. The heart in my breast was light
as the wind itself while all day the timbers shook
and the wind sang in the ropes as if in a reed pipe.
Then Helios descended in his fiery chariot behind us and soon
there appeared the she-bear who waits for Orion, and the Pleiades
fleeing the great net he flings over the sky.

No moon was showing so that every twinkling knot,
each gleaming crease of that web burned into my eyes
and pressed into my spirit the pattern you see me weaving always.
Never do I tire of sprinkling borders and hems with its beauties,
though soon I was to struggle urgently against the hardships
its sea-borne magic brought me. For after the day's run
was ended, I stood away alone to admire those lights
and the gleam that the surface of the sea gave back.

· XXI ·

THEN HELMSMAN Apollytos came to me. He took my hand
in his and leaned to kiss my wrist. He spoke to me, saying:
'O my queen, how I wish that the winds and my ship's running
could carry us close to towering Krete in the day's watches.
For I have heard you say that you long to see the cities
around the seas, and those of Krete are among the greatest
for splendor. Never have I journeyed up the stream of Aigyptos,
preferring to keep to the wine-blue seas and my spacious vessel.
But I think not even Thebes, nor all the lofty palaces of Egypt
are more imposing in design, nor richer
than Krete's. Still better than this would be the time
when you would loose your hand from its stiffened grip
and say to me: "My helmsman, take me far across
the sea and show me what I've never seen, for without you
I will never see it." For then I would willingly grasp the steering oar
and take care of your life, and you could see every land

around the margins and all the delightful islands of men,
and many whose peaks are wooded and home only
to flocks of land and sea creatures and soaring birds.
Never would you tire of the endless wonders I could show you.'

    I addressed him, saying: 'O helmsman, how I wish also
I could see all this you speak of. For always as a girl
I watched from my father's house while the lovely ships
and gritty working skiffs came and went on the swells
of the harbor. I envied my brothers, for they could go down
to the beaches to listen to the sailors' tales and hear the latest songs
of many lands from the wide-ranging singers there
on the breakwater. How I longed to ride the lusty waves
wherever the winds and the currents would take me. But before this
my only sea-voyage was that straight and brief one
to Ithaka when I married my husband, stately Odysseus.'

    Then he chided me, leaning his head close to mine
so that none of the other seamen might hear him: 'O, Penelope,
do not think by speaking that name you will hold me
back from telling aloud the desire in both our hearts.
For I divined these secret thoughts long before you let them pass
your lips. And I know also what other desires are brimming
in you, for they crest in your eyes, they kindle in your voice,
they beat in your light footsteps on the beams and timbers of my ship
as you tread the deck sore, like the heart in my breast. O Penelope,
lady of my wandering, come. Let me take you where already
you longed to go.' He spoke thus while the net of stars wheeled
around the sky. I turned away, speechless and deeply troubled.

    Beside me a knotted rope-end shivered in a breeze, tapping wildly.
At long last I found the words to speak to him in answer:
'I will not deny what you say you know of my desires.
It is foolish to babble empty words when two people
see clearly, each into the other's heart. I see this
now. But I have many other desires in my heart
and these I would not easily give over. If only
I could never have to choose between one way or the other
but always have all possible. Now it seems

that the journey I would make to be with my friend at her homecoming
is a weight on my breast. I must find her and join her.
O do not say it will not be accomplished, for the spirit within me
has chosen this way, forsaking my family, my homecoming to Ithaka,
my husband. Hard-hearted, do you not remember your vow
to him and to me, and would you now divert me from my purpose?'
'Never, unwilling, O queen.' He spoke no more
but nodded crisply as I stepped into his forfeit dwelling-space
and drew the door bar in its thong. The night was long
before sleep drifted over me and slackened my limbs at last.

    And when fresh-faced Dawn arose from her couch I too
arose, to a brisk wind, the steady lift and slap
of the ship upon a sea of deepest blue, with foam
creaming and slipping along the vessel's sides
and under her carven beak. And all that day the sails filled
and the wind sang in the ropes like a chorus of sea-birds
while the ship cut easily through the racing waters like a ball
expertly lifted and tossed among well-practiced dancers.
And my helmsman answered all the questions I thought to ask him
about the high-decked vessel, the workings of the sails in the wind
and the currents and how she shuddered in the chop and troughs,
the intricate knots and fastenings, and the men moving in rhythm with their mates.

    For the whole length of the day wind drove the ship
onward while Helios played on the spray and birds swam
and fishes soared. My helmsman laughed and the spirit within me
brimmed to my eyes and lips with little cries of joy.
When night approached on her dark-tipped wings, the winds fled
for land and our spacious vessel lolled on a sheen the color
of pomegranates, I wished that day and the journey would never
end. My helmsman came near and spoke to me solemnly:

    'I had thought, my queen, that before now you would see
the little ship that carries your friend toward green-mantled Aigyptos.
I have steered my *Sea-Swift* the best way to cross
her course. But catching her depended always on winds both steady
and strong, winds my ship was built and rigged for.
I do not think we will find her, but she will make port

before us and soon make her way tracklessly up the river.
You must not think to follow along so blind a path.
Rather come with me and range the delightful seas.'

    'My helmsman, please do not speak these words of blandishment.
For while it is true that I delight in the pleasures of voyaging, my journey
has a course to follow; there is a beach that awaits my footfall.
The next thing the spirit within me urges me to accomplish
is to know my companion Mabantha's country, its customs and its people.
For there the women are as skilled as goddesses in weaving cloth,
and their work is rich and strange. They use dyes unknown
to the women who live along the margins of the seas. They stud
and adjust their looms to make the patterns intricate beyond
those of other women. They have more arts
to show me also. Nor did I willingly suffer my friend's departure.
I meant to go with her and was not eager to part from her.'

    'My queen, I no longer think that this can be accomplished.
Soon your companion's faster ship will make its way
inside some breakwater there where spreading Aigyptos
meets the surge of the sea. And next she can arrange quick passage
on some one of the numberless vessels that breast
the current beside the wondrous stone-carved mountains
made by men, by Thebes and the other glorious cities.
She is experienced in travel. You cannot hope to catch her.
Nor should you journey alone among treacherous men
and guileful women. You do not know them. One
could betray you and deliver you to some evil man to use
for his dalliance. Shamefully you would lose your homecoming, your family
and friends would lose you forever. It is useless.'

    He caught me to him and held me and named me,
speaking harshly and with pleading in the same voice:
'O Penelope, never would I be a man if I let this thing
be accomplished. Nor will I help you to do it. Rather I would leave
my ship, my life, and journey with you to care for your life.
Come, let us be together, for I know you desire it also.
Let me go with you, and be beside me always, my queen.'

    'O helmsman, all this you offer me teases and troubles

the fraying heart within me. I cannot ask you for my sake
to be someone other than who you are. And yet there is delight in what you say.'
'But Penelope, my dove, I offer it. Besides this, you *have*
asked it. In your heart, which I know like my own, you wished
for this. It is useless to deny it. Come. Together. . .' I began:
'My helmsman, do not say it, for Odysseus. . .' But he
would hear no protest. 'Do not invoke that hateful name
to me. I will not allow you to wear it like a cloak
around your shoulders.' He spoke in my ear so the breath from his mouth
stirred my hair.
                         'Odysseus' name goes wide
across the seas for resourceful ways and cunning.
But Odysseus was a fool to permit you to leave your city to roam
the seas without him beside you. He cannot value the treasure
he possessed since he let it escape. Never, once you are mine,
will I let you go out away from me. Rather I will cherish you
and share with you my ship and every day of my life, endlessly
riding the tossing waves with the long-tailed sea-birds following
and favoring winds always, since we ride them as they will it.
Never will you need to journey alone; never will you feel
the division in your mind between which is best, the journey or the homecoming.
Come then, put away your other designs and let us two
go up into my bed so that lying together
in a bed of love we can have faith and trust in each other.'

    Now it seemed like years since Odysseus had spoken such words
of persuasion, since words of naked urging had grazed my ear
and glazed my eyes with thick desire. Since Odysseus. . .

    I answered him again and said to him: 'Apollytos, how can you ask me
to be forgetful with you? For do you not remember your oath
to both of us? Do you not think of the disaster that befell
so many for Helen's sake, and Paris, who carried her away
from her wedded husband and her country with just such words of love?'
He waved his hand in dismissal and his upper lip curled.
'That slut Helen was never the prize you are.
But now you have spoken my name to me. Take what you own.'

    'Apoll – Helmsman, you speak of unthinkable things. My spirit

batters the cage of my breast like a dove. My heart
and mind are divided, for my heart inclines also toward my homecoming.
I cannot choose tonight. My mind unravels with confusion.
Let me go to bed alone in your compact cabin.
I beg you, do not urge me now when my spirit storms
within me and terror eats my heart out. There would be no
pleasuring in it.' He answered: 'Not like this, my queen.
I would not be willing to take you to my bed unless
you can bring yourself, my goddess, to submit to me in love.
That is how I desire you; then you will be my queen.'

    He released me then and stepped away into the shadow
of the great mast-pole. I felt the night wind
like cold hands gripping my burning arms
and shuddered for the lack of Odysseus' great sea-purple mantle,
which I sent with Ailanthis to be a shield and herald on her journey.
I stepped into Apollytos' cabin in turmoil, drawing
the door bar in its thong. *O Ithaka, Odysseus, rocky homeland,*
how far I am from your shores and still how far
I thought of going on my journey. First
there was one friend who persuaded me to go with her to be locked
away in the land whose people know nothing of the sea.
Now this one would take me endlessly roaming the seas
and far from land. And with neither would I ever be queen
of my own life, but always inclining to someone else.
O Ithaka, Odysseus, rocky homeland, loom weight, anchor,
sea-bird's cleft and driver who laid aside the reins,
you are my journey's end, my hidden harbor revealed,
endless fame and timeless name on the ribs of my weaving.
In this moment I discovered my mind's deepest purpose.

    Now I could not sleep, for intent had tightened the sinews
of my spirit and would not let the joints in my body loosen.
Nor could sweet slumber come upon me before the dawn came.
And when she spread her saffron robes upon the sky
I arose, impatient, with serious words to speak to Apollytos.

    But my helmsman stayed by the steering oar and avoided
my words. He never turned his gaze to meet mine,

nor would the strong-limbed oarsmen speak to me in answer
to my questions, nor show me sea-wonders as they had before.
They shuffled over the decks with a surly aggrieved air.
I put out my hands to the bread and dried fishes
a grave seaman brought me alone in my place at the stern
of the heaving ship. Helios set beside us, the evening
came on, the starry net was cast on the sky, but still
the ship groaned and pitched, so I made my way early
to the helmsman's dwelling space and drew the latch to
on its thong. Next I prayed to Athene for the gift of slumber
and a sleep drifted over me like a mist, loosening my joints
and dissolving the tumult in my mind like foam in the trough of a wave.

But then my ears rang with a high squeal and the rasp
of bronze on bronze. I started awake. Another creak
sounded over the slap of waves on groaning timbers.
Someone approached. No scream came to my throat,
no chance of escape by the door flickered in my mind.
I lay awaiting each creak and shuffle with dread
like a hare pinned with an arrow awaiting the hunter's grasp.

Apollytos had given his word that this room was mine inviolate
as long as he gave me conveyance, but here came a hand groping
for my mouth. Next an arm pinned my shoulders
to the pallet beneath. Green fear seized me. I twisted
despite myself, shedding regretful tears for how,
at last, after so many trials of heart and mind, I knew
I wanted my husband, my homecoming, my only lord.
After all the years I held away from my heart and my couch
so many arrogant suitors, all of them better men
than these on board Apollytos' ship, was I now spoil
for a faceless cur? The spirit within me rebelled and I reached
for the sharp bronze hairpin I ordered from the smith, Pherisos,
on Ithaka so many seasons ago. I kept it tipped
with poison. As I started, the hand relaxed its grip.

It moved to my eyes and brushed at the tears.
I pulled it away roughly and screamed aloud. My forearms
were squeezed to my sides. The hand clamped on my mouth again.

A body heaved onto my breast and stopped my breathing.
I stiffened. It pulled away. *It pulled away*.

    Then I heard shuffling, and bronze clashed on cold bronze.
For the whole of the night remaining I did not sleep
until mist-shrouded Dawn peered through the crack by the door bar.

    Before I arose from my bed to dress, my helmsman banged
loudly at the door bar and demanded entry. I pulled the bolt
and he thrust his way in to stand before me like a mighty bull
before a young Naiad. We stood there this way, we two,
conversing with one another by questioning looks. He
was the first one to speak, saying: 'My temptress,
I come for your answer now. I can no longer hold
the turmoil in my breast for I have seen that your spirit is knit.
O, answer me now – that you come with me willingly, eagerly.
Then, queen of my seas, you will set me free of torment,
free of the weight I carry with me, always ranging
on the misty face of the seas, seeking the gift of oblivion
to the evil that men do. Already the spirit within me
submits to your hand on my steering oar. The wind shifts;
we could soon be adrift in the dry swelter from far Aithiopia.
Tell me your answer quickly.' So Apollytos spoke
and in his words I heard and knew in him both
a man who loved and would shelter me forever and the conqueror
who next would take and render me his helpless thrall.

    I answered him, saying: 'O helmsman, never did I wish
to speak to you this way. Some things that pass between a man
and a woman should be never spoken, for some words, once spoken,
are like a treacherous west wind that suddenly
blasts the sails secured for quiet seas and bursts them.
But had it never caught them, they would have gone on
easily billowing the ship into many harbors afterward. . .'

    He stopped me, saying: 'All this cavils and is foolish,
for you yourself have said it was useless to deny my words.
It might be sufficient answer for some man among men
but not for me. For not only with lustrous eyes
did you speak to me long ago, but with your touch. You stroked

my arm so desire and daring seized me again.
Never will they let me go, whether you come with me, always
caring for my life, or whether you leave me to veer endlessly
on restless waters, alone and unredeemed. Answer.'

At first I could not. Then a voice stirred within me
and I answered him, saying: 'Helmsman, never would I intend
to snare you by this, you who have shared my trials and counseled me
as no other man save Odysseus could. Never did I scheme
to enmesh you in my designs by such a gesture. When you told me
the story of your wife and daughter ravished, and you
as father, husband, formerly loved but shamed in their eyes
as a man among the rest, you stirred my spirit to pity.
I touched you with the hand of a friend, like this. . .

'As for redeeming, only you can accomplish it. For each of us
must care for his own life, spin her own web, and this
is why I say that I would return to Ithaka.
For there is my loom – Odysseus, my palace, my children, my unfinished weaving.
Nothing is more sweet in the end than husband and family, ever.
They are my life, my web, and I must care for it myself.'

Now he was stricken to silence. Roughly
he shook my hand from his arm and turned his handsome face
away. We stood there as if stunned and no words
passed between us for a time. Then he spoke:
'O Penelope, I'm too filled with you to speak – perhaps
it will be easier soon, but right now I wish you were not
anchored in my thoughts. How I wish you were far away.
I must now go back to work and set my course,
hoping that my ship will bear me up, since I cannot catch myself.
My voice is silent for the first time in this matter, or almost.
But never, as I have given my oath on it, never will I
convey you to Ithaka. I will not be the one to see you returned
to Odysseus, undeserving as he is. Fare well, O queen.'
He turned aside from me then and left me haughtily.

I dressed slowly. It was painful to leave that room
for my seat at the stern of the ship. For two more days
I was held on his ship among the sullen seamen, who spoke to me

arrogantly now. Apollytos neither spoke nor dined with me,
nor did he set the awning to shield my reddened arms
from the scorch and the dry wind. And on one day Helios was before us
all the day long, and another, always behind us.

   On one day Helios rose and sank on our right
and the next he rose to our left, though I could scarcely keep track
for the fear I endured in the deep of those nights, never knowing
whether an end to my suffering was near or if I would be carried
on the tossing seas for long days, denied my homecoming.
Always the terror was with me as to what sort of country
this man would choose to set me free in and whether
the people there would be violent, savage and without courtesy,
or would speak the language of the Achaians and be hospitable to strangers besides
I dared not question the unyielding helmsman, but pondered by day
with dread in my heart for what might be the outcome of each night.

· XXII ·

WITH SO MANY thoughts crowding my mind, this seemed
to me to be the best way: to show no fear
and to act in the way women do when in company
with noble men and good ones, secure and confident, and calm.
So all that day I bore the yoke of my fear, pretending,
while wondering what evils lay in store for me to suffer next.
But then across the misty face of the water I saw land
lying very close to us. As welcome as the return of a sea-faring husband
or son, so the sight of land was delightful. We ran on
toward the land, though soon I could hear the terrible pounding
of the sea on jagged rocks, and foam and sea-spray hissed
toward us. It seemed the *Sea-Swift* drove like a fish-eagle straight
for ragged boulders thrust up in the wash. I stole a look
at helmsman Apollytos and saw that his face was set in a grim
unseeing mask like that of Dionysos' wheeling dancers.

   He saw the fear I could no longer hide as the crash
of surf and the suck of sea-troughs dashed the vessel
forward wildly toward snags and splintering doom.
He turned and shouted to the oarsmen and they dipped their cocked oars
smartly into the churning maw and pulled us hard away.
We drove along the sheer of the cliffs beside shadowy mountains
and stayed so close to the land I could see
women carrying water. But when we had run that way
for some time we came to the end of a promontory and the *Sea-Swift*'s
course now carried us straight away from the desired landfall
and toward the open main. Alarmed, I went quickly
to the helm and spoke to Apollytos in words of blandishment saying:
   'O helmsman, I do not think this is Ithaka, nor any land
I have seen in my journeying, yet the sight of it is welcome to me

as to anyone unaccustomed to go forever wandering the seas
without the sight of land. What land is it? Who
are the people who live there? Have you decided to return me to my country
and family after all, since we seem to be sailing away
from the land we approached just now? Or have you devised
some other hurt against me? Surely such a man as you
can never be contented this way.' He drew his brows
together, and stiffened with an effort of will against his fury.
He growled: 'O queen, do not think that you move me
by these cunning words or that you change my mind's course.
For there are oaths that I have sworn and these weigh heavier
by far with me than your words. And one of these
I say again with all of my men hearing it: never
will I be the one to return you to Odysseus. As for this island,
you yourself will have to find out what land it is,
for each city is singular and receives every man or woman
differently. And now, see, we have come to the deep channel
that leads straight into the harbor, and there I will leave you.'
    He shouted and signaled to his men and the ship turned sharply,
dying in the water. The railing under my hand shivered
and rattled against the stanchion. The men leaped to the lines
and drew in the sails like freshly washed clothing snapping.
They put away the running gear and beat the waves
with their oars toward the harbor on the far side of the cutwater. The sea birds
left us and winged away toward the wider reaches.
No land birds ventured toward us in the blast of side-sweeping winds,
nor did any dolphins crest in the trough or swell
around us, but on we ran, ever away
from our own dark shadow, heading for the land. We stopped, however,
outside the breakwater, near its very end, and the oarsmen
put away their oars and made fast the anchor cable.
    I entered the cabin that had served as my refuge and prison
to see to my chest and gather my bundle. Apollytos shouldered
his way in the door. Shutting it he spoke to me, saying:
'My siren, you see how I keep to my word, both those
that were spoken in anger and those that escaped my heart

in love. When you are at home, if you come there, and lie
in your husband's bed, remember how I was the one who nearly took you
away to the ends of the seas.' He bowed and I answered him, saying:
    'Helmsman, Apollytos, if only I could *never* think of you
whenever I return home. Wait – I would give you a gift, something
to remember me by.' I handed him the tunic I had woven
for Telemachos to wear on the occasion of his marriage. I had carried it
with me for a charm. But now I was eager to make a show
of thanks to this heartstrong hero, and of the lingering division within me.
    He thrust it back to me, saying: 'How could I ever wear
this cloth next my skin? For I would always feel your fingers
touching my shoulders as I fastened the pins, your arms against my chest,
imagine your hands lingering as they smoothed the folds along my thighs.
No, I would take from you something else, a token
that belongs to that vile Odysseus. I would have you give me
the fabled honey cup of heroes, the one he received from Menelaos
before he sailed with the Achaians in the hollow ships to Ilion.
I have seen you draw it many times from your coffer to pour
a libation. For this is the splendid cup Hephaistos wrought,
that Jason gave to Medea, and Theseus had it next
from hapless Phaedra before it passed to the house of Atreus.
Surely of all the possessions in Odysseus' palace this
is esteemed at the highest value, beside his circumspect queen.
Yet clearly he gives it no thought. But then he is a fool, or he would not
send away from him together his two greatest treasures.
Now always whenever I pour the honeyed wine into it I will lift it
to you as to a goddess, and to Odysseus whom I bested and let off.'
    'Helmsman, I, for my part, see it differently. Still,
although I vowed to myself that I would never lose it, you
shall take it. I hope that it may turn from a bitter cup to a sweet one.
Fare well.' His oarsmen approached and carried my belongings
to the skiff. Sinking Helios was spangling the wavelets inside
the cutwater, so the little figures of men on the shore and scrambling
the decks of ships were pulling long shadows with them.
Two oarsmen made the waters flash with their broad oars
and carried us quickly to the strong wharf at the end

of the harbor where numberless stone posts ranged with ships
tied up there. They spoke no words but unloaded my bundles
quickly. I went afterward to climb the slippery, well-worn steps.
Immediately they turned the little craft back
seaward, and as I watched they rowed straight on toward
the *Sea-Swift*. As if by some magic the wind died.
The sea flattened to a lurid sheen. The ship sprouted
sails from the mast pole, then moved away without any wind.
Suddenly a mist drifted between us and followed her course
toward the steep promontory. Nor did she appear again,
though the strange mist soon lifted away from the face of the sea.

    I stood there long, watching and yearning deep in my spirit
for those never-to-be-accomplished desires that vanished with her. A buzzing
of jeers and laughter seized my attention. I looked about me.
Leering seamen were gathered to look me up and down.
'This is a comely prize the sea throws back on land for us.'
'Sure must'a been some pretty rows 'board
that ship over her purple couch and those rosy arms.'
'By the gods, th'r' must. Else why'd they go away so quick
and leave us such a juicy duck for the pluckin'?' I held
my veil and picked up my bundle then. I stood to my full
height and assumed all my bearing and stature. The spirit
within me urged me to show no fear but to cast over me
a mantle of dignity as if I still had Odysseus' flowing cloak
about me. At this a young man with a new-grown beard,
in the most graceful time of young manhood,
came out to meet me and spoke to those others and me, saying:
'Where are you going, unhappy queen, alone along the wharves?
You are some innocent, or else you have come from far away.

    'Come in silence while I lead the way for you and do not
meet anyone's eye, nor ask them questions
for they have not respect for lone women from the outlands.
But you are not like the ordinary women who voyage alone
on the open seas. No, wonder takes me when I look at you,
since for poise and bearing you resemble one of the goddesses
who hold wide heaven. Come and I will take you to the house you seek.'

He picked up my possessions and I followed behind him, walking in his footsteps.
Dread was in my spirit for the unknown hosts about to receive me;
what people were they whose land I had come to, and were they
violent and savage like our mountain kinsmen near Pytho
or hospitable to strangers and with godly minds like Nestor's seed
and gracious Helen? But soon awe for the fair and orderly
city overtook me, for the clean streets, the wide thresholds,
and public springs. The women filling their water jars glowed with
health. Their robes were expertly woven and their calls to their children
were cheerful, their donkeys well-fed and their fowl thriving.

    Soon we came to flourishing orchards and abundant vineyards,
and below them rows of lush greens. We walked
along a road of crushed seashells so no dust rose up
to settle on the leaves or fruits, and approached the wall
of a high-roofed house with sunlight shining from it as from
the spangled wavelets of the morning sea in a fresh breeze.

    My guide vanished from beside me. I stepped across the threshold
of bronze, and wonder took me. I walked on into the courtyard
through the portico, the brazen walls and silver columns
just as in my dream, seeing all and seeing nothing
until I came to the hall where the king and queen of the country sat
beside the hearth in firelight. Women of the household followed
and manservants turned from their tasks. I knew the queen at once.

    It was Arete of the distinguished counsel. She rose from her chair,
letting her handiwork fall into her basket. She came to me herself
moving majestically, yet her light step and the warmth in her voice
told that she knew me at once also. She addressed me, saying:
'Welcome at last, Penelope, select among women.
A woman's greeting. You honor our house, which has had much
honor even before this, since your husband, splendid Odysseus,
came to us lately. Your son Telemachos is even now
with us in the palace, sent by your far-seeing husband
to be a sweet light to guide you toward your longed-for homecoming.'
And now she folded me in her arms, as tears welled in my eyes.

    For there is nothing better to urge on the release of clenched tears
than the proffered shoulder. I gave myself over to relief

as Arete led me through the palace and up the doubled staircase
to her high chamber. There we could speak, and I began it,
saying: 'Arete, gracious queen, I thank you for your greeting
and above all for the sweet news of my dear son.
But tell me more so that I may know the full truth;
how is the terrible wound which the boar inflicted upon him
with its dreadful tusk? And which others of my family are with him?
What news does he bring of Odysseus and my two daughters?'
    Arete, daughter of Herakleite and Rhexenor, spoke to me then:
'Penelope, daughter of Aramantha, they are far off on Ithaka
and the mainland. But your son is well and firm, an enchantment of grace
about him so that wonder takes me when I look on him. I think
I never saw such a likeness as he has to his father, great-hearted Odysseus.
Still, I think you will be more contented to hear
the story from your son's own lips, nor is it fitting
to tell another's story when he is close by and will tell it
soon himself. I myself first have a question to ask you.
Whence have you come, and who gave you this clothing? From the look
of the pattern and weave, this is not the glorious handiwork of your own loom,
but rather a web from Helen's loom. Did you speak to our sister,
Helen, and did she send with you any words for me?'
'Arete, my friend, all that you have guessed is true. Here
is a splendid robe from Helen's hands for you also.
But where is my son now, and when shall I clasp him to my breast
and see him for myself, and kiss him on his head and eyes?'
'My friend, all this shall be accomplished presently.
But come, wash with water and put clean clothing upon your body.
And let us know each other while I myself bathe you.'
She helped me with my silver shoulder pins and unwound the fringed
girdle. Next she added water to the tub of carven white stone,
both hot and cold just as I wished it.
    She bathed me with a firm sponge, adding perfume to the water
from a luminous jar of cobalt swirled with gold, and rinsed
away the salt scurf of the sea from my hair, piling it
high on my head. And after, she poured out fragrant oil
from a golden flask to anoint my thirsting skin and laid out

a robe and beautifully worked skirt for me to wear,
fine-woven and thin like the wing of a moth, and gleaming.
And while I took my ease we conversed as old friends
about our homes, our families and people, and our customs.
We continued this way, exchanging ideas about all manner of tasks
and all ways of accomplishing our duties and living skillfully.
We found that we held much in common between us and twisted
strong threads of friendship. Presently Nausikaa, her daughter,
came with her attendant women to greet me, saying:

    'O Queen Penelope, wonder takes me as I look at you,
for although your fame is told around the restless seas,
it is more for your steadfastness and loyalty to your wedded husband
than for your beauty and stature and your own excellent gifts.
But it is easy to see why even such a man as he is,
endlessly suffering hardships on malevolent seas, should hold out
for his homecoming, striving for it urgently, always single-mindedly.'

    The women combed my hair and put on my golden circlet.
I dressed and fastened the triple eardrops with mulberry clusters
fashioned in gold. We laughed like girls, as long ago in the house
of Ikarios my father, my sister Iphthime and I used to prattle
down the shadowy hallways on our way to the feasts and dancing.
Descending the staircase, we passed along the brazen walls
with their cobalt frieze and between the dogs made of gold and silver
by the golden door with the silver lintel above. And here
young men fashioned of gold were holding flaring torches
in their hands. And when Alkinoös, the hallowed king,
saw us he arose from his throne. He came and took me
by the hands. He set me in a polished chair, next to his wife's
own silver-studded chair, and then he himself placed
a footstool at my feet. A maidservant brought water
and poured from a splendid pitcher, holding it above a silver basin
for me to wash, and she pulled a polished table
before me. A housekeeper brought in the bread and served it to me,
adding many good things to it, generous with her provisions
while a carver lifted platters of all kinds of meat and set them
on a table in front of me beside my golden goblet.

But meantime Alkinoös went to powerful Laodamas, his son,
who had been sitting next him and who was the son he loved most.
He spoke to him quietly. I noticed what he did, and understood.
My heart was a storm within, but I put my hands forth
to the things that lay before me. I watched the portal as I ate.

· XXIII ·

THEN LAODAMAS returned, and with him my beautiful son,
Telemachos, looking like one of the gods. An enchantment of grace
was about his head and shoulders. He stood taller and straighter
than before and walked with a confident gait. My spirit soared.
I rose and embraced him. He clasped me to his breast as I spoke, saying:
'You have come, Telemachos, sweet light. I feared I would never
see you again when we left in the ships for Pytho and on to Pylos
and Sparta, searching always for the cure for your wound. But now
here you are before me, healthy and firm, looking like a leader
of men. Wonder takes me as I look at you. But come now,
tell me news of your father, and how all this was accomplished.'
   'My Lady Mother, I will tell you the whole story.
But first I give you my father's loving kiss with which
he sends you words of his heart's urgent longing for your
safe homecoming. He says he has foreseen it all in a dream, with you
beside him. He says: "Tell her all our house and her loved ones

213

long for her." He is like a sword without a scabbard, rattling
loosely in an oaken chest carried from room to room
though thick fleeces and heavy cloaks surround it.'
But then he stopped, for Nausikaa came in from a side door
in the brazen wall. She carried a splendidly worked pitcher,
and held it above a silver basin for him to wash.
She pulled a polished table before him. His eyes blazed
as he looked at her. Nausikaa, with a goddess' poise about her,
went and stood beside the pillar that supported the roof
with its joinery and gazed upon him with pensive eyes and admired him.

 My heart stirred within me for Odysseus' youth and mine,
lost forever to jealous gods, but I put away
the tumult in my breast to ponder later in solitude. Now
great Alkinoös spoke thus: 'Son of Odysseus,
what you say is fair and orderly. For nothing is more sweet
than home and a consort who shares in everything. This, for a man
is always best. And in a son it is best by far
to be thoughtful, and respectful toward the lady who is his mother.
Men see this and admire it, and to the young girls
it gives confidence that he will be a gentle husband.
But now, O queen, it is fitting that you be the first to tell us
your story, since you are his senior and this takes precedence in storytelling.
Whence have you come, and how, and whom have you heard and seen?'

 I began with how we had made our way first to Pytho
and the strange magic by which three days passed
while we lived only one long night of questioning
under the priest's watchful eye, how then we were inducted
into The Pythia's own city of women where industry,
graciousness and sisterhood abounded in secret. I told how Nerianne
found her glad calling there and Mentor arranged
our escape before he died at the hands of hateful kinsmen
of Odysseus' own line. The task of telling the story
set the framework for me, like the sturdy posts
of a loom from which the threads suspend, and the hands are inspired
by the loveliness of the pattern to weave it firmly, more brilliant
with each pass of the shapely shuttle. But always a story

depends on the words that unwind it in their deliberate
sequence, so I chose my words with care. Since often the song inspires
the singer, the words came readily. I told of our journey to Pylos
where Nestor's daughter and sons received us kindly and gave us
hospitality, driving us themselves in their well-wrought chariots
to far Lakedaimon. I told how Helen knew me at once
and treated me like her own dear sister, and how she taught
Ailanthis many secret ways of plants and potions,
giving her cuttings and jars from her own abundant plantings.

    I told of the return to Pylos, of Nestor's death, how Mabantha
lay ill, but you, Phemios, left her with me,
and made your way to Ithaka with Ailanthis and Helen's treatment.
I told how next Mabantha escaped in the night and how
I sailed quickly after her with the helmsman Apollytos, and much
of the story of how he deceived and tried me, detaining me with him
several days aboard his ship on the watery wastes
of the ocean with never sight of land. I told how, after
much suffering, I reached Phaiakia and was guided to the palace.

    At once Euryalos stood up, Naubolos' son, a man
like treacherous Ares himself, with a raging in his breast, first
at Odysseus and now at Telemachos. For before them,
Eurylos had been first among the Phaiakian suitors for Nausikaa,
her hand in marriage, and he thought he would have her. He spoke craftily:
'Surely there are many things left out of this queen's story.
How are we to believe that she did not know
of this sea captain's leanings toward her when wantonly, it seems,
she went alone aboard his ship, with no attendants.
There is no trusting such a woman. For in this
she resembles Helen, that other faithless queen, whose recklessness
brought about the doom and destruction of many.'
So he spoke and all about the palace were shocked.

    Looking at him darkly, my Telemachos answered:
'You sot, that was reckless speech, not at all seemly.
Was it not enough to insult my father when he was a guest here
not long ago? My mother's faithfulness
is well known, and she is one on whom the goddesses

and gods have bestowed a smirchless reputation. She foiled
the designs of many powerful men who vied for the privilege
of lying beside her. I myself witnessed this,
but then a child I could not always see
a way to defend her. Now I am a man. I set
the choice before you – either fight me here or run.
This time you will know the wrath of Odysseus.'

    He drew his sword and rushed at Euryalos, raging
as if to kill. Euryalos screamed and ran under his guard.
He clasped Telemachos' knees and groveled, a kid bawling.
Telemachos grasped him by the hair and shook him off like a puppy
or a snake whose head he would dash against a rock.
He bent Euryalos backwards, brandishing his glinting sword.
In a stroke he thrust the point straight down till it struck stone
and splinters clattered to the floor, but not before Euryalos
shrieked like a pig at butchering or an ox in sacrifice.
He writhed from Telemachos' grip, whimpering, and lurched away,
shamefaced, shown for a coward – blusterer that he was.
The sword clanged on the floor. Telemachos tore off his scabbard.
He approached Queen Arete and dropped the scabbard, clinking, at her feet.
He leaned his forehead to her knees and spoke, saying:
'Sorry am I to spoil the feasting here in your palace
by this show of unruly fighting. But this man stirred up
anger deep in my breast by his wild speaking. I had to strike out
for my mother's honorable intentions, her reputation.'

    Now Alkinoös straightened on his throne and addressed Telemachos:
'Young man, it is not outrageous for you to act thus among us,
since this way you show us the strength you are endowed with.
A manful son knows to defend his parents.
Rare is the man who stays his hand from anger
when such a churl speaks out to him thus in assembly.
Euryalos must return to make amends to your mother,
with words and gifts, for having spoken out of reason.
I think it must be wine to his head that makes him rash.'

    But Arete laid a hand ever so lightly
on her husband's shoulder and leaned forward to speak, saying:

'My husband, all that you have said is reasonable, but the mind
within me is outraged. Are not the sword and scabbard
Telemachos wore the same ones Euryalos gave to Odysseus,
to make amends for the insults he flung
at Odysseus also? See its silver nails and handle, the scabbard
of fresh-sawn ivory rings. Was this not the gift of greatest value
Euryalos could bestow? Of what use, then,
could another gift be? The youth is unworthy. Let him
go back to the house of his father Naubolos to tend his pigs.'
The queen spoke urgently and the king was persuaded.
At once he spoke to the best of the Phaiakians, who were assembled there:
'Hear me, leaders of the Phaiakians, and men and women of counsel;
you have heard what I judge the best course. And we ourselves
will make amends to our guests with lavish treatment.
Let someone quickly bring Demodokos with his clear-voiced lyre.
Our guests will see how far we surpass all others
in the speed of our feet in dancing and singing, and remind Odysseus of it.'
        The herald led in the blind singer, Demodokos, with his lyre.
Demodokos led them out to the dancing ground, and about him
gathered young men in the flush of their youth who beat the floor
with their feet. Then Alkinoös asked Laodamas and Telemachos
to dance by themselves, nor did they refuse him and despite
Telemachos' new-healed wound none could challenge them for beauty
and grace of movement in tossing the ball and leaping to catch it.
And when they were finished Telemachos tossed the scarlet ball
Nausikaa's way and she, springing lightly on slender ankles,
easily caught it, and so led the women's
dancing. And she, white-armed, and lithe as tall grasses
by a river or as Artemis, who moves on the mountains and shines
above all her nymphs, and is easily marked among them, though all are lovely,
so this girl shone among her handmaidens, a virgin unwedded.
I turned my head toward discreet Arete. She had seen it
also and nodded to me with her brows. I could not hold
a smile within me, and turned my head so that none might see.
        But still within my heart was a longing for more news
of Odysseus and the full story of my son's amazing cure.

I would have to wait until the bright dawn, for only
then could I question him and learn everything. Finally we arose
to pour the last libation and all went home to bed,
each to his own house, or to her own room. And I went up
to Nausikaa's fragrant room, where she herself led me,
bedding down in the antechamber while Arete lay beside her husband.
And for Telemachos the maidservants had made up a bed on the porch.

    But when Dawn of the fair hair showed again
I dressed myself at once in the richly worked robe from Arete's
hands, the one that Odysseus carried homeward
in the polished chest, cutting the knot before I could work it.
All about the palace I could hear the lovely morning sounds.
Serving maids flitted through the halls, murmuring like the birds as they whirled
from their nests in the eaves. I heard soft rustling in the chambers
around the balcony as doors opened and closed gently.
I slipped past lovely Nausikaa, drowsing on her couch,
and out through the close-fitting doors with their double panels. I descended
the tall stair and made my way quickly to the great hall
where Arete was already looking after her household, speaking
to her housekeeper and going over everything to see that all was in order.
'Penelope, my friend, a woman's greeting on this awaited day.
Come, sit beside me near the fire while I spin my new yarn.
For your son also is risen early and gone out with Alkinoös
and our sons to the place of assembly in the city, next to the harbor.
And now, while my daughter sleeps and we can converse together
so none may hear, I myself first have questions to ask you.

    'Did we not both notice that Telemachos burns for Nausikaa, how she
admires him with her eyes? This is a sight that gladdens
the heart of a mother when she sees it. While always a man wishes
for his daughter to bring him honor as his sons will, her mother
prays for her happiness also. And always Nausikaa paid no heed
to her own youthful neighbors although many,
besides Euryalos, courted her. And this was so even before
that handsome stranger, your Odysseus – whom I helped as I promised you
long ago that I would – finally came and the spirit
within her decided to find herself a husband from elsewhere.

But tell me truly about Helen and glorious Lakedaimon.
How does her proud husband treat her now she is restored to him?
Is she as sweet as she was when we were mere girls
and we played together beside Eurotas' stream – before
Apollo of the silver bow struck down Rhexenor, my father?
Did she remember to send me her greeting?' Arete questioned me
thus and I spoke to her in answer, saying: 'Arete, my friend,
her way is graciousness itself; the very air that moves
behind her in her wake closes in wonder at her kindness and spirit.

　'For she is no longer merely a beautiful woman, that is,
one who is seen by the mindless for her beauty and stature only.
Rather she is grown to true womanhood, much as the callow
unbearded youth becomes at last reasoning and mature,
but under his father's patient example. And since Menelaos
was away from Sparta on still more warring, plainly
he trusts her once more; she moves in freedom and is sovereign
of her own pursuits, which is always best for strong women.
Indeed she sends you her woman's greeting, along with the robe
I gave you, that in its sheer weaving and pattern is the same
as my lovely garment that your sharp eyes observed before this.
For on them both is told the wondrous tale
of the siege of fallen Troy; here are the hollow ships
of the Argives, their decks bristling with men eager for battle.
But here also are the far-off homelands, the strong-founded houses
and rude hearths of the greave-wearing heroes, with patient wives
and sweethearts, mothers and children, carrying on their living.

　'All who see this pattern and weave it patiently
on their own looms will also know of many other lives
and the hardships endured by those the singers never sing of.
And the wearers also. Woman shall pass them to woman in this way.
The children who come to stand beside their mothers and watch
the loom weights swaying and figures emerging thread by thread
will pattern their songs on the tinkling weights and the thumping beaters.
So this story too will be handed down the generations.
Such are the gifts from women's hands.' I spoke and gave it
and next there arose within us the desire for exulting.

Now the light of the sun would have lifted and set on our talking
had not Arete spoken a quick word to me, saying:
'Shall I say something to you or keep it hidden within?
Very soon Nausikaa will arise and come down,
so we must take our pleasure in confiding now. Your Telemachos
follows her all about the palace and she is eager
for him also. Alkinoös understands what they feel, and has noticed.
Since she cannot stay long unmarried, it is better
if she goes out and finds her own husband from elsewhere.
For she is not like those two shining daughters you bore
to glorious Odysseus after he left in the black ships
for ill-starred Ilion. Nausikaa delights in giving comfort
to her brothers and parents and kinfolk. She is especially patient
with little ones and foundlings, and skilled in fine handiwork besides.

'But Telemachos is only just come to maturity, although
his measured words and thoughtful ways belie his youth.
Odysseus knows nothing of his casting up here, since he sent him first
to Pylos in search of you. And it is the custom, in matters
of young people's marrying, to listen to their fathers' words
and know their will. Before this, Alkinoös favored
that one of Naubolos' sons who is sent away to his father,
since he spoke out rudely to you last night. But among
the Phaiakians Naubolos is far the most powerful, and he
desires a marriage of kinship. He has given many gifts
so one of his sons may win her. Can we not hasten a marriage
and prevent his winning my husband's favor again?'

'O my friend, what you say is fair and orderly. No mother's eyes
are needed to know the truth of what you say; any one
can see it for herself. I myself will speak
for Odysseus, if this is needed, and if my son will ask me.
First I must test Telemachos and see what his thoughts are.

'But tell me this truly, O Arete, so I may know
the weave of it: how is it you come to sit alongside
your husband, a man who gives you pride of place, and you
dissolve quarrels so the people look toward you as to a god?
And Alkinoös listens and shares his thoughts and plans with you fully,

which is the dream of many women, but few accomplish it.'
'Penelope, sister, how is it you are questioning me
in this matter? For have you not also wielded Odysseus' power,
raising your children and taking care of his household until
his return? And did you not decide on your daughters' journey and choose
your own course afterward? Have you not lived
as I have? Therefore you know: it is in granting yourself
power that power is granted.' She spoke and I answered her, saying:
'All this rings true. Wonder takes me as I think
upon your wisdom, your knowledge of my innermost thoughts.
And is it not strange that we knew each other's thoughts and dreams
even before meeting?' She answered me next, saying:
    'Those were no dreams, but a shared vision. Did I not know you
at once when you slipped between the columns at the far doorway?
But put in your mind also this thing that I tell you. Still
we are accomplishing separately and yet we also strive together
with men. But no man's mind can work like a woman's, and you
have seen that sometimes I must be like a goddess for
designing and common sense where Alkinoös is lacking in thoughtfulness.'
We continued conversing until my son Telemachos strode in,
stepping over the bronze threshold. The first to see him approach
was Arete. She silenced me then with a look, and calling
Telemachos to us she spoke to the two of us in words of endearment:
'Penelope, my friend, and Telemachos, my spirit calls me to speak out,
for someone may come into the hall and interrupt your time
together. Always between a mother and her sons there come
many concerns and other people. We mothers can rarely
be alone with our grown sons to speak with them for a moment.
And we see many things, and can still advise them.'
    So speaking she left us together, and we turned to each other
with delight. I was the first to speak after seating him near me
on a lion-footed settle: 'O my son, how proud
I am to be called the mother of such a son as you were
last night in this very hall when that arrogant young man
spoke out to shame our name. When you were still a child
you had to permit such insults in our palace, but now you are grown

to manhood you rival even your father for courage
and persuasion. Now I am eager to hear from your lips the story
of all that has happened, any welcome news
of your father and sisters, and what truly came to pass
on that not-to-be-mentioned Neritos. It is so strange;
what kind of boar could get near to a hunter as skilled as you are?
How was it your excellent dogs did not bring him down for you?'

    'My mother, that was not some ordinary beast,
but rather, by some magic, a boar and sow together,
for I saw clearly the great teats swaying heavily
as she closed upon me with the tusks of a colossal boar, and his male parts
also. And there was yet a further horror –
a third tusk, yellowed and twisting, sprouted from the brow,
and this was stained dark at the tip from rooting in a pit.

    'That was the spear to my wound, for although I drove for it
straight on, my shaft was glanced aside as if from a brazen
shield strong-forged by Hephaistos himself, and the brute
bore in craftily under my guard as if
it knew which way I would dodge. I thrust again and again
but my blows were turned aside. It raged and twisted
swiftly and slyly for me, leering foully. It lunged me
back to the sheer of the narrow cleft; my arm clashed
against the rock face, nor could I lift the spear high
to stab, but the beast pierced me here where you see the well-healed
scar. Next it veered away and was swallowed by a mist
that swirled over and removed me from the land of the sensible,
casting me into the clutch of darkness. Writhing shadows
held me until my sister Ailanthis bent over my couch
with her soothing medicine from Helen's own hands.

    'Dear Mother, my life belongs to Helen and Ailanthis, and to you
above all, who managed everything, risking so much to save me.'
So he spoke, but I smiled on him and stroked him with my hand and spoke to
him, saying: 'Telemachos, your mind and thoughts seem once again
as steadfast as before, when you were yourself. But now that you are come
to your maturity you must put in your mind this other thing I tell you:

    'Your life belongs to no one but yourself – that is, until you choose

the lady, your wife, to share it. For each man girds himself
afresh to a challenge, and every woman refills her own vessel,
even as she pours out life-giving water
from the golden pitcher, or else she must return many times to the spring.
Nor was our journey accomplished for your sake only, but rather,
long before that time it was decreed by the goddess Athene
that I take Nerianne and Ailanthis to The Pythia at Pytho. I pledged to.
And I had my own purpose in accomplishing this as well.'

· XXIV ·

'BUT NOW, sweet light, the heart within my breast rejoices
at the welcome sight of that smooth scar, and delights in your renewed strength.
Come now, tell me any news of your father.
What words do you have from Odysseus for my ears only?
And tell me of Ailanthis, and how your father now receives her.'
    'Mother, I will answer all that you ask me.
But first I must tell you another strange thing, and sad.
I was told this wonder; I did not see it for I was in darkness.
The moment my sister Ailanthis laid upon my festering wound
the healing herb from the great jar of Eurotas' water,
Grandfather Laertes fell stricken and weak. It was as if
some god had seized the life in him to breathe it
into me. For next I took a deep and even breath,
and soon my body loosened from its coils. I slept and healed
like a pup beside its dam after it has given suck at every teat,
and falls into a contented drowse at last.
    Ailanthis tends him now, nor does she count his sickness
can be cured. Rather he slowly weakens and by now old age
may have taken him down into Hades. My father told me
not to tell you this, if I did not find you still at Pylos.
For he told me that he dreamed that you were gone on
from there on your own journey and he urged me never to try
to divert you with stratagems or pleading for his sake. Next
he told me, should I find you gone, to seek some word of you
here at Arete's knees in Phaiakia, in Alkinoös' house.
So I think that his dream must have come to him from the goddess herself
for here you are, Mother, and here, too. . .'
                                        But now,
just as Odysseus had dreamed my life, I saw his.

Through the dream's gateway now came a vision I remembered
from the night before, a dark image becoming light
again in my mind. The dream figure was the image of Ailanthis.
She stepped into my bedchamber, passing beside the thong of the door bar,
came and stood above my head and spoke to me:
'Dear Mother, you are sleeping, so peaceful in your heart.
I do not wish to trouble your ease, since soon enough
you will have your homecoming and know all of it. Then perhaps
in your weeping you will remember that I came to you to tell you
these things. My kindly tutor, dearest grandfather Laertes,
will soon die and go down to Hades to join his dear wife.
Words came from Pylos of Mabantha's flight homeward,
and Phemios is eager to follow, to search for her with their child.
Nor can I long resist the urging from deep within me
to journey with him to far Aigyptos' banks, to Thebes,
great seat of knowledge, especially in herbs and medicines.
There Helen urged me to journey one day – there
I might learn for myself the cures and uses of many plants
and bring back to the Achaian homeland my skill honed.

'To Phemios himself permission is granted, but my father,
though he says he will no longer thoughtlessly ordain his loved ones' lives,
begs me to wait for your return before I go.
O Mother, how I long to see you again before
I go so far away. But Phemios will not wait long.
When Phemios goes, I go too. I do not know
if I will see you soon, or ever again in our lives.
I give you a daughter's, a woman's greeting, Mother. Fare well.'

I told Telemachos the dream and the image faded. Once again
I was with my son before me, his mouth open in amazement.
'O Mother, surely some goddess is with us – for as you spoke
I saw Ailanthis here before us both and heard her voice.
So now there is little time for me to tell you more.
We must make our way quickly homeward. But the *Ktimene*
is far away on Ithaka. No one here dares
give us conveyance since the god, Poseidon, in his anger
over my father's blinding of his brutal offspring, the Cyclops,

forbade conveyance for ordinary strangers. The god smashed
the ship that brought my father here on his way homeward.
He rooted the ship there as a rock in the harbor. And this
was a prophecy of old brought to completion, Alkinoös said,
so he stopped the conveying of travelers who make their arrival here,
as Poseidon ordered. This is what I would have you consider.'

    I spoke no words in answer, though I saw the way. First
I made a test of my son – although in my heart I was reluctant
to give him up to another, so recently were we
restored to each other. I spoke in a teasing manner:
'And now you will tell me it is easy for you to leave this place,
for nothing in it pleases you, and lightly you return to your father
with no thought except of the excellent hunting you give up?'

    He looked at me thoughtfully then, and his eyes were dark
with feeling. He spoke to me softly, saying: 'Mother dearest,
what you say is far from the truth. For here I have found
the bough my spirit needs to perch and rest upon.
Here I have found the scabbard for my sword, the rack for my spear,
the shield for my pillow and the laces of dyed purple oxhide
to bind my sandals to my feet. And this, I know now,
my Mother, was your meaning when you spoke of the lovely girl who would be
my wife, for she is in my eyes each moment of every day,
whether she is near or not. Nausikaa
will be my wife or I will cross the seas to Dodona or Pytho
to hear the will of the gods before I take another.

    'But, Mother, I see by your smile you know this already.
I know you to be wondrously skilled in the reading of hearts,
for I remember now how you comforted me when last we left
the house of Laertes and my twin playmates, never to be known
as my own sisters until my father Odysseus' homecoming.
It was hard for me not to be angry when I thought of all I missed
while you in your wisdom and cunning kept their true identity
secret from all the world of men, and the gods were generous
in their complicity. But now I think of you, how always
you were on your own, devising wiles against the suitors' urgings,
and me a child, unable to see my way to the wise course,

nor to understand your struggles without my father.

   'But now he is returned, I must speak to my father first
to tell him that I plan to marry. For never before has he
been close by to share the joyous occasions of my life
and his is the right to give permission.' I was choosing my words
to try to dissuade him when Alkinoös and his sons came in,
and with them the best men of Phaiakia. And Arete
of the wise counsel came down from her upper chamber with Nausikaa.

   Manservants came in. They took the spears from the men to fasten them
in the racks beside the pillars. Maidservants, thronging,
held for them golden pitchers and poured water over silver
bowls for them to wash, and the men sat on the chairs
and benches all around the walls of the lofty hall.
The first to speak was Alkinoös: 'It is a hard thing,
O queen, to imagine how even such a man as Odysseus
could ever be followed by such a son, one who equals
or excels him in all skills as well as in size and beauty.
But Telemachos is this son. And since Odysseus was urgent
to make his way homeward quickly after suffering hardships ·
and long years tossing on the angry seas, now
I will keep you both with me to enjoy the pleasures of friendship,
putting off your homeward journey until we have had our fill
of feasting and hunting and games.' I spoke to him then, saying:

   'O great Alkinoös, how I wish that we could stay
in your palace and receive your hospitality, feasting long days
and enjoying the dancing and singing and the stringed lyre.
And how I wish that I could always sit beside Arete,
your gracious wife, to share our skills, our joys and sorrows.
But I, too, am eager to make my way quickly
homeward, with Telemachos. For my daughter Ailanthis, the one
who is with Odysseus, appeared to me in a dream. She spoke to me, saying:
"Laertes will die soon and go down to Hades." I pray
that I may see the old man before he dies,
and already I have been away for ten and eight days.'
Alkinoös answered, saying: 'O Zeus Father, now I wish
that being the man he is and thinking the way that I do,

Telemachos could marry our daughter and be called our son-in-law, staying
here with us. But since he has a father who is far away
and he was my guest and my friend, I cannot give her to him
without Odysseus to sanction it. For this would be unseemly.
Neither, my guests, can we give you a ship, as compassion would urge us.
For Poseidon has given his oath that he will smash our ships and hide
our city under a mountain if ever again we give
conveyance to outlanders. And there in our beautiful harbor is accomplished
the first part of his oath, the ship he stunned to stone
with a flat stroke of his hand. And our city lies beneath
a shuddering mountain, always anxious lest the god fulfill
the prophecy and bury us. Not one more ship may give
convoy to strangers, and the ships that brought your son and you
have fled, in fear of some disaster. I can see no way.'
    But I saw another way it could go and spoke to him, saying:
'O Illustrious, since you are willing to let Telemachos have
your daughter in marriage, there is a way that all can be accomplished.
For I was long the power in my own palace and to me
fell all the devising and deciding. Therefore, I can speak
and appoint the marriage for our son. And see the clear proof
of Odysseus' intent before all; it was he himself who put it
into your mind, Telemachos, to come here to seek me,
although he thought I was in Pylos.' So I spoke
and Alkinoös had no opposing words for an answer. Next Arete:
'My husband, is not all that she says fair and orderly?
Have you not said that I speak for you?
Therefore do not count Odysseus less wise, for his fame
is sung far and wide for resourcefulness, as Penelope's is for prudence.
    'And listen to this other thought that I have; this is the only way
to unravel the knot that binds these our guests
unwilling on our shores. For never did Poseidon swear in his oath
that we Phaiakians must cease conveying our own upon the seas.
If we give our permission for a wedding feast and appoint it
for tomorrow, Telemachos will be our son-in-law, Penelope, our cousin,
no longer ordinary strangers given conveyance.
Then our ships can convey them to Ithaka swiftly

without constraint, and return safely home to us.'
  Telemachos stood then, tall and erect, a wonder to behold.
'O queen, surely goodness and wisdom are with your people
always since yours and your husband's is the power in this district.
But I would never be the one to take your daughter for wife
and carry her far across the seas unless she
wills it. For only is that woman happy who gladly
shares her husband's bed and the chamber of his mind also.
In this I follow my father's wisdom, such as
he has taught me since coming home at last from Ilion.
So now she must speak for herself.' He spoke and all in the palace
stirred with amazement. But Nausikaa, with a goddess' wits about her,
moved away from the pillar that supported the roof with its joinery.
She gazed upon Telemachos with pride in her eyes and gave him her hand.
She spoke to him aloud and addressed him in measured words, saying:

  'Hello, friend. It seems I have known you ever since
that day when first I saw your father standing by the river
and he also was too thoughtful to compromise my life.
Or perhaps it was the goddess, who spoke to me in a dream urging me to go
to the washing place, saying I would not be long unmarried,
who first put your image in my mind, for I paid no heed to my own
Phaiakian neighbors but always yearned for some other one.
I can share the bed of such a one as you are,
a hero handsome as your father and willing to share your mind
and spirit also as our parents have done before us.
So I will take you, that is, with the good will of my mother
and father, having made friends with you, to be formally married.
And then, I will carry you safely over
the restless seas to our life together in Ithaka.'

  There was a murmur of approval among all gathered in the palace.
But among them now came Naubolos, Euryalos' father. He approached
Alkinoös and spoke to him and asked him a question:
'Alkinoös, do you have it in mind or do you not to call back
my son? For he has gone, and taken my ship and he says
he will spread evil words of this man's mother, Penelope,
to her husband in Ithaka, stirring trouble among the people

there, and so prevent any marriage of Telemachos with Nausikaa.
With bitter heart I come to you myself, for he is my own
son, and the fault in his behavior lies first with me
though I tried to stop him. Always it is best for a father to recognize
faults in his children and help his neighbors hold them to account.'
So he spoke and all were stirred; we had not thought
of further evils. Hallowed Alkinoös was the first to speak:
'Naubolos, all that you say is sensible. Never
will I be the one to visit the sins of the son upon the father
when he is innocent. As for the marriage, so these may depart soon
I appoint it for this night. Let all preparations be made at once.'
So he spoke and all of us within the hall rejoiced.

    Next it was wise Arete who continued the discourse, saying:
'Phaiakians, what do you think now of this man before you
for poise and character, and for feeling well balanced within him?
He and his mother are our guests, but you may have a part in their honoring.
Though we hurry to send them off, do not cut short their gifts,
especially on the lovely occasion of our daughter's marriage to Telemachos.'
Alkinoös spoke also, addressing them all and saying:
'Now I too lay this charge upon each of you. We will store away
clothing for our guests and for our daughter in the polished chests.
Come, let us man by man, and women also, give a great tripod
and a cauldron, or a silver-handled cup, or a golden bowl
and pitcher, a polished chair and footstool, ladles, lamps,
loom weights and fleeces, mantles or tunics, yarn and purple dyes,
bracelets and ear-pendants of gold, silver, ivory, carnelian –
all that is proper to send with a king's daughter when she marries.
Each one of you, go to your own house and return in haste.'

    So Alkinoös spoke and his word pleased the rest of them.
They all went home to do it, each one to his own house.
While they were going, all about the palace many maids
and manservants busied themselves preparing for the feasting to come.
And the men brought in the oxen and sheep and fat porkers
to be sacrificed, and wood for the singing fires. The women cleaned
the tables with sponges and set out bowls and stemmed goblets.
They laid fleeces on the polished chairs and drew up footstools.

Soon flowers bestrewed the floors and wood filled the cressets,
wine the mixing bowls and bread the baskets, with olives
and figs. Demodokos came and tuned his lyre and played for them
so they sang even as they did the tedious tasks.

    Thus when old Helios in his fiery mantle sank again
the Phaiakians returned to the palace, and their wives with them, wearing
their colorful hoods and bearing gifts of well-washed cloth
and elaborately worked robes. And the men brought lavish
gifts, and Arete, the revered queen, herself coming up to me,
signaled me to undo the intricate knot of my travel-worn chest.
She leaned her head close and spoke so none might hear us:
'Shall I be imagining it, or shall I speak of it and tell you what I know?
Is this not the same knot that Odysseus used
to fasten the polished chest we sent along with him
with many gifts of clothing and gold, the one he learned
from the witch Circe, on her enchanted island? She told him
that none other could ever learn it; it was too intricate.
So tell me, where did you learn it and how do you know it?'

    'Arete, my friend, this is indeed a strange tale.
For this was the knot whose knowledge I always shared with Odysseus
and with him alone. He must have forgotten its secret workings
during the long years of warring in Ilion and the hardships
he suffered, tossed by the spiteful seas. I will ponder
forever the meaning of this strange coincidence as I make
my way homeward and take up caring for my life again.'
She spoke aloud, saying: 'Here is a gift for you, my friend,
something to remember from Arete's hands, to wear
beside your husband wearing his own purple mantle.
Nor shall you want for protection without his cloak to shield you.'
Arete held out a cloak of deep purple worked
in sea-blue threads with ships crossing rippling seas
on raised oars within a border of curling waves.

    I reached into my chest and addressed her, saying:
'I would give you a present also. This bobbin
is from the loom on which I wove Laertes' shroud.
But never shall I weave a web of so many threads, no pattern

so complex; my designing will always be simpler, more direct
and I will take pleasure in thinking of you, moving expertly
up and down your loom as I do at mine.'
I turned again, since Arete's words, echoing Helen's,
reminded me of Helen's gift to my son and his bride.
'I give you this gift also, my son; it is the gift
from Helen's hands, for your wife to wear on the lovely occasion
of your marriage. Until my journey it lay away in the palace
in my keeping. Perhaps some goddess put it into my mind
as a talisman, to bring us together again, while she kept you waiting
for me at home in Ithaka. Or perhaps I was always meant
to find you here. My new daughter, it is yours to wear.'
    Telemachos took it then and gave it to Nausikaa. Wonder
took the company as the shimmering cloth fell in lustral folds
from hand to hand but a silence held as he pleated
and draped it from the pins with golden dolphins on her lovely shoulders.
Then a shiver of amazement, a sigh, rose from us all.
Demodokos struck his lyre. Chords of unbridled delight
spiraled to the eaves like bright birds from our hearts.
The tables were pulled close, cups were lifted, the thigh pieces
portioned out and all the joys began to flow
in a rainbow of colors and motion and lovely faces before me.
    I felt a wonder that came of knowing all that went before
and all that will come hereafter, for both old and young.
No longer could I keep my tears within me,
and taking my veil in my hands, I drew it over my head
to enjoy my fill of weeping. Arete alone noticed,
since I was sitting next her and she heard me sighing heavily.
At once she spoke to me, saying: 'Penelope, my friend,
how many thoughts must crowd your mind now that such joy
is come at the heels of so many trials. But I think also
that you must be longing deep in your spirit for your dear husband
to share in this lovely occasion. Perhaps the goddess
will hasten the dancing and singing for you while also holding back
the long night at the outward edges for me and the rest of us
here in the palace.' I spoke to her then in answer, saying:

'O Arete, let us not wish for it to hasten away
like an owl winging out into the night, but rather,
like swallows in the courtyard soaring and swerving, golden and bright
as arrows or little swarming fishes that dart and flash,
we may linger close to the light of the joyous fire and the torches
while the maidservants refresh them, one kindling another, on
'til first light. For I would never be the one to say
it was only days ago that Telemachos was still an infant;
rather, I have a sense that much time has passed
in bringing all this to completion. Therefore I know
there will be time for Odysseus and me to enjoy all
we have missed. I shall not be the one to wish
for this time to be past, but savor it fully in the present.'
    And so I did, and perhaps the goddess heard me or perhaps
not, for it swept on toward its happy conclusion in singing
and dancing, in light and laughter until the last libation
which Alkinoös appointed just as Dawn of the golden tresses
spread her locks upon the sky before rising. Alkinoös addressed us:
Now, Pontonoös, mix the wine and serve it
to all so that with a prayer to our father Zeus
we may send our dear ones on their way back to Ithaka.'
So he spoke and Pontonoös did it. And Arete
came and stood next to me and spoke softly, saying:
'Fare well to you, Penelope, sister and friend, and until
we meet again keep in your heart my woman's greeting.'
At the last we walked out over the threshold
and great Alkinoös sent his herald to go along with us.
    Laodamas drove Nausikaa in her bridal cart, she
wearing her veil and decked with blooms and carrying the vase
of barley. A maidservant went before her carrying a golden distaff
and silver loom weights inlaid with curved-horn sheep
all of ebony. And others were sent along with us to carry
my battered chest, and more bearing food and red wine.
But when we had come down to the sea where the ship was
we all went aboard silently, looking seaward past
the great stunned ship of stone where storm clouds gathered.

We prayed for Poseidon's mercy toward the daughter of the Phaiakians.
We took our seats at the stern of the ship and the expert seamen
slipped the cable free from its hole in the stone post
and sat down, each in his place at the oarlocks in order.

    Now the harbor bore none of its former menace; these seamen
looked upon us respectfully. I looked thoughtfully
upon that lovely harbor which at first seemed so strange
and hostile but now was suffused with light not only
from the sun but also the light of friendship. I resolved
to relish every moment of the journey ahead,
however lightly the ship ran on the creaming waves, or even
if the storm winds caught us and tossed us, heaving, amid the savage
peaks of a churning sea, for this was no dream,
this longed-for homecoming, but a vision shared with my husband, Odysseus.

    But now, as if when we passed that stone-struck barrier
while speeding from the harbor's mouth some sentinel there
had lit a signal fire to vengeful Poseidon, a scud
of clouds gathered into one blue-black shroud overhead
and bore upon us. The sea went eerily flat.
A scum of yellow foam hissed over the sea's surface
which was black as charred wood. We smelled brimstone, felt
a fitful wind soughing and heard that treacherous song of the Sirens.

    Telemachos leapt from his seat beside me, a wildness
in his eyes. He strode to the midst of the oarsmen, shouting orders
to heave for shore. The oarsmen stared, for they heard nothing
but a hollow sound like wind in the cave of a cliff,
all the while the sea, calm, and the dark cloud swelling.
The oarsmen lifted their oars in confusion. The ship shuddered.
I stood and hurried to speak to the Phaiakian helmsman:
'This is only a spell from Poseidon, sent as a trial.
Do not heed my son's words, for he was recently ill,
and is not himself. Nor think of returning to the harbor,
but press forward.' And the helmsman, seeing the sense in my words,
answered me, saying: 'Indeed, O queen, yours is the power here.'

    My son tore off his mantle. He rushed toward the prow
and stretched landward, but the voices called from all sides

like the four winds of a storm whirling together. Only this
was a storm in his mind only, for while I too
heard the sinuous calls as once I heard them voiced
by my own Nerianne, they did not unhinge me. At once
I thought what to do next, for surely Goddess Athene
never intended our story to end here, after the trials
we all had endured, and now so close to our homecoming.

    'Nausikaa! You are the one who must act now. Go to him.
Stand beside him, you two at the prow of the ship.
Remind Poseidon that here is no ordinary stranger
given conveyance, but now we are kinfolk to the Phaiakians.'

    Nausikaa sprang from her seat where, until I spoke, she sat,
rooted, in horror. She clung to Telemachos, turning his face
to look into hers. The roiling cloud lowered over, mute
like a vulture gliding with no sound over picked bones.

    Telemachos started as from a trance and flung his mantle
into the filthy sea. 'Here, Cloud-Gatherer,
is all you shall have of me.' Arm in arm, he
and his bride defied the cloud above, and the voices ceased.

    The sea cleared, the cloud dissolved, and a breeze arose.
The seamen bent to their rowing and with their oars
they tossed up a lively spray. As if the ship itself understood,
it surged ahead, leaving perils behind. I sank into my seat
at the stern, giving thanks to Athene in my spirit. Now if only,
whatever lies Euryalos spread on Ithaka, he never
persuaded my husband not to welcome us home. . .

    Ithaka, O homeland, loveliest island among them all —
the rough-hewn rocks that girdle the loins of Achaia —
lap of my longing, seat of my pleasure, image in my mind's eye
turned inward in eager remembrance, in anticipation.
With what delight I left you. With a spirit that was open
to all those shores that floated within the cast of my mind's net
I set my course and never, yet always, looked back,
never, yet always, saw you there, behind, ahead of me,
hovering like the goddess, considering all the dreams that I lived.
You were always with me, always beside, or behind or above

those places, those palaces, those people and practices, weaving ever
stronger the devising of my equally longed-for homecoming.
Now in the distance I search for your outlines, hidden away
behind Doulichion's high jagged headland
and Same's out-thrusting bluff pointing to it, gates
to my inner, sea-worn, enduring Ithaka, with your summit
hidden still. O I will forgive you the evils that befell
my son on your slopes if only you will appear behind
the spit of Same, over the shielding sea mist that lies
on the face of the water behind those pillars. Appear, O soon.

    And next from a blue that cannot be told from the sky or the sea,
as if in the blurring of the eye, it was there, first pale and low,
then rising to meet the slope of the waves and the crest of my eagerness,
frothy and light-flecked and moving toward me as in the best of my dreams,

    O here the rocky finger pointing me home, here
the steep cliff with slanting path, there a curved inlet,
narrow bay, the ragged shore where waves
crash and cream on great rocks and caves suck in
and expel the spume. And now a bluff and now a hollow,
there a sea-bird, next a swallow. O, what will I find
when I round the little grove of poplars and pass through the gates
into the courtyard of my own house? How
will I find my garden, my vines? Will there be fat grapes
hanging in abundant shade, or has Aktoris neglected
the water jars? And what of my nine downy goslings,
the ones that were hatched just before that never-to-be-forgotten night
when Telemachos was stricken? O may I come home in time
to embrace old father Laertes before he dies,
and take Ailanthis to my breast to give her my greatest gift,
my woman's fare well, before her own journey. And may I soon
mount the surpassingly sturdy bed of my husband
and linger there in love and murmurings.

                    But now the glide
past the cliffs of Neritos' sheer plunge into the water,
and the coasts of Doulichion, Same, Asteris and even Zakynthos
wheeling around the stern in order as we leaned and turned

on the favorable wind toward Ithaka's fairest harbor and shore.
And next we faced that first headland where Laertes had stood.
There in Helios' slanting rays was a pillar of white stone
with a shine on it that glistened. It stood where Laertes stood
and I felt it welcoming me home. And next we rounded
the bluff and I saw the curve of the harbor unfurl from behind
the folds of the hills, gleaming walls, the breakwater stretch
and ships laid up on the beach. A hundred fires lined
the shore with smoke and dancing flames. People were gathered
as if for the hecatombs Odysseus had promised to Athene
to acknowledge her help in bringing him safely home from Troy at last.
Soon I was to learn that indeed Laertes was gone
to Hades, and these rites I joined were to honor him.

    With my eyes straining I strove to see, in all that multitude
of moving figures, the few – no, truthfully, that one,
that one majestic figure, broader than the rest
and godlike in stature. For at once I divined Ailanthis, too,
already gone, departed that morning with Phemios, bound
for the banks of Aigyptos. My spirit faltered then, and an ache
invaded my breast. Then I searched for the hateful face
of that wretch, Euryalos. *Did he ever arrive? Did Odysseus listen,
and was he deceived?*

    Then there was my husband, standing lion-like
on the rocky shelf of the shoreline with the sunlight glinting in his beard
and his dancing eyes, and the flames leaping behind his erect
and expectant form. Surely no man could match him
for strength and beauty, not even Telemachos, for all his youth.

    Nor could anyone match him for insight, for there on the shore –
where last I stooped to retrieve the stone I carried with me
on all my journey – pulled onto the shingle and bedecked
with garlands and cloths from my own loom, was the ship I had longed for,
my own vessel. It was *Ktimene*, now named *The Penelope*.

    Our Phaiakian oarsmen pulled in their oars and stowed them away.
They made all fast on the ship, and threw the anchor stones
over the side. And then we were going ashore, our skiff
headed straight for that waiting figure like an arrow for the round

knob of a bronze shield, or a gannet for her own nest
among all the others on the rocky ledge above the surf.
My Odysseus stepped forward. He took me by the wrist,
those thoughtful gray eyes piercing my heart and mind,
and helped me step out beside him on the whispering stones
of our island home, and soon I made my desired homecoming.

But you, Phemios, were already gone, with my vanished Ailanthis.
Neither has godlike Nerianne returned to the dear home
of her well-settled parents to hear our tales and take up
her lyre to sing the rest of the story among the listeners –
that is, what we know to this point, since stories never end –
so it may go down among the generations of women and men.
So you, Phemios, must sing it for her whenever she comes:
how Odysseus had already dispatched the evil-mongering Euryalos,
how he knew me at once as our alien ship rounded the headland
and approached the harbor, how he proudly clasped his son
and new daughter to him and gave them his fatherly blessing,
and to me, hearty approval. How he tenderly undid the knot
on my battered chest and fastened it firmly again with our binding.
How at last I take my place beside him whenever he calls the people
to gather at the place of assembly by our strong-founded house,
yielding me precedence in certain matters, and listening to my counsels.
Of how Telemachos, following in the goddess' footsteps, accomplished
the land journey that blind Teiresias foretold for his father,
granting to us enjoyment of what remained of our youth together
until we came to the threshold of old age.

GLOSSARY

Note: most of the characters in *The Penelopeia* are well known from Homer's ancient tales, *The Iliad* and *The Odyssey*, and from Greek mythology. Those names with asterisks appear for the first time here, in Penelope's own story.

Ach'ior*: *see* Akaion
Achai'a/Achaians: Another term for the Greeks
Achil'leus: Greatest warrior of the Greeks at Troy, father of 'Leus*
Adme'te: A maid to Penelope
Adre'ste: Helen's maid
Agemem'non: King of Mykene, leader of the Greeks at Troy
Aida'mis*: Mabantha's* mother, queen of her African homeland
Aigy'ptos: The river of Egypt, i.e., the Nile
Ailan'this*: Twin daughter of Penelope and Odysseus sister of Nerianne*
Aithio'pia: Ancient Nubia/Ethiopia
Akai'on*: Realm of A'khior*, Apollytos'* father, to the West
Ak'toris: Penelope's personal maid
Alkan'dre: Wife of Polybos of Thebes; Egypt, host to Helen
Alki'noös: King of Scheria, i.e. of Phaiakia
Amphin'omos: Penelope's friend among the suitors
Anchi'ses*/Klos'tios*: Brothers of Timenos*, kinsmen of Odysseus
Antikle'ia: Mother of Odysseus, wife of Laertes
Anti'lochos: Nestor's son killed at Troy
Apoll'ytos*: Sea captain on Penelope's voyage with her daughters
Araman'tha*: Penelope's mother
Are'te: Queen of Phaiakia/Scheria
A'res: God of war
Ar'gos/Ar'gives: Name for area of Northern Greece; also Greece/Greeks
Ar'temis: Hunter goddess of chastity
A'treus: Father of Memlaos and Agememnon, Greek leaders at Troy
Askle'pios: Renowned early Greek healer

239

As'teris: Tiny island between Ithaka and Same

Atha'lia*: Daughter of Apollytos*

Athe'ne'/Atryto'ne/Tritogenei'a: Goddess of wisdom, daughter of Zeus

Auto'lykos: Maternal grandfather of Odysseus, whom he visited as a boy

Boö'tes: Star constellation, used for navigation in *The Odyssey*

Celen'dre*: Cohort of Penthesilea, the Amazon Queen

Cha'lkis: Site on the way to Pythos

Clytemne'stra: Wife of King Agememnon, killed for his murder

Dan'aans: A term for the Greeks

Demo'dokos: Blind singer at Alkinoös' court in Phaiakia

Dio'kles: Penelope's host between Pylos and Sparta, also Telemachos' in
  The Odyssey

Diony'sos: God of wine and revelry

Dodo'na: Sacred site in the Northwest of Greece

Do'lios: Faithful retainer of Penelope and Odysseus

Douli'chion: One of the islands, near Ithaka, in Odysseus' realm

E'chios*: Friend of Peisistratos; Penelope's driver to Sparta

E'lis: Area of the Western Pelopennese

Epei'ans: People of Elis

Eso'pus: River in Lakedaimon, near Sparta

Eume'los: Penelope's brother-in-law

Eumai'os: Odysseus' faithful swineherd

Eury'alos: Youth in the court at Phaiakia, son of Naubolos

Eury'bates/Rbatha*: African companion to Odysseus; brother to Mabantha*

Eury'dike: Wife of Nestor; Queen of Pylos

Eurykle'ia: Childhood nurse to Odysseus

Eury'machos: A chief suitor and antagonist of Penelope; also lover of Melantho

Eury'nome: Housekeeper to Penelope

He'len: Helen of Troy, Queen of Sparta, famous throughout history as the
  most beautiful woman in the world, daughter of Zeus

He'licon: Beginning of the route to Pytho

He'lios: God of the sun
Hel'las/Hel'lenes: Greece, Greeks
Hephai'stos: God of the forge
Heraklei'te*: Mother of Arete
Hermi'one: Daughter of Helen; married away
Hyrmi'ne/Kro'unoi/Phe'ai: Coastal sites North of Pylos

I'lion: Troy
Ika'rios: Penelope's father
Iphthi'me: Penelope's sister
I'thaka: Penelope's and Odysseus' island realm, off Western Greece

Ja'nys*: Pharoah's chariot driver
Ja'son: Legendary, earlier Greek hero, also famous for journeying

Ka'mylos*: Itinerant singer
Kary'methe*: One of Penelope's household women
Ka'sti*: Wife of Timenos*, Odysseus' kinsman near Pytho
Ki'tios*: Tender of Penelope's geese
Klo'stios*: Kinsman of Odysseus near Pytho
Krete/Keftieu: Island kingdom south of Greece
Kri'sa: Harbor of Mt. Parnassos, near Pytho

Laer'tes: Odysseus' father
Lakedai'mon: Kingdom of Sparta
Lao'damas: Alkinoös' favorite son
Le'da: Helen's mother, at Zeus' caprice
'Le'us*: Son of Penthesilea and Achil'leus

Maban'tha/Maban'da*: Penelope's friend, African princess, wife of Phemios
Malei'a: Southern tip of the Pelopennese
Mede'a: Consort of Jason
Melan'tho: Treacherous serving maid of Penelope
Me'don: Herald to Penelope and Odysseus
Menela'os: King of Sparta, Helen's husband
Men'tor: Respected advisor to Odysseus' household

Meo'tis (Lake): Location of Amazons' city
Myke'ne: City of King Agememnon, Menelaos' brother
Myr'sinos: Promontory on Northwestern Pelopennese

Narce'the*: Wife of Diokles at Pherai
Nau'bolos: Father of Eurylaos
Nausi'kaa: Princess of Scheria, daughter of Alkinoös and Arete
Nepto'lemos: Son of Achilleus, married Hermione
Nerian'ne*: Twin daughter of Penelope and Odysseus, sister of Ailanthis*
Ner'iton/Ne'ritos/Ne'ion: Mountain of Ithaka
Nes'tor: Sage warrior at Troy, King of Pylos
Nom'bril Stone: Name of the sacred icon of Pytho

Odys'seus: Penelope's husband, long absent King of Ithaka
Oidi'podes/Oedipus: Legendary King of Thebes, consulted the oracle at Pytho
Ompha'los: Term for the Nombril Stone at Pytho, meaning 'Navel of the World'

Païe'on: Legendary healer
Pal'las/Athe'ne: Term for the goddess
Pa'ris: Prince of Troy, abducted Helen, leading to Trojan War
Parnas'sos: Hallowed mountain in Northern Greece, near Pytho
Parrha'sia: Region in the Pelopennese
Peisis'tratos: Prince of Pylos, friend of Telemachos
Pelopennese': Southern part of Greece
Pene'lope: Queen of Ithaka, wife of Odysseus
Penthesile'ia: Queen of the Amazons, reputedly killed at Troy
Pera'ios*: Hunting companion of Telemachos
Phæ'dra: Kretan wife of Theseus, legendary earlier hero
Phaia'kia/Sche'ria: Kingdom visited by Odysseus in *The Odyssey*
Phe'mios: Court musician at Ithaka
Phe'rai: Way stop between Pylos and Sparta
Pher'isos*: Blacksmith in Penelope's household
Phoe'bus: Alternate name for the god Apollo
Phthi'a: City of Achilleus
Phy'lo: Helen's maid
Plei'stos: River near Pytho

Polydam'na: Healer friend of Helen in Egypt

Polykas'te: Princess of Pylos, Nestor and Eurydike's daughter, sister to
    Peisistratos

Polyphe'mos: One of the Cyclopes, son of Poseidon; blinded by Odysseus

Ponto'noös: Alkinoös' herald

Posei'don: God of the Sea

Pri'am: King of Troy

Py'los/Pylians: City of Nestor, on the West coast of the Pelopennese

Py'thia/The Py'thia: Oracle priestess at Pytho

Py'tho/Delphi: Original name for sacred shrine to Apollo; later 'Delphi'

Rba'tha*: Given name of Odysseus' comrade, Eurybates, Mabantha's* brother

Rhexe'nor: Father of Arete

Ru'mor: Personified by the Greeks as a deity

Sa'me: One of the islands in the realm of Ithaka

Si'don: Phoenician city

Sika'nia: Thought to have been Sicily

Spar'ta: City of Helen and Menelaos in mainland Greece

Taÿ'getos: Mountain range between Pylos and Sparta

Teire'sias: Blind Theban seer

Tele'machos: Son of Penelope and Odysseus

Thebes: City in Northern Greece

Themiscy'ra: Legendary city of the Amazons, near the Black Sea

The'seus: Legendary hero of earlier generation

Thrina'kia: Island of Helios, sun god

Ti'menos*: One of Odysseus' kinsmen, husband of Kasti*

Triple Ways: Crossroads between Thebes and Pytho

Troy, Tro'ad: Ancient city made famous by *The Iliad*, Homer's tale of the
    Trojan War, fought over Helen, abducted wife of the king of Sparta

Zakyn'thos: Island in realm of Ithaka

Zeus: Capricious king of the gods, father of Athene and Helen

Acknowledgments

This tale has been fashioned as a continuation of Penelope's story from *The Odyssey,* as if it had been told to, let us say, 'Demodoka,' and translated by Richmond Lattimore. Therefore I have made fair use of aspects of his translation of *The Odyssey* (Harper Collins, 1965), which I think is the best for language and style.

I do thank the many people who read *The Penelopeia* and offered critique, advice and encouragement: Cornelia and Robert Gates, Eleanor Hasbrouck Rawlings, Betty Neogy, Alice Moir, Florence R. Gardner, Irene Bromberg, Constantin Mattheos, Alicia Ostriker, Molly Peacock, Robert Fagles, my colleagues in US 1 Poets' Cooperative in Princeton, New Jersey, and most especially, my own wandering hero, Captain Robert P. Odenweller.

A Note on the Text

As my models for style are Richmond Lattimore's translations of *The Iliad* and *The Odyssey*, I have followed his spelling of names, chiefly using 'k' for 'c' (as in Ithaka) and forms such as 'Achilleus' and 'Menelaos' for Achilles and Meneleus. As Lattimore explains, this is to keep the diction closer to the Greek, archaic and modern, rather than to the Anglicized Latin forms many of us are used to. Like him I have made exceptions for names we are very familiar with, for example: Odysseus, Helen, Apollo, Troy.

I have also used 'Ilion' (whence *The Iliad*) and 'the Troad' interchangeably with Troy, as Lattimore did throughout *The Odyssey*. I feel that these uses render the text more historical, more 'authentic' in feeling, as if translated from a 'recently found text' by a 'Demodoka.'

'Akaion' I imagine west of Sikania (Sicily?), perhaps at the present Marseilles or Barcelona.

J.R.

A Note on the Type

THE PENELOPEIA has been set in Bodoni Book, a face based on the designs of Giambattista Bodoni (1740-1813). The son of a Piedmontese printer, Bodoni began his career as superintendent of the Press of Propogation of the Faith in Rome. In 1768, he was named head of the ducal printing house in Parma, where he carried out his most important work as printer and typographer. Innovative in both type design and printing technique, Bodoni's books were widely admired for their meticulous presswork, opulent production, and generous formats – though his reputation as a printer of scholarly works was diminished by poor proofreading. ¶ While Bodoni's early work was executed under the influence of the Fourniers, the family of French typefounders and printers, it was the work of the English typographer John Baskerville that would most profoundly color his later output as a punchcutter and designer of books. The types Bodoni cut at the Stamperia Reale, considered the first "modern" faces, are widely admired for the pronounced contrast between thick and thin strokes, for their fine serifs, and for their openness and delicacy.

Design, composition & cartography by Carl W. Scarbrough